Freedom and Emergency Powers in the Cold War

ROBERT S. RANKIN
Duke University

WINFRIED R. DALLMAYR
Purdue University

New York

APPLETON-CENTURY-CROFTS
Division of Meredith Publishing Company

614-1

Library of Congress Card Number: 63-21213

PRINTED IN THE UNITED STATES OF AMERICA

E72850

To the memory of

EDWARD S. CORWIN

an inspiring teacher and scholar

and

JOHN F. KENNEDY

who in his high office combined
courage and strength with prudence,
reason and humanity

Preface

THE PRESENT STUDY was begun in the summer of 1961 at the height of the Berlin crisis; it was completed in its major portions in fall of 1962 in the wake of the Mississippi debacle and in the midst of the Cuban conflict. Since then, crises and tensions seem to have multiplied rather than diminished. Perhaps the immediate dangers of the cold war have been somewhat lessened by the partial test ban agreement reached in Moscow in summer of 1963; but domestic conflicts have increased in intensity. Automation and related changes continue to inject a particular vehemence into labor disputes and, in one instance, Congress was forced to legislate compulsory arbitration. The struggle over segregation has become a full-scale battle during 1963 whose fronts reach into all areas of social life. Thus, the basic concern underlying this study has certainly not been lessened and, regrettably, can be expected to trouble our minds for many years to come.

Since the purpose and scope of the study are explained in the introduction, this preface can be brief; however, it cannot be brief to the point of showing a lack of gratitude. The writers have many reasons to be thankful to many people. Both writers have benefited from the generous financial support which they received in the form of a research grant from the Ford Foundation. The authors also should like to express their appreciation for the permission given by Professor Charles Fairman and the Industrial College of the Armed Forces to cite material of regularly limited circulation. The Holifield Subcommittee of the House Committee on Government Operations was kind enough to make available to the authors hearings and reports, sometimes in advance of their public release. There are numerous other people from whom the writers have benefited through conversation and general encouragement.

Special thanks should go to Mrs. Ilse Dallmayr, a loyal wife, who spent many hours typing and retyping the manuscript. Without her interest and help, the study would not have progressed and certainly not have been completed in this short period of time.

                                                                        R.S.R.
Durham, and Lafayette, October, 1963   W.R.D.

Contents

Table of Cases

FREEDOM AND EMERGENCY POWERS IN THE COLD WAR

Quod enim necessitas cogit defendit.

"We must never forget that it is a constitution we are expounding . . . a constitution intended to endure for ages to come, and consequently, to be adapted to the various crises of human affairs."

Chief Justice John Marshall,
McCulloch v. *Maryland* (1819)

I

Introduction

IN SEVERAL STATEMENTS and addresses made during May of 1962, the national chairman of one of the great American parties identified as the central issue of the year, and as one of the major political issues of our time, the growing power of the president. As the chairman observed, presidential authority, already greatly increased as a result of war and postwar crises, has recently been further expanded due to personal ambition. "The president," he asserted, "is an ambitious man and Americans applaud ambition. But when ambition feeds on the individual liberties which were guaranteed to all of us under a free and representative form of government, it is time to call a halt. This is the big issue of 1962—the issue that must be met head on" during the election campaign. According to the national chairman, the growth of presidential power endangered the maintenance of our constitutional system and of civil liberties. Unless the president's "relentless drive for more and more power over the people is checked," he claimed, "the time is not far distant when the United States can no longer call itself a republic." [1] Under the impact of expanding executive authority, individual citizens and their rights tended to be assigned a secondary role, "a role which clearly subverts the intentions of the founding fathers and the basic principles of all Americans whether they are Republicans or Democrats." [2]

To be sure, these statements were not intended as an entirely objective assessment and were inspired in large measure by the political dictates of an election campaign. To this degree, the

[1] *Milwaukee Journal* (May 25, 1962), p. 1, col. 1. (Representative William E. Miller of New York).

[2] *Ibid.*, p. 19, col. 1.

chairman's observations do not require very serious analysis and attention. Obviously, partisan charges of power lust and dictatorial ambitions have not been reserved to the Kennedy administration. One has only to recall the invectives hurled against President Truman's steel seizure in 1952 and against President Eisenhower's actions in the Little Rock episode of 1957. Nevertheless, irrespective of any partisan charges and commitments, the fact of expanding executive powers in recent decades and especially in the postwar period is undeniable. This expansion is not—at least not primarily—the result of any personal ambition of individual office holders. It seems much more appropriate to say that expanded functions and responsibilities have been thrust upon individual office holders, regardless of their party affiliation, by the extremely unstable and hazardous world situation and by the domestic implications of the nuclear age. Ever since the United States decided, during World War II, to abandon the policy of isolationism and to enter the world community in a position of leadership, her governmental institutions have been faced with an ever increasing multitude of problems and dangers of unprecedented proportions. The cold war confronted this country with a hostile system of government in which all the resources of society are constantly geared toward one massive common effort. It is hardly surprising that an age of almost permanent crisis and emergency in which small incidents may lead to a rapid warming-up of the cold war and possibly to a nuclear holocaust, should have produced the response of growing governmental emergency powers and responsibilities.

The realization of cold war needs and requirements, however, does not entirely resolve the issue of the growth of governmental powers. In a constitutional system dedicated to the preservation of individual liberties, expanding emergency functions of the government raise problems of grave importance and magnitude. The basic and inescapable question is, How can a democracy face the challenge of the cold war and still remain a democracy? or to put it differently, How can constitutional liberties be preserved in an age in which strong governmental powers seem required to guarantee their very existence? Obviously there is no easy formula or solution to this question. The present study is an attempt to examine how the conflicting objectives have been reconciled—(if indeed they have been)—in the postwar period and what lessons may be drawn from postwar experiences in this field. It would be less than candid to say that the study is conducted in a completely neutral spirit. The writers of the study are deeply committed to the principles of individual liberty and dignity and to the over-riding goals of civil and social justice. Guided by this perspective, their examination assumes a basic tenor which necessarily differs from a position dedicated to the concept of authority for au-thority's sake. The results of their examination and some general evaluations with respect to emergency authority and its relation to our system of separation of powers are presented in the conclud-ing part of the study.

Despite the obvious importance of the problem, the growth of governmental emergency powers in the cold war period has not received its proportionate share of public or scholarly attention. This fact may be due in part to the understandable human inclina-tion to ignore or repress, as far as possible, the horrible dangers implicit in our nuclear age. This comparative neglect may also reflect an undesirable tendency to consider the problem merely as the business of the government and to leave the worries to public officials. There are, of course, some excellent studies on presiden-tial emergency powers and on the topic of martial law. Most of these, however, were written some fifteen or twenty years ago and were not yet conceived in the light of cold war developments.[3] In more recent years, only a few studies have been devoted to the problem of emergency powers. In one instance, an analysis was made of presidential powers in times of crisis; but the analysis was not specifically directed to postwar or cold war developments and ranged broadly over the field of congressional authorizations and administrative responsibilities since the New Deal period.[4] In another instance, the functions of the president in the field of civil rights and race relations were the object of scholarly inquiry;

[3] Compare, e.g., Clinton L. Rossiter, *The Supreme Court and the Com-mander in Chief* (Ithaca, 1951), and *Constitutional Dictatorship* (Prince-ton, 1948); Edward S. Corwin, *Total War and the Constitution* (New York, 1947); Louis W. Koenig, *The Presidency and the Crisis* (New York, 1944); Bennett M. Rich, *The President and Civil Disorder* (Washington, D. C., 1941); Robert S. Rankin, *When Civil Law Fails* (Durham, 1939); Charles Fairman, *The Law of Martial Rule* (Chicago, 1930; 2d ed., Chicago, 1943).

[4] J. Malcolm Smith and Cornelius P. Cotter, *Powers of the President Dur-ing Crises* (Washington, D. C., 1960).

but the inquiry was only incidentally concerned with executive emergency powers.[5] There have been numerous articles and essays dealing with emergency powers in industrial disputes or other specified and circumscribed areas;[6] however, little or no attempt has been made to integrate these experiences in a general analysis and conception of cold war emergency powers.

The scope and emphasis of the present study are limited in several respects which should be pointed out here. The study does not intend to review the growth of any or all governmental powers in our time; its purpose is to grasp the expansion and present status of extraordinary or emergency powers. Moreover, this explanation should be further specified to the effect that the examination is really and primarily concerned with executive emergency powers, in particular with the powers of the president and state governors. The inclusion of state chief executives is based on the realization that our constitution establishes a federal system and that, despite the progressive obliteration of state boundaries in a time of jet travel, there is still a certain analogy between presidential and gubernatorial powers. The examination of executive emergency powers should also reveal the extent to which contemporary changes in federal-state relations have tended to circumscribe the opportunities of state governors to exercise their otherwise legitimate authority. While concentrating on the development of executive powers, the study certainly cannot ignore the role of the other branches of government in our constitutional system. Many of the executive emergency powers are derived from legislative enactments; others—sometimes called "inherent" powers but more appropriately described as implied powers—are independent of statutory authorization and are based directly on federal or state constitutions. In addition, the role of the courts has to be considered and especially the question whether and to which degree resort to executive emergency powers is subject to judicial review.

Even with the mentioned specification, however, the range of the study is not yet adequately delimited. The inquiry does not

---

[5] Richard P. Longaker, *The Presidency and Individual Liberties* (Ithaca, 1961).

[6] Many of these articles and studies are referred to subsequently in the various chapters.

deal with all types of executive emergency powers, but only with those powers which are in some form characteristic of our postwar period. The study does not deal with military powers strictly speaking, especially with the powers of the president over the nation's military forces in time of war or warlike emergency. Strategic planning and the conduct of military defense are part of the president's traditional authority over the nation's military establishment under the constitution. Although the nuclear age has greatly enhanced the urgency of military defense preparations, executive authority in this field poses few or no problems of a novel character. Other customary or perpetual emergency functions are disaster relief and similar responsibilities in the event of natural catastrophes. Natural disasters show little regard for the course of human history and hurricanes or floods strike irrespective of the existence of distant early warning systems or Conelrad devices. In this sense, disaster relief powers are of a timeless or ahistoric quality and can be expected to be exercised in times of peace, cold war or military conflict. The present study, on the other hand, is definitely concerned with human history and more particularly with the twilight zone of executive powers which are somehow influenced by or are a peculiar feature of the cold war and of an age haunted by the eschatological visions of nuclear destruction.

In portraying the growth of executive emergency powers during this period, the study delves into three major problem areas which the writers considered particularly typical or instructive: the areas of nonmilitary defense, industrial disputes, and race relations. The choice was guided in part by the conviction that it would be preferable to examine in detail the experiences made and the lessons learned in a selected group of areas rather than to skim over the surface of a great variety of mingled and ill assorted emergency responsibilities. Moreover, it is believed that the choice and presentation of the selected problem areas reflects in a fairly illustrative manner developments of the cold war period. From the beginning, the cold war has been, and continues to be, a physical power contest between two blocs of nations. This aspect is reflected in nonmilitary defense preparations and in the growth of executive emergency powers over the civilian population and domestic resources in case of a sudden deterioration of cold war relations. Despite the obvious and perhaps primary significance of the contemporary power contest, it is clear that the cold war is also a conflict between two economic systems. This aspect of economic competition has steadily grown in importance since the death of Stalin in 1953, especially with the rise of Khrushchev and the recent adoption of ambitious, far-reaching economic plans in the Soviet Union and the communist bloc. In the face of this economic challenge, domestic efforts to maintain a stable economy and the expansion of executive powers over industrial disputes endangering the national welfare become readily understandable. Apart from the aspects of military and economic competition, one cannot overlook the fact that the contest between the two blocs is part and parcel of the broad, social revolution of our time. At least since the middle of the last decade, the cold war has acquired a third dimension with the emergence of underdeveloped, uncommitted countries as a result of the rapid advances of former colonies in Africa and Asia toward independence. Irrespective of the question of cause and effect, one of the tasks of the present study is to explore certain parallel developments in this country during recent years and to review the application of executive emergency powers to the field of race relations and constitutional equality.

2

Nonmilitary Defense

THE MOST revealing and unique form of emergency authority in the cold war period has its basis in the area of civil defense and defense mobilization. As a permanent institution or organization, nonmilitary defense in the United States is entirely a postwar phenomenon. The precise limits and ramifications of this new phenomenon are perhaps hard to establish; but whatever its exact definition,[1] it obviously constitutes a novel combination of military and civilian preoccupations either in the form of an extension of military standards to the life of the civilian population or in the sense of a greater impact of the requirements of civilian survival on military operations. As one observer has pointed out:

Civil defense is by nature a hybrid, making use of military measures adapted for civilian use, and therefore may not seem natural to either military men or civilians.[2]

[1] "Nonmilitary defense" has been defined as follows: "Civil defense and defense mobilization encompass the entire field of nonmilitary defense as distinguished from military defense, which is the function of the Armed Forces. Civil defense and defense mobilization together involve all preattack and postattack activities undertaken to save lives, marshall the resources of the Nation, mobilize production, stabilize the economy, control the distribution of goods and services, restore communities, and repair industrial plants and facilities of all kinds." Executive Office of the President, Office of Civil and Defense Mobilization, *The National Plan for Civil Defense and Defense Mobilization* (hereinafter cited as *National Plan*), Annex 4: "Authorities for Civil Defense and Defense Mobilization" (Washington, D. C., August, 1959), p. 1. For a definition of "civil defense" as distinguished from defense mobilization or the mobilization of resources see Section 3(a) of the Federal Civil Defense Act of 1950, as amended; 64 Stat. 1246 (1950), 50 U.S.C. App. 2252 (1958).
[2] Dr. Merle Tuve, Chairman of the Committee on Civil Defense of the National Academy of Sciences and the National Research Council, in Hear-

Endowed with this "hybrid" character, nonmilitary defense, and civil defense in particular, is clearly a manifestation of the international cold war with its blending of wartime and peacetime standards and its constantly shifting emphasis from one to the other set of rules. More particularly, the conception of a permanent civil defense organization is a telling demonstration of the postwar revolution in arms and weapons and of the horrible threat of potential destruction posed by these weapons for military forces and civilian population alike. A very compelling illustration of the danger in recent months was afforded by the Cuban crisis of October, 1962, which suddenly opened up the prospect of a thermonuclear holocaust.[3]

The curious mixture of military and civilian aspects in the area of nonmilitary defense has serious implications for the development of executive emergency powers. The president has the constitutional mandate to act as commander-in-chief; but, at least in peacetime, this authority extends only to the armed forces and not to the civilian population. In wartime, the authority of the president under this clause is greatly increased; in fact, together with his functions in international relations, the "war powers" of the president are usually considered examples of his independent or "inherent" prerogatives. However, the range of war powers has traditionally been linked with the dictates of military necessity and military defense. In any event, since the Civil War, the population of the United States has not been seriously exposed to the threat of attack and never to a danger of such enormous proportions as implicit in our nuclear age.

It is at least debatable whether and to what extent the authority of the president over the nonmilitary population under a civil defense program can be derived strictly from his war powers. By necessity, an effective civil defense program must comprise long-

---

ings before a Subcommittee of the Committee on Government Operations, House of Representatives, *Civil Defense for National Survival* (hereinafter cited as *Investigative Hearings*), 84th Cong., 2d Sess. (1956), pt. 2, p. 205.

[3] The danger has been reduced somewhat by the partial test ban treaty, outlawing nuclear tests in the atmosphere, outer space and under water, which was initialed by the representatives of the United States, the United Kingdom and the Soviet Union on July 25, 1963 and which, after ratification by the Senate and the president, went into effect on October 10, 1963. However, one should perhaps not forget that previous test suspensions have been unilaterally terminated or abrogated.

range preparations and planning, that is, activities which cannot be limited to the attack or immediate postattack period but must extend into "peacetime"—as far as the cold war permits such a designation. Reliance on war powers to cover these activities clearly involves a considerable modification of the usage of the concept. Unless the term "cold war powers" is adopted, it may be preferable to qualify the functions of the president in the nonmilitary defense field as a combination of traditional war powers and his prerogatives as chief executive and law-enforcement officer. The situation is somewhat different on the state level; for although state governors are usually empowered to act as commanders-in-chief of the state militia, states are regularly deprived of the capacity to wage war and thus, of war powers. On the other hand, states are traditionally endowed with the so-called "police power," a power which is not as such inherent in the federal government. Nevertheless, an extension of the police power to nonmilitary defense programs injects an element of war emergency into the concept which is not regularly found in police actions.[4] Thus, while transforming the war powers of the president in the direction of a greater emphasis on "civilian" operations, nonmilitary defense modifies the police power of the states by adding the aspect of "defense" measures.

There can be no doubt that the blending of military with civilian standards and other emergency measures prompted by the cold war pose a grave challenge to the maintenance of civil government and the protection of civil rights. As early as 1947, Professor Robert E. Cushman pictured the far-reaching implications of atomic energy on traditional American concepts of civil liberty.[5] This sobering warning was written, however, before the advent of the hydrogen bomb and the development of intercontinental ballistic missiles. The increase in the destructive power of weapons and the speed of delivery has in the same measure increased the urgency of the problem of constitutional freedom.

[4] For a derivation of civil defense authority on the national level from war powers see *National Plan*, Annex 4, pp. 3-4. For a discussion of the concept that civil defense at the state and local level is based upon the police power of the states see *People* v. *City of Chicago*, 413 Ill. 83, 108 N. E. 2d 16 (1952).

[5] Robert E. Cushman, "Civil Liberties in the Atomic Age," *Annals of the American Academy of Political and Social Sciences*, 249: 54 (1947).

The prospects of the establishment of a sound balance between civil liberties and emergency preparedness depend to a large degree on the constant vigilance of public opinion. Only if this vigilance is preserved is it possible to find validity and promise in Clinton Rossiter's statement "that a democratic, constitutional government beset by a severe national emergency can be strong enough to maintain its own existence without at the same time being so strong as to subvert the liberties of the people it has been instituted to defend" and that "merely because we are to have a government strong enough to deal with the Atomic Age does not mean that we are henceforth to be slaves." [6]

Quite apart from the problem of maintaining civil liberties is the question of the wisdom of civil defense measures designed to counteract the potential threat of nuclear attack. There is a segment of public opinion which believes that any form of civil defense preparations tends to foster a false and unwarranted feeling of security and thereby to decrease public hostility to military ventures and increase the likelihood of nuclear war. This belief appears to be quite sincere, although it may be difficult to gauge accurately the impact of civil defense measures on public opinion and on the likelihood of attack or the threat of war. Certainly if the belief were correct, the consequences would be not only deplorable but disastrous. In fairness, however, one should mention that most efforts in the field of civil defense have been inspired by the opposite assumption or expectation, namely that civil defense preparedness may act as an additional deterrent to nuclear attack or war. Preventive measures against an evil do not and should not imply a desire for the evil to occur.

1. THE ADMINISTRATIVE PROTEUS

There is hardly a function or agency in the government which has been subject to more frequent alterations and reforms than nonmilitary defense. The alterations appear to be due, in equal measure, to changes in the international cold war climate and to the fact that nonmilitary defense is a comparatively new feature in the national administrative machinery. Obviously, civil de-

[6] Clinton L. Rossiter, *Constitutional Dictatorship* (Princeton, 1948), pp. 1, 3, 14.

fense and mobilization authority has always been located in the executive branch of government. Congress has passed some legislation regulating the assignment and exercise of this authority; congressional regulations, however, have not always been sufficiently clear or specific, a fact which has encouraged the chief executive on various occasions to exercise considerable discretion in respect to administrative organization and performance of functions. Executive discretion amplifies the already vast range of emergency powers bestowed by Congress upon civil defense officials and agencies. In view of this range of executive prerogatives and congressional delegations of authority, it appears desirable at the outset to review the development of nonmilitary defense organization and to examine the extent to which existing administrative arrangements insure or encourage the responsible exercise of emergency powers.

Plans and Programs

Although, as stated before, nonmilitary defense properly speaking is a product of the atomic age and thus mainly a postwar phenomenon, experiences with civil defense were not entirely lacking in the United States during the first and second World Wars. Nevertheless, the influence of these experiences on later developments was greatly limited due to the absence of a serious threat to the American homeland. The first World War witnessed little or no serious preoccupation with civil defense problems. In the Council of National Defense which was established in August of 1916, the Secretary of War supervised only certain minor activities which later came to be viewed as civil defense functions.[7] Concern with civil defense problems was more pronounced during World War II. On May 20, 1941, more than six months before Pearl Harbor, President Roosevelt created the Office of Civilian Defense within the Office of Emergency Management which was a part of the Executive Office of the President. Following the entry of the United States into the war and in view of British air

[7] See Elwyn A. Mauck, "History of Civil Defense in the United States," *Bulletin of the Atomic Scientists*, 6: 265-270 (1950); Carey Brewer, *Civil Defense in the United States: Federal, State and Local*, Library of Congress, Legislative Reference Service, Public Affairs Bulletin No. 92 (Washington, D.C., February, 1951), p. 9.

raid experiences, the program of civilian defense was strengthened. On April 15, 1942, the president expanded the responsibilities of the Office of Civilian Defense and appointed a full-time
director for its management. At the same time, a Civilian Defense
Board was established consisting of the Secretaries of War and
Navy, the Attorney General, and the Director of the Office of
Defense, Health and Welfare Services. The range of functions
within the purview of the Office of Civilian Defense was broadly
conceived to encompass all activities of civilians whether directly
or indirectly related to the war. However, the primary task of the
national office was supervision and coordination rather than
planning or implementation. Beginning in the spring of 1944, the
functions of the agency were gradually curtailed and the office was
finally abolished on June 30, 1945.

At the end of World War II, the feeling was prevalent that the
world had once again been made safe for democracy and that
peace was here to stay for an indefinite period of time. A rapid
program of demobilization was initiated in the United States.
However, clouds soon began to gather in the sky as conflicts developed between the former wartime allies. On November 25,
1946, only eighteen months after the Office of Civilian Defense
had been abolished, the Secretary of War established a Civil
Defense Board within the War Department under the direction
of Major General Harold R. Bull. The function of the Board was
to study the problem of civil defense and to formulate policies
concerning the administrative allocation and organization of civil
defense functions and the possible role to be played by the War
Department. The "Bull Report" of February 15, 1948, based its
findings primarily on civil defense experiences in the United States
and other countries during the second World War, although it was
recognized that civil defense as organized and directed in World
War II would be inadequate for the future.[8] Concerning administrative arrangements, the report recommended that civil defense
be organized in a hierarchical manner ranging from local self-help
groups to protective service units on the municipal and state
levels. The task of the federal government was conceived primarily
in terms of guidance and coordination and, in order to achieve the

[8] National Military Establishment, Office of the Secretary, *A Study of
Civil Defense* (Washington, D.C., February, 1948).

desired uniformity of action, the establishment of a single civil defense agency was proposed. The report concluded that, pending final allocation of civil defense responsibilities, some agency should immediately be designated to initiate coordinated planning and that, under prevailing circumstances, such an agency might best be located within the War Department or the proposed Armed Forces or Defense Department.

Acting in accordance with the recommendation of the Bull Report that interim planning be conducted, Secretary James Forrestal of the newly established Defense Department, created the Office of Civil Defense Planning on March 27, 1948. The Office, placed under the direction of Major General Russell J. Hopley, was ordered to prepare a program of civil defense including a plan for a permanent federal civil defense agency and for state and local subdivisions. After intensive investigation of all previous foreign and domestic civil defense experiences, the Office submitted its findings to the Secretary of Defense on October 1, 1948. The study, often referred to as the "Hopley Report," outlined and recommended for adoption a "sound and effective peacetime system" of civil defense which could "quickly and easily be expanded in the event of an emergency a program that will bridge the gap by providing the link that is missing in our defense structure." Like the previous Bull Report, the study of the Hopley group proposed a comprehensive civil defense structure including federal, state and local organizations. The basic operational responsibility was placed in the states and the communities. On the federal level, the Hopley Report recommended the establishment of a permanent National Office of Civil Defense which was to have only a small staff mainly to furnish general guidance, training and coordination. The report considered the question of whether the national office should be located in the Executive Office of the President or in the Defense Department; it decided in favor of the latter alternative "since a very large part of the civil defense program will require continuous coordination with all agencies responsible to the Secretary of Defense." [9]

The recommendations of the Hopley Report concerning the

[9] U.S. Office of Civil Defense Planning, *Civil Defense for National Security* (Washington, D.C., October, 1948), pp. 1, 2.

establishment of a national civil defense office were not immediately translated into reality. Possibly, there was some hesitation
to expand the authority of the Defense Department, although the
Hopley Report had emphasized that the proposed national office
was to be strictly under civilian control. Moreover, President
Truman appeared to be opposed to the idea of a permanent civil
defense office, stating that emphasis at the moment should be
placed on peacetime planning and preparation rather than operation of a full-scale civil defense program with a definitive administrative structure. As a result, the president, on March 3, 1949,
assigned primary responsibility for civil defense planning to the
National Security Resources Board, an agency which had been
created on the basis of the National Security Act of 1947. Under
the 1947 act, the National Security Resources Board was to advise
the president with respect to the coordination of military, industrial, and civilian mobilization, including policies and programs
for the maximum use of material, manpower and production resources in time of war and for the stabilization of the wartime
economy. Later, in 1949, the Board was transferred into the
Executive Office of the President. The function of civil defense
planning which previously had been exercised primarily by the
Department of the Army and the Defense Department was thus
unified with the defense mobilization function and placed more
directly under the control and initiative of the president.

Prior to the assignment of new functions in March of 1949, the
National Security Resources Board had undertaken numerous
studies related to nonmilitary defense: primarily studies on manpower, industrial dispersion, available water power, housing,
transportation and communication facilities. Beginning in October of 1949, the Board conducted an intensive information ex-
change program with state governors and other agencies, a
program designed to establish policies for relationships with state
and local governments, to clarify federal objectives and activities
and to promote state civil defense legislation. On September 8,
1950, the chairman of the National Security Resources Board
submitted to the president a new master plan for civil defense
against air and atomic attack.[10] The plan, generally known as the

[10] U. S. National Security Resources Board, *United States Civil Defense,*
NSRB Doc. 128 (Washington, D.C., 1950).

"Blue Book," followed previous recommendations by placing operational control of the civil defense system in the hands of the state governments. The functions to be performed at each level of government were outlined in the report and the organizational structure of state and local operations was specified. The federal government was made responsible mainly for policy direction, information and general coordination. The most significant suggestion on the federal level was the proposal of an independent agency, a Federal Civil Defense Administration, in the executive branch of government.

Congress Decides to Act

At the time when the report of the National Security Resources Board was issued, the danger of nuclear attack directed against the United States was no longer a mere hypothesis or distant possibility. On September 23, 1949, the president had announced that the Soviet Union had exploded an atomic device. The impact of this elimination of our nuclear monopoly was soon heightened by the intensification of the international cold war struggle. On June 25, 1950, the Republic of South Korea was invaded by North Korean armies, a challenge which was countered by the immediate resolution of the United States, acting in conjunction with the United Nations, to resist aggression with armed force. These developments dispelled any optimism which may have existed previously with regard to prospects of an enduring peace and contributed a new sense of urgency to nonmilitary defense programs. Congressional hearings were held to determine the effects of atomic attack and the preventive measures which might be taken to reduce the effects of such an attack. Scientists attempted to describe the magnitude of the problem under the new set of circumstances and to elucidate possible counter-measures to decrease the country's vulnerability.[11]

The preoccupation of the administration with civil defense problems was reflected in President Truman's message to Congress of September 18, 1950, in which he transmitted the plan of the National Security Resources Board, stating that "this report

[11] Compare Eugene Rabinowitch, "Civil Defense; The Long-Range View," *Bulletin of the Atomic Scientists*, 6: 226 (1950).

presents a sound and workable outline of the civil defense problems we face, and what the federal, state and local governments should do to meet them." Congress immediately set to work and hastily drafted civil defense legislation was introduced on the same and following days. After revision and more careful preparation, comprehensive civil defense bills were submitted to the House of Representatives on November 30 and to the Senate on December 1. Before the bills were sent to committee, President Truman, on December 1, established a temporary Federal Civil Defense Administration within the Office of Emergency Management and transferred the civil defense personnel and facilities of the National Security Resources Board to the new agency. The creation of this temporary body injected new life into an almost defunct part of the Executive Office of the President and placed civil defense into the same administrative position which it had occupied during World War II. Congressional hearings on the proposed civil defense legislation began on December 4. After differences in the respective draft bills had been ironed out in conference between the two houses of Congress, the Federal Civil Defense Act was approved by the president on January 12, 1951.

Both in congressional hearings and in debates on the floor of the two houses, the urgency and importance of an adequate civil defense program was stressed by proponents of the bill. As Senator Kefauver pointed out in opening the Senate debate, "The Senate Armed Services Committee and the Joint Committee on Atomic Energy are agreed that there is no more pressing problem facing the country today than is the prompt enactment of legislation in this field." At the same time the novelty of the proposed emergency legislation and of its implications for civil government was emphasized by several speakers. "If the bill becomes law," Senator McCarran objected, "it will be one of the most drastic and far-reaching laws ever placed on the statute books of our country. It goes further toward curtailing the rights and liberties of the individual than any act Congress has passed, to my knowledge." A similar, although somewhat more favorable assessment of the bill was voiced by Representative Price on the floor of the House:

It is no exaggeration to call this civil-defense legislation a revolutionary departure in our jurisprudence. We are entering upon waters still in good part uncharted; we cannot be sure that the measure now before the Congress is the final answer to our problem—the field is too new for final answers. But I am confident that this legislation gets us off to a good start and I know that the Congress will keep our civil-defense preparations under constant review.[12]

With regard to allocation of functions, the Federal Civil Defense Act did not constitute a drastic deviation from earlier plans and recommendations. Primary responsibility for civil defense was vested expressly "in the several states and their political subdivisions," while the federal government was given mainly the tasks of overall guidance, planning, coordination and only modest operational functions. The character of the proposd federal civil defense agency was a matter of controversy during congressional hearings and debates. Basically, three forms of organization were suggested: the new service could be established either as a part of the Executive Office of the President, or as a branch of another department, especially the Defense Department, or as an independent agency. The first alternative did not receive very serious or extensive consideration. The main objection to this form of organization was apparently that the proposed agency was to exercise not only supervisory but also some operational functions which could not properly be performed within the Executive Office of the President.

The second alternative gave rise to more animated debate. The idea that the civil defense agency should be established as a fourth branch within the Department of Defense, a branch coequal with the three military services, was sponsored primarily by representatives of the American Municipal Association.[13] The proposal was predicated on the assumption that the character of modern warfare and modern defense preparations required close cooperation between military authorities and civil defense officials, and that this type of cooperation could only be achieved through the coordination of military and civil defense branches within the Defense Department. The idea was opposed not only by a majority of congressmen and representatives of private and civic groups, but also by spokesmen of the Defense Department who argued that the military establishment was fully occupied

[12] See 96 Cong. Rec. 16924, 17091, 16838.
[13] See Federal Civil Defense Administration, *Legislative History, Federal Civil Defense Act of 1950* (hereinafter cited as *LH 1950*), Advance Copy, vol. 1, pp. 42, 48-52.

with the performance of its primary duties and should not be burdened with additional functions. Behind this controversy loomed the larger question of military versus civilian control of the civil defense administration, although the sponsors of the departmental idea did not seem to endorse military supervision. The concept of civilian control was persistently stressed by many speakers and witnesses, especially in view of the considerable emergency powers granted by the statute. As Representative Harlow observed with regard to the appointment of top civil defense officials:

The thinking that I had in bringing this subject up was this: that when this process takes form in the time of an emergency, as contrasted to all other branches of the Government, the authority vested in the Administrator and this organization will be stupendous, far beyond anything ever before exercised in the country, and in line with the practice of this committee in all of its military legislation in the past as in connection with the Secretary of Defense and the Deputy Secretary of Defense, even with their relatively limited powers compared to the powers of this gentleman when there is an emergency, the committee very insistently wrote in "from civilian life" in order to make sure that civilians were in those positions.[14]

The Federal Civil Defense Act, as finally passed, established an independent agency—the so-called "Federal Civil Defense Administration"—whose director, subject to presidential supervision, was endowed with a vast range of powers in civil defense emergencies.

During 1950, another law was passed by Congress whose provisions were in many respects related to the problem of nonmilitary defense. The law, known as Defense Production Act and enacted on September 8, was also prompted by the Korean crisis and international cold war developments. The central aim of the act was to gear American industry for defense and to back up the defense effort with a stable economy. To accomplish this aim, the law established a system of priorities and allocations for materials and facilities, authorized the requisitioning and condemnation of such materials, provided for wage and price stabilization, for the settlement of labor disputes in defense industries, and for tightened control over credit operations. Partly on the basis of

[14] *Ibid.*, p. 56.

the Defense Production Act and partly on his own authority, President Truman, on December 16, 1950, created the Office of Defense Mobilization within the Executive Office of the President. This step was undertaken on the same day which witnessed the president's proclamation of the existense of a national emergency.[15] The director of the new defense mobilization office was given authority, on behalf of the president, "to direct, control and coordinate all mobilization activities of the executive branch of government, including but not limited to production, procurement, manpower, stabilization and transport activities." The office was designed as a small policy-making and coordinating, rather than an operating agency. The following year saw the mushrooming of several advisory boards and agencies under the office's general supervision.

Decline and Confusion

While the Korean war was in progress, the newly established agencies made a determined effort to live up to their assigned tasks, although the growing proliferation of functions and services boded ill for the development and implementation of a concerted program. With the termination of the war and the passing of the cold war crisis in the Far East, public concern with civil defense problems faded rapidly. The incoming Republican administration was dedicated to the resumption of peacetime standards and the reduction of governmental activities and services. The initiative and vigor of federal agencies operating in the civil defense area declined. A telling illustration of this decline can be found in the fact that in 1954 the major facilities of the Federal Civil Defense Administration were transferred from Washington to Battle Creek, Michigan. At the same time, the efficiency of nonmilitary defense programs was reduced by a growing rivalry between major agencies and by a prolific delegation of functions and services. On the top level, confusion prevailed primarily with respect to the functions of the Federal Civil Defense Adminis-

[15] This state of national emergency is still in existence today, mainly because the Korean war was ended by an armistice only and not by a peace treaty. Compare U.S. Congress, House of Representatives, Report to the Committee on the Judiciary, *Provisions of Federal Law in Effect in Time of National Emergency*, 87th Cong., 2d Sess. (January 25, 1962).

tration, the Office of Defense Mobilization, and the Defense Department. Apart from the problem of military rule in a post-attack situation, the Defense Department was concerned with military use of production resources, while the civil defense office required resources for civilian relief and the defense mobilization agency was supposed to mobilize and allocate resources to meet both military and civilian needs.[16]

The confused state and inaction of the nonmilitary defense machinery contrasted sharply with frightening new developments in arms and weapons. On November 1, 1952, the United States had exploded a thermonuclear device during Operation Ivy at Eniwetok Atoll in the Pacific Ocean. On August 8, 1953, a Russian announcement confirmed that the United States no longer had a monopoly of the hydrogen bomb. Full-scale thermonuclear tests conducted by the United States in the Pacific during 1953 and 1954 disclosed that the destructive effect of hydrogen bombs was far more widespread than had previously been assumed or imagined. In addition to the tremendous initial effects of shock, blast and heat or thermal radiation, the tests demonstrated the additional effects of initial nuclear radiation and of long-range residual radiation or radioactive "fallout." A test conducted at Bikini Atoll in the Pacific in March, 1954 showed that the radioactive fallout from a twelve to fifteen megaton explosion covered an area two hundred twenty miles long and twenty to forty miles wide. It was reported that a single hydrogen bomb could release more destructive energy than all the bombs dropped on Germany and Japan during World War II. At the same time, the armaments race was steadily intensified by the development of faster and more efficient delivery systems, including air and submarine launched missiles and intercontinental ballistic missiles. In the light of these changes, existing nonmilitary defense plans became increasingly unrealistic and outmoded. The extent of the radiation effects of thermonuclear explosions cast doubt on the value of a civil defense program founded predominantly on state and

[16] A modest attempt to reduce the existing confusion and duplication was made by the president in the Reorganization Plan No. 3 of 1953, effective June 12, 1953, which abolished the National Security Resources Board and the Office of Defense Mobilization and vested their assorted functions in a newly created Office of Defense Mobilization within the Executive Office of the President.

local government services. Also, the development of more rapid delivery systems reduced the significance of early warning methods and challenged the adequacy of policies geared to evacuation.

Despite the frightful prospects of a thermonuclear war, public attitude remained at the beginning strangely unaffected. Probably the very magnitude of the potential destruction produced a feeling of individual helplessness and apathy. It must also be said that the executive branch of government did little to stir the public from this apathy. The first attempts to re-evaluate nonmilitary defense programs were made by private and civic study groups. A review committee of the so-called "Project East River" acknowledged in 1955 the difficulties of industrial dispersal and emphasized the danger and fallacy of a program relying exclusively on evacuation as single civil defense technique. The report of the committee also urged a closer relationship between defense mobilization and civil defense activities and pointed to the need of new congressional legislation and greater federal leadership.[17] In a similar spirit, the National Planning Association examined the existing nonmilitary defense structure and found that lack of central direction and federal guidance rendered the system cumbersome and ineffective.[18]

Partly under the influence of these studies, Congress decided to take another hard look at the existing nonmilitary defense program. The first major investigation was conducted by a Subcommittee on Civil Defense of the Senate Armed Services Committee between February and June, 1955. In the course of these hearings, testimony was received from a great number of representatives of the administration, the military establishment and civic organizations. The testimony elucidated the effects of the

---

[17] Associated Universities, Inc., *1955 Review of Project East River* (New York, 1955). The original "Project East River" was a research program undertaken by a study group under the chairmanship of General Otto Nelson and jointly sponsored by the Federal Civil Defense Administration, the National Security Resources Board and the Defense Department. The major portions of the group's original report were issued during 1952. Compare Joseph E. McLean, "Project East River—Survival in the Atomic Age," *Bulletin of the Atomic Scientists*, 9: 247 (1953).

[18] See U. S. Senate, Hearings before the Subcommittee on Civil Defense of the Committee on Armed Services, *Civil Defense Program* (hereinafter cited as *Senate Hearings*), 84th Cong., 1st Sess. (1955), pt. 2, p. 815 (Exhibit 11: National Planning Association, "A Program for the Nonmilitary Defense of the United States").

new nuclear weapons and indicated the doubtful value of existing civil defense preparations. Representative Chet Holifield,
chairman of the Military Operations Subcommittee of the House
Committee on Government Operations, was invited to testify and
expressed strong disapproval of the administration's inactivity.
"I believe," he stated,

at this time only the President can give us the leadership that is necessary to this program. Only the President can give to our people the
sense of urgency necessary to secure the support of public opinion.
Only the President can break the log jam of public confusion and indifference on the part of an uninformed populace. . . . The responsibility under our Constitution for the preservation of our Nation lies at
the door of the President who is also our Commander-in-Chief. . . . In
the face of this undeniable set of facts I cannot understand the apathy
and indifference on the part of the President of the United States in
bringing to the American people the facts about the impact of these
weapons and I cannot understand his failure to take leadership, federal
leadership, in the formulating of target area defense plans.[19]

Congressman Holifield also criticized the lack of congressional
initiative and urged the speedy enactment of new civil defense
legislation. The Senate subcommittee agreed that the civil defense program was in need of reform, but voiced the opinion
that the Civil Defense Act of 1950 might lend itself to this task
as its potentialities had not been fully realized.

During the following year, the nonmilitary defense problem
was subjected to the most thorough and comprehensive congressional examination of the postwar period. The examination was
undertaken by the Holifield subcommittee of the House Committee on Government Operations. During the hearings which
lasted from January to June of 1956, over two hundred witnesses
appeared before the subcommittee including representatives from
the fields of science, engineering, and medicine, public officials
at the federal, state and local levels of government, the chairman
and members of the Joint Chiefs of Staff and other military witnesses, and private citizens, civic leaders, and spokesmen of
national organizations. The public transcripts of the testimony
comprised seven impressive volumes. From the evidence presented at the hearings, the subcommittee concluded that a poten-

[19] *Ibid.*, p. 661.

tial enemy was able to strike the United States with high-yield nuclear weapons and that the threat of such attack required a national program of civil defense, under federal leadership, to insure survival of the nation. In the words of the subcommittee report, issued at the termination of the hearings:

As weapons grow larger, so do the requirements of planning and with nationwide fallout as a hazard, the geographic limits on the planning problem are the nation itself.[20]

In order to improve the existing nonmilitary defense program, the report formulated a series of concrete proposals, including the recommendations that federal legislation should be redrafted to vest the basic responsibility for civil defense in the federal government, "with the states and local units of government having an important supporting role," and that the new legislation should create a permanent Department of Civil Defense, combining the civil defense functions of the Office of Defense Mobilization and of the Federal Civil Defense Administration. As the report further specified, the Department of Civil Defense, in consultation with the Defense Department, was to formulate a master plan for nationwide civil defense, a plan which was to be based on the key civil defense measure of shelter protection against the blast, heat, and radiation effects of nuclear explosions.

Following the issuance of its report, the subcommittee began the drafting of legislation to implement the described proposals. In January of 1957, this legislative measure was introduced by Representative Holifield with the endorsement of every member of the subcommittee and similar or identical bills were soon submitted by other members of the House. The Holifield bill revised congressional policy by affirming, in its declaration of objectives, that "civil defense is an integral part of national defense and a direct responsibility of the Federal Government in keeping with its constitutional duties to provide for the common defense and to protect the states against invasion." The declaration added that "Congress recognizes that the states and their political subdivisions have an important supporting role and should be assisted

---

[20] H. Rep. 2946, 24th Intermediate Report of the Committee on Government Operations, *Civil Defense for National Survival* (hereinafter cited as *Subcommittee Report*), 84th Cong., 2d Sess. (July 27, 1956), p. 45.

and encouraged to perform appropriate civil-defense tasks consistent with the national plan of civil defense provided for in this
act." With regard to administrative organization, the bill envisaged the establishment of a new executive department, to be
known as Department of Civil Defense.[21] This department was
to exercise the functions of the existing Federal Civil Defense
Administration and also those functions of the Office of Defense
Mobilization which the president determined to be of a civil
defense nature, a provision which was designed to eliminate
inter-agency rivalry and duplication of services. In addition to
the creation of the new department, the bill provided for the
establishment of a Military Liaison Committee as a bridge to the
military, of a Scientific Advisory Board as a bridge to science,
and of a Civil Defense Advisory Council as a bridge to local,
industrial, labor, and civic interests. The Holifield bill also revised
the emergency provisions of the 1950 act, mainly by stipulating
a congressional intent to retain civilian control of civil defense
measures and by strengthening the powers of the departmental
secretary to requisition supplies and to direct state and local
operations.

During February and March, 1957, hearings were held by the
subcommittee on the Holifield bill and related measures and testimony was again received from federal agencies, private organizations, and state and local civil defense officials. Although
various amendments were suggested at the hearings, the subcommittee's proposed legislation was endorsed in whole or in part
by virtually all national organizations and by most government
witnesses. Nevertheless, some spokesmen close to President Eisenhower, especially representatives of the Bureau of the Budget,
expressed strong reservations or disapproval. Actually, the sub-

[21] In drafting the bill, the Holifield subcommittee examined several alternate or counter-proposals such as the establishment of the federal civil defense agency in the Executive Office of the President or as a branch of the
Department of Defense. The first alternative was found to weaken the
agency's capacity to exercise operating responsibilities and its accountability
to Congress, while the second proposal was discarded as jeopardizing the
independent status of civil defense and the principle of civilian control. See
H. Rep. 839, 80th Report by the Committee on Government Operations,
Status of Civil Defense Legislation (hereinafter cited as *Status of CDL*),
85th Cong., 1st Sess. (July 22, 1957), pp. 26-27.

committee was well aware of the reluctance of the administration to exert leadership and of congressional hesitation to appropriate the necessary funds. Despite an earlier admission by President Eisenhower in July, 1956, that "our whole civil defense effort needs both strengthening and modernizing," [22] it had become increasingly obvious that the policy aims of the administration did not coincide with the views of the Holifield group. Already on February 8, 1957, a draft measure was introduced in the House of Representatives by the Federal Civil Defense Administration, a measure which was approved by the Bureau of the Budget and apparently reflected the current views of the administration. Whereas the Holifield bill envisaged a complete revision of federal civil defense legislation, the draft measure contained only a number of moderate amendments to the act of 1950. The chief effect of these amendments was that the policy declaration of the 1950 act was changed to read that "the responsibility for civil defense shall be vested jointly in the Federal Government and the several states and their political subdivisions", a change which departed both from the original bill which placed this responsibility primarily in the states and localities, and from the Holifield bill which placed it primarily in the federal government. During the hearings on the Holifield measure, the Assistant Director of the Budget testified that the amendments submitted in February constituted the total legislative program of the president at the time. The Assistant Director also criticized the proposal of the Holifield bill to create a new civil defense department and indicated presidential disapproval of the idea:

It has been concluded that from the executive standpoint this step is not necessary at this time. The problems and inadequacies of civil defense appear to stem largely from those factors such as dramatic development of weapons capability . . . rather than from organizational difficulties. As a result the President does not propose at this time that the Federal Civil Defense Administration be made an executive department.[23]

[22] Letter of the president to Federal Civil Defense Administrator Peterson, of July 17, 1956; see U.S. Congress, House of Representatives, Hearings before a Subcommittee of the Committee on Government Operations, *New Civil Defense Legislation* (hereinafter cited as *Legislative Hearings*), 85th Cong., 1st Sess. (February-March, 1957), p. 185.

[23] *Ibid.*, p. 187.

Reorganization of 1958

While the amendments introduced in February of 1957 comprised the legislative changes which the president considered at the time desirable, the administration was not adverse to further organizational reform of the nonmilitary defense system. Later in the same year, the Bureau of the Budget contracted with McKinsey and Company, a management consultant firm, to study the problem of administrative reorganization. Under its contract, the firm presented a study in two volumes which were submitted respectively in December, 1957 and March, 1958. The McKinsey report agreed with the Holifield subcommittee that the existing nonmilitary defense system invited rivalry, confusion and duplication, especially with respect to the functions of the Office of Defense Mobilization and the Federal Civil Defense Administration. As possible methods for overcoming the existing confusion, the report explored the executive department concept recommended by the Holifield subcommittee, and the idea that civil defense be constituted as a part of the Executive Office of the President. As major drawbacks of the Holifield proposal the report mentioned the aspects that older departments would not readily accept direction by a new department in the field of civil defense activities, that departmental status would tend to freeze the organizational structure, and that the president's ability to make quick adaptations would be retarded. The advantages of the Executive Office arrangement, on the other hand, were found in the prospect that it would promote an integrated and consistent civil defense program, that the stature and publicity of the agency would be enhanced, and that the president would have flexibility in changing delegations and modifying the administrative structure quickly to meet changing needs.

On the basis of the McKinsey findings, President Eisenhower, in his budget message for 1958, drew attention to the outmoded character of the existing nonmilitary defense structure and to the need of administrative reform.

The rapid technical advances of military science have led to a serious overlap among agencies carrying on these leadership and planning functions. Because the situation will continue to change and because these functions transcend the responsibility of any single department or agency, I have concluded that they should be vested in no one short of the President. I will make recommendations to the Congress on this subject.[24]

On April 24, 1958, the president submitted to Congress a reorganization plan which followed almost literally the recommendations of the McKinsey report. Under the provisions of the plan, all authority in the field of civil defense was transferred to the president. At the same time, the Office of Defense Mobilization and the Federal Civil Defense Administration were abolished and replaced by a new agency in the Executive Office of the President, called the Office of Defense and Civilian Mobilization; finally, the president was authorized to delegate or reassign nonmilitary defense functions vested in him to the new agency. As the reorganization order was not rejected by either house of Congress, the plan became effective on July 1, 1958.[25] On the same day, the president delegated to the director of the new agency all the functions transferred to him by the reorganization plan. Congress supplemented the reorganization of the civil defense structure by the enactment of two statutes. On August 8, 1958, a law was passed which contained most of the legislative changes proposed by the administration in February of 1957. Among other things, the law changed the declaration of policy of the 1950 act by making civil defense a joint responsibility of the federal government and of the states and their political subdivisions. Another statute of August 26 changed the name of the new federal agency to Office of Civil and Defense Mobilization.

The reorganization plan was open to criticism on several counts. As the Holifield group noted in the course of a subcommittee investigation, the most questionable aspects of the plan resided in the president's exercise of an almost unprecedented reorganization authority and in the location of the new agency in the Executive Office of the President with the result of a limited accountability to Congress. Shortly after its establishment, the

---

[24] See H.Rep. 1874, 26th Report by the Committee on Government Operations, *Analysis of Civil Defense Reorganization* (hereinafter cited as *Analysis*), 85th Cong., 2d Sess. (June 12, 1958), p. 18.

[25] Reorganization Plan No. 1 of 1958, 23 Fed. Reg. 4991 (July 1, 1958); 72 Stat. 1799 (1958).

new Office of Civil and Defense Mobilization made a moderate
effort to implement at least some of the earlier recommendations
of the Holifield subcommittee. In May of 1958, the director of the
federal office announced a "national shelter policy" which was
sponsored by the administration. The program did not envisage
strong government initiative, but merely intended to encourage
large scale private construction of fallout shelters. In the opinion
of the Holifield subcommittee, the policy provided merely for a
"demonstration program, not a shelter construction program." [26]
In October of the same year, the president announced the so-
called "National Plan for Civil Defense and Defense Mobilization," a master plan which, amplified by forty-one annexes, set
forth the basic policy guidelines of the administration's civil defense program. Annex ten of this program, issued in December,
contained the "national shelter plan" which, again, was based
mainly on the principle of stimulation, information and self-help,
and did not provide for direct and substantial federal assistance
for shelter construction.

In August, 1959, the Governors' Conference at its meeting in
Puerto Rico adopted a resolution urging the several states to in-
form their citizens on the dangers of nuclear fallout and to
encourage individual shelter construction. At the request of Governor Rockefeller of New York, a special White House Conference
on Fallout Protection was held in January, 1960, at which the
civil defense committee of the Governors' Conference met with
federal officials to consider possible ways of stimulating the construction of fallout shelters. Although the agenda of the meeting
included suggestions for several new federal activities to support
state programs, the Governors' committee departed with no firm
commitments of increased federal assistance. New hearings on
federal civil defense operations and shelter planning were conducted by the Holifield subcommittee in March, 1960. The testimony received at these hearings convinced the subcommittee that
little progress had been made since 1958 in the field of shelter
construction, a finding whose significance was highlighted by the
breakdown of the Paris Summit Conference in May, 1960.

[26] H.Rep. 2554, 34th Report by the Committee on Government Operations,
Atomic Shelter Programs (hereinafter cited as *AS Programs*), 85th Cong.,
2d Sess. (August 12, 1958), p. 12.

There is a curious kind of unreality in American life today associated with civil defense. The unreality lies in the enormous distance which separates the need and the means of fulfilling it. Civil defense planning is rudimentary, decentralized, uneven, often irrelevant, despite the growing nuclear threat. . . . The subcommittee reaffirms its view, first expressed in 1956 and restated in subsequent reports, that any effective national plan for civil defense must be based on the key measure of shelter protection. The setting forth of desirable objectives and the listing of functions which various levels of government and the public are expected to perform, in the absence of an effective shelter construction program, cannot properly be represented as constituting a national plan for civil defense.[27]

Reorganization of 1961

When President Kennedy took office in January 1961, international relations were characterized by ferment and mounting tensions. The Congo crisis had been developing ever since that country achieved independence in June, 1960. Policies of the United Nations in the Congo had led to Soviet attacks on Secretary-General Hammarskjold and to proposals of a "troika" or three-man secretariate. On January 1, 1961, the United States had called upon the Southeast Asia Treaty Organization to check communist invasion of Laos while, on January 3, President Eisenhower had broken off diplomatic relations with Cuba. In his State-of-the-Union Message of January 30, President Kennedy pointed to the many perils facing the nation abroad and called for a bolder approach to these problems. In March, the president urged a rapid missile build-up and a drastic increase in the military budget. On June 3 and 4, President Kennedy, during his tour of Europe, held talks with Soviet Premier Khrushchev in Vienna where nuclear testing, disarmament and the unresolved situation of West Berlin were among the many irritating items on the agenda. From this time on, international relations deteriorated rapidly. Shortly after the Vienna meeting, the nuclear test-ban negotiations in Geneva broke down. Premier Khrushchev began to insist on the speedy conclusion of a peace treaty with Germany during the current year, announcing that failure to reach such a

[27] H.Rep. 2069, 21st Report by the Committee on Government Operations, *Civil Defense Shelter Policy and Postattack Recovery Planning* (hereinafter cited as *CD Shelter Policy*), 86th Cong., 2d Sess. (July 1, 1960), pp. 2, 37.

settlement would lead to a separate peace treaty between the Soviet Union and East Germany. On July 8, the Soviet Premier cancelled scheduled cutbacks in armed forces and increased the arms budget to prepare for potential conflict.

The described cold war developments and especially the explosive Berlin situation prompted President Kennedy to make a broad reappraisal of the nation's defense posture. In this reappraisal, considerations of military defense clearly overshadowed the civil defense aspect. Nevertheless, the requirement of maximum civilian survival in the case of nuclear attack loomed large in governmental planning of the time. In any event, the policies of the administration reflected a conviction that only expanded Pentagon leadership could impart new vitality and vigor to the nation's nonmilitary defense program. The first clear indications of the president's plans with regard to nonmilitary defense were contained in his Civil Defense Message to Congress of May 25.[28] In this message, the president observed that "one major element of the national security program which this nation has never squarely faced up to is civil defense." In order to overcome this deficiency and strengthen national security as a whole, the president urged the speedy "initiation of a nationwide long-range program of identifying present fallout shelter capacity and providing shelter in new and existing structures," a program which "would protect millions of people against the hazards of radioactive fallout in the event of large-scale nuclear attack." The president emphasized, however, that the implementation of this program required not only new legislative authority and more funds, but also new organizational arrangements. As solution to the administrative problem, the president suggested the assignment of operational responsibility for the program to the Defense Department although he added that "it is important that this function remain civilian in nature and leadership; and this feature will not be changed." At the same time, the message proposed the reconstitution of the Office of Civil and Defense Mobilization as a small staff agency with coordinating functions, under the name of Office of Emergency Planning.

At the beginning of July, government planning was stepped up and studies on the availability of manpower and production

[28] H.Doc. 174, 87th Cong., 1st Sess. (May 25, 1961).

facilities in the event of emergency were conducted by military, civil defense, and economic agencies.[29] Following a series of White House discussions, the director of the Office of Civil and Defense Mobilization on July 7 submitted to President Kennedy a memorandum which endorsed and amplified the president's earlier civil defense message. "It is my belief," the director stated,

that such assignments as are herein proposed offer promise of an invigorated, meaningful, nonmilitary defense program, if supported by a larger commitment of Federal resources, and buttressed by a continuation of the Presidential concern, leadership, and support which you have demonstrated.[30]

On July 20, the proposed administrative changes were implemented by an executive order of the president.[31]

The executive order relied very heavily on the reorganization plan of 1958 which had stipulated a continuing power of delegation and reassignment of functions by the president. Under the terms of the order, the Secretary of Defense—subject to the direction and control of the president—was delegated virtually all functions contained in the Federal Civil Defense Act of 1950 and vested in the president pursuant to the reorganization plan of 1958. These functions were to include the development and execution of a fallout shelter program, an adequate warning system, emergency assistance to state and local governments in postattack situations, and the protection of emergency operations of state and local government agencies in accordance with plans for the continuity of government. The order also transformed the Office of Civil and Defense Mobilization into a strictly advisory branch within the Executive Office of the President. Although the old name of the office was retained in the order, it was understood that legislation would soon be introduced to change its name to Office of Emergency Planning. Among other things, the new

[29] For details of various studies and reports preceding the 1961 reorganization, see H.Rep. 1249, 9th Report by the Committee on Government Operations, *New Civil Defense Program* (hereinafter abbreviated as *New CD Program*), 87th Cong., 1st Sess. (Sept. 21, 1961), pp. 12-25.

[30] See U.S. Congress, House, Hearings before a Subcommittee of the Committee on Government Operations, *Civil Defense 1961* (hereinafter cited as *CD Hearings 1961*), 87th Cong., 1st Sess. (August, 1961), App. 2, p. 379.

[31] Exec. Order No. 10952, 26 Fed. Reg. 6577 (1961); reproduced in *CD Hearings 1961*, App. 3A, pp. 379-381.

agency was directed to advise and assist the president in planning, directing and coordinating the nation's civil defense and defense mobilization program; in reviewing and coordinating civil defense activities of federal departments and agencies with each other and with the activities of states; and in enlisting state, local, and private participation. The agency was also called upon to develop plans and to coordinate preparations for the continuity of federal, state, and local government operations in order to insure "effective functioning of civilian political authority under any emergency condition." The order was to become effective on August 1, 1961.

The president's order was accompanied on the same day by a White House press release and by statements of the director of the Office of Civil and Defense Mobilization and of the Secretary of Defense. The press release quoted the president as saying that "in calling upon the resources of the Department of Defense to stimulate and invigorate our civil defense preparations, I am acting under the Federal premise that responsibility for the accomplishment of civil defense preparations at the Federal level is vested in me." The release also stated the president's intention to submit to Congress in the near future a request for increased federal support for the civil defense program. The statement of the civil defense director observed that the expanded federal commitments implied in the reorganization were

indeed encouraging developments to those state and local government leaders, civil defense officials, and selfless dedicated supporters of civil defense who have labored these many years against such discouraging odds to bring about a state of civil defense preparedness in this country.

Secretary of Defense, Robert S. McNamara, pointed out that civil defense would be organized in his department "as a civilian function, drawing where necessary on the military departments for available support" and that "civil defense must be integrated with all aspects of military defense against thermonuclear attack." [32] On July 25, the president addressed the nation over the radio and television stressing the necessity of military build-up and civil defense reform in the light of international tensions and especially the Berlin crisis. On the following day, legislative re-

[32] See *ibid.*, App. 3B, p. 382; App. 3C, p. 382; App. 3D, p. 383.

quests were submitted by the president to Congress, requests which included additional appropriations for military and civil defense, and an increase in the manpower of the armed forces. The legislative measures were passed by Congress with unprecedented speed. On August 1, an Office of Civil Defense was constituted in the Defense Department to carry out the responsibilities assigned to the Secretary of Defense. The reorganization was completed on September 22 by a legislative change of the name of the federal civil defense and mobilization agency to Office of Emergency Planning.

There can be no doubt that the reorganization of 1961 posed serious questions with respect to the proper allocation and exercise of emergency powers. As in the case of previous reorganizations, the new arrangements established in 1961 were subjected to extensive scrutiny by the Holifield subcommittee. Somewhat surprisingly, the inquiries and comments of the subcommittee displayed a very tolerant and obliging attitude toward the policy decisions of the new administration. The attention of the subcommittee appeared directed entirely at the clarification of assigned roles and functions, rather than the basic propriety of the new arrangement itself.

In his opening statement at the beginning of hearings conducted by the subcommittee in August, 1961, Chairman Holifield observed correctly that "the Military Operations Subcommittee, under my chairmanship, has been a sharp critic of civil defense," adding that "we intend, as a subcommittee, so long as I am chairman, to maintain our friendly and sympathetic but critical eye on civil defense;" however, the critical faculty was not used significantly in subsequent inquiries. In an appreciative mood, the chairman stated that

I, for one, find it encouraging and fortunate that President Kennedy understands the importance of an effective civil defense program, and has declared it a key element in his recommendations to strengthen our defenses and our capability to resist Communist aggression.[33]

In the course of the hearings, a considerable amount of time was devoted to the problem of the precise responsibilities of, and the relationship between, the Defense Department and the new Office

[33] *Ibid.,* pp. 1-2.

of Emergency Planning. Secretary of Defense McNamara pointed out that, especially with the assignment of the shelter program, his Department exercised major control over civil defense while the Office of Emergency Planning was to function as an advisory and coordinating agency without operational authority. According to the director of the old Office of Civil and Defense Mobilization, the reorganization order—apart from the assignment of other, specific tasks—conferred upon the Office of Emergency Planning a mandate to set policy, assign duties, and coordinate functions, including those of the Defense Department. Chairman Holifield stressed the importance of the coordinating and planning responsibility without which the Emergency Planning Office would very likely be "engaged in a futile exercise." [34]

The subcommittee report of September, 1961, commended again the president for his executive leadership and for his recognition of "the vital importance of an effective civil defense." The basic effect of the reorganization measures was described in the report as follows:

These actions would mark a full turn of the wheel in two cycles of Government operations: One is the return to the Defense Department of civil defense planning functions which had reposed there in earlier years; the other is the revesting in two separate agencies of civil defense and resource mobilization planning functions which had been consolidated in the Office of Civil and Defense Mobilization in 1958.[35]

As the report continued, the reorganization of 1961 re-established "the pre-1958 division of labor between civil defense and defense mobilization with this important difference. For the first time since the early planning work after World War II, civil defense will be housed in a regular Cabinet department of the Government—and in the biggest department of them all, the Department of Defense." The subcommittee was not unaware of the fact that the reorganization raised "problems old and new;" however, these problems were viewed mainly in terms of a reconciliation of conflicting functions and objectives and not as a challenge to the underlying premises of the reorganization. "Civil defense, it was commonly said," the report stated,

[34] *Ibid.*, pp. 5-13, 23-24, 51-61, 65, 66.
[35] *New CD Program*, pp. 5, 9.

is and must remain essentially civilian in nature. At the same time it must be integrated with military defense to take advantage of the great resources of the Department of Defense and to signify the essential unity of military-civil defense in the nuclear age. Yet civil defense must not encroach upon nor interfere with the performance of vital military missions. Conflicting values or objectives such as these would have to be reconciled. Furthermore, civil defense encompasses many functions and involves many agencies of the Federal Government. Which functions were suitable for transfer to the Department of Defense? Which should remain with the new Office of Emergency Planning? Which should be delegated or redelegated to other Federal departments and agencies? What assurances would there be that the bifurcation of civil defense and resources mobilization would not give rise to the overlapping, duplication, and confusion that characterized FCDA-ODM operations for the largest part of a decade?[36]

Concerning the transfer of civil defense functions to the Defense Department, the report recognized that "the committee proposed at one time that the importance and urgency of civil defense justified a separate department of Cabinet rank. The assignment of civil defense responsibilities to the Department of Defense is a compromise." Whatever doubts the subcommittee might have had concerning the propriety of this compromise were apparently outweighed by the advantages of the new arrangement. One of these advantages was the prospect that the arrangement would put an end to the "low status, meager financial support, and limited accomplishments" of preceding civil defense agencies. "The Department of Defense," the report observed, "with its huge budget, its great and varied resources, and its far-flung network of organizations could easily absorb civil defense functions. Undoubtedly a Department-sponsored program would command more public attention and inspire more confidence in the Congress that civil defense would be a serious concern of the Government." Another advantage was discovered in the commanding position of the Secretary of Defense.

As far as military agencies and resources are concerned, despite the immense difficulties of coordination, the Secretary will have this advantage: That he is the civilian "commander" of the entire defense establishment. His word will be law to the responsible military department heads and military command chiefs. In this position of overriding

[36] *Ibid.*, pp. 29, 10.

authority and command, the Secretary of Defense will be able not only to coordinate military resources and services for civil defense work but to prevent major military policy decisions and actions which conflict unnecessarily with civil defense objectives.[37]

With regard to the functions of the new Office of Emergency Planning, the report admitted that "more than a little confusion has been created by the Executive order concerning OEP's role in civil defense." This confusion was found to derive primarily from "differences of understanding as to the 'advisory' or staff role of OEP" and from the "rather chaotic situation in 'delegations' to Federal departments and agencies." The report observed that the Office had no significant statutory powers in its own right and that civil defense functions withheld from the Secretary of Defense were reserved to the president and not to the director of the new Office. "Whatever policy, supervisory, or coordinating functions OEP performs in the civil defense field," the report concluded, "will be done by virtue of its mandate to assist and advise the president. Except in this advisory role, the OEP Director is expressly relieved of civil defense responsibilities delegated to his predecessor by the president in 1958." [38] The role of the new Office was considered stronger in areas outside the civil defense field, especially in defense mobilization or resources management. Moreover, apart from the advisory function to the president, the Office was expressly assigned the task to develop plans for the continuity of government operations in the event of attack. The civil defense field was the object of additional hearings conducted by the Holifield subcommittee in February, 1962 which, however, were concerned primarily with the national shelter program.[39]

The hearings and reports of the Holifield subcommittee served the very valuable purpose of clarifying functions and responsibilities resulting from the 1961 reorganization. Without detract-

[37] *Ibid.,* pp. 30, 9, 31.
[38] *Ibid.,* pp. 32-33.
[39] See U.S. Congress, House, Hearings before a Subcommittee of the Committee on Government Operations, *Civil Defense 1962* (hereinafter cited as *CD Hearings 1962*), 87th Cong., 2d Sess. (February, 1962); also H.Rep. 1754, 16th Report by the Committee on Government Operations, *National Fallout Shelter Program* (hereinafter cited as *National Fallout Shelter Program*), 87th Cong., 2d Sess. (May 31, 1962).

ing from this accomplishment, one may legitimately wonder whether, in this instance, the subcommittee has lived up to its role to act as the "conscience" of civil defense. The main objective of the reorganization was obviously a more rapid and efficient development of the fallout shelter program and related civil defense measures. Despite the urgency of this goal, however, there are many arguments speaking against the new arrangement, arguments deriving from a concern with constitutional safeguards in emergency situations. Actually, some of these arguments had been stated very ably by the Holifield subcommittee on previous occasions. The major problems posed by the new arrangement involve the president's reorganization authority and the administrative structure of nonmilitary defense. The executive order of July, 1961, reaffirmed the premise of the reorganization plan of 1958 according to which basic responsibility for civil defense is vested in the president himself, and reassigned various functions to the new agency in the president's office and to the Department of Defense. It is not established that the reorganization plan of 1958 or other orders constitute a sufficient basis for such a broad transfer of responsibilities without the benefit of prior change in the enabling legislation. As the Holifield subcommittee observed in 1958, "it is doubtful that the Congress intended the reorganization authority to permit the transfer of major functions to the President himself." It is also useful to recall the subcommittee's remark that "the vesting of functions directly in the President is bound to create an area of uncertainty regarding his accountability to the Congress for administrative performance." [40] Similar doubts apply to the president's power of continued reassignment and cross-agency delegation of functions in the executive branch outside congressional control.

Regarding the administrative structure established in 1961, it appears that the reorganization combines the disadvantages of two alternative arrangements previously considered by the Holifield subcommittee. During the preparation of civil defense legislation in 1957, it was pointed out that the transfer of major functions to the Defense Department would have the probable effect of reducing the status of civil defense, subordinating civil defense considerations to military requirements and of jeopardiz-

[40] *Analysis,* pp. 5, 6.

ing civilian control over civil defense activities.[41] In its analysis
of the administration's plan of 1958, the subcommittee argued
that a civil defense agency located in the president's office would
tend to be limited to advisory and coordinating rather than operating responsibilities—an assessment which was fully borne out
by the reorganization of 1961. The major deficiency of the presidential office arrangement, however, was found in the likelihood
that "shrouded in the aura of his high office," the president's subordinates might "plead a confidential relationship to the President
and stand silent before the Congress." [42] The absence of full
accountability to Congress—especially if coupled with the possibility of military supervision of major functions—must be a matter
of concern in view of the vast emergency powers vested in the
nonmilitary defense administration. In the event of all-out nuclear
war or in cases of overpowering necessity, the president and his
subordinates may well be entitled, under the president's war
powers, to take all necessary action even without congressional
authorization or control, although the president's finding of necessity would remain subject to judicial review. However, nonmilitary defense activities are not so narrowly limited, and comprise
also preattack and postattack situations where the emergency may
be less compelling and where "inherent" executive powers would
not apply. In reference to these situations, a nonmilitary defense
organization would appear preferable which followed more
closely existing legislative assignments of power and in which the
exercise of functions remained more fully subject to congressional supervision.

2. NATIONAL EMERGENCY POWERS

The powers which the president and other executive officers
may exercise in implementing nonmilitary defense programs are
based in part on congressional statutes; other independent powers
are likely to be invoked in cases of civil defense emergency
depending on the urgency of the situation. The major pertinent
statutes in this area were enacted by Congress in 1950, in the

[41] *Status of CDL,* p. 26.
[42] *Analysis,* p. 5.

form of the Defense Production Act and the Federal Civil Defense Act.[43] Both acts have been amended on numerous occasions. The Defense Production Act reflected congressional preoccupation with the impact of the Korean crisis on the nation's economy and defense preparedness. As the declaration of policy of the act states:

In view of the present international situation and in order to provide for the national defense and national security, our mobilization effort continues to require some diversion of certain materials and facilities from civilian use to military and related purposes. It also requires the development of preparedness programs and the expansion of productive capacity and supply beyond the levels needed to meet the civilian demand, in order to reduce the time required for full mobilization in the event of an attack on the United States.

The governmental activities authorized by the Defense Production Act were allocated by the statute, in large measure, to the president himself. Most of these functions were subsequently delegated to the Office of Defense Mobilization and later to the Office of Civil and Defense Mobilization. Today, the major powers seem to be vested again in the president and, through him, in the Office of Emergency Planning and in other agencies and departments.

The governmental powers granted in the act are regularly of a long-range character and are not directly geared to an immediate defense emergency. Moreover, some of the more drastic emergency functions were revoked after the termination of the Korean crisis. The latter functions related primarily to the condemnation and requisitioning of materials and facilities, to price and wage stabilization, and to the settlement of labor disputes. In its present form, the act contemplates primarily the implementation of certain long-range preparedness measures by the president and other officers to whom functions have been delegated. These measures include the establishment of a system of priorities and allocations for materials and facilities, the granting of financial assistance for the expansion of productive capacity, and the activation of pro-

[43] Other statutes related to the area are the Trade Agreements Extension Act of 1958, the Federal Disaster Act of 1950, the National Security Act of 1947, and the Strategic and Critical Material Stock Piling Act of 1946.

grams to facilitate the production of goods and services necessary for national security.[44]

The first title of the act authorizes the president to require that performance under certain contracts or orders which he deems necessary for the national defense shall take priority over performance under any other contract or order, and to allocate materials and facilities in such a manner as the national defense may require. These powers are not to be used, however, unless the president finds that a material is scarce and essential to the national defense and that the defense requirements cannot otherwise be met without creating a significant dislocation of the material's distribution in the civilian market to such a degree as to cause appreciable hardship. According to another section, the president, in order to expedite production and deliveries or services under government contracts, may authorize federal departments or agencies to guarantee in whole or in part any public or private financing institution; he may also make provision for loans to private business enterprises for the expansion of capacity, the development of technological processes, or the production of essential materials. Both functions may be exercised without regard to the limitations of existing law. If the president finds that high-cost sources of nonprocessed material will result in a decrease in essential supplies, he may provide for subsidy payments on any such domestically produced material; also, upon a certification by the Secretary of Agriculture or Interior that a particular strategic product is likely to be in short supply in time of war or other national emergency, he may initiate programs for the development of substitutes for such strategic products.

More important in the present context are the powers derived from the Federal Civil Defense Act. As originally passed, the act allocated virtually all functions to the Federal Civil Defense Administrator. Under the terms of the reorganization plan of 1958, however, all civil defense powers were vested directly in the president, only to be delegated, in large measure, to the director of the Office of Civil and Defense Mobilization and, in 1961, to the Office of Emergency Planning and the Defense De-

---

[44] For the text of the act as currently in effect see S.Rep. 1124, *11th Annual Report of the Activities of the Joint Committee on Defense Production,* 87th Cong., 2d Sess. (January 23, 1962), pp. 393-405.

partment. Nevertheless, final supervision and control of all functions, and in some cases exclusive responsibility, remains in the hands of the president.

The act distinguishes between general "powers and duties" and "emergency authority," apparently with the understanding that the former could be used in all situations, even in the absence of emergency, while the latter would be exercised in case of large-scale catastrophe. Among the regular "powers and duties," the section dealing with governmental acquisition of private property deserves brief mention. Due to the basic operational responsibilities of the Defense Department under the reorganization order of 1961, this power seems to be vested today mainly in the Secretary of Defense, subject to presidential control. The section grants the authority to procure by condemnation or otherwise, construct, lease, transport, store, maintain, renovate or distribute materials and facilities for civil defense, with the right to take immediate possession thereof. Acquisition "by condemnation" obviously refers to the taking of private property through regular condemnation proceedings in a court of competent jurisdiction. However, the authority granted by the act is much broader as suggested by the phrase "or otherwise" which signifies that, apart from contractual transfer and condemnation, the government may under certain conditions requisition private property for public purposes without judicial proceedings. Nevertheless, it must be added that, at least in this particular section, the authority of the government is carefully circumscribed and qualified. Above all, the procurement power can only be exercised in accordance with the requirements of existing law in the sense that statutory provisions concerning negotiations, transfer of title and determination of compensation must be observed. Moreover, the act adds the proviso that the procuring officer may only lease real property, but cannot acquire fee title to this property unless specifically authorized by act of Congress.[45] Also, the acquiring officer is required to

[45] This proviso was specified by an amendment to the act of June 25, 1952. In August of 1956, a further proviso was added according to which the acquiring officer must come to an agreement with the Committees on Armed Services of the Senate and House of Representatives before entering into real property transactions involving the lease, acquisition of fee title, or a transfer of real property belonging to the United States, if the estimated annual rental, price, or value is more than $25,000.

report at least quarterly to Congress all property acquisitions made under this section of the act.

The broadest latitude of powers is granted in the title of the act dealing with "emergency authority." The powers were originally attributed to the Civil Defense Administrator; but under the reorganization order of 1961, the entire stand-by authority of this title is expressly vested in the president.[46] During congressional hearings and in debates on the floor, apprehension and concern were expressed primarily in reference to the emergency provisions of the act. As Representative Short observed on the floor of the House: "In the case of an atomic attack the power of the Administrator would be almost unlimited." In the course of the House hearings, Representative Vinson seconded this observation by saying:

I doubt whether you have ever seen language as broad as this. It makes this man a complete dictator. He can take over all the realty of the United States. . . . I do not find any objection to the objective. Nobody could find objection to that. But your broad latitude: If it was administered according to the authority here, you could just run the whole country. Absolutely.

Representative Kilday added: "It is more power than was granted to the President in the War Powers Act." [47]

As the act stipulates, the provisions of the emergency title become operative only during the existence of a state of civil defense emergency. The existence of such an emergency "may be proclaimed by the President or by concurrent resolution of the Congress if the President in such proclamation, or the Congress in such resolution, finds that an attack upon the United States has occurred or is anticipated and that the national safety therefore requires an invocation of the provisions of this title." The act also provides that the emergency may be proclaimed with respect to a designated geographic area or areas when the president determines that an attack has been made upon or is anticipated within such area. It should be observed that a civil defense emergency does not necessarily arise with a presidential declaration of a

[46] Exec. Order No. 10952, 26 Fed. Reg. 6577 (July 20, 1961), Sec. 3(b). Compare *CD Hearings 1961,* p. 38; and *New CD Program,* p. 35.
[47] See *LH 1950,* pp. 263, 277, 279.

national emergency and that a special proclamation or at least notification is required in order to put the provisions of the title in operation. Also, it may be useful to point out that the existence of a civil defense emergency does not necessarily coincide with a declaration of war or actual warfare. Possibly, there may be a declared war without the existence of a civil defense emergency due to the absence of an attack or anticipated attack upon the United States. On the other hand, the proclamation of a civil defense emergency in case of an anticipated attack does not seem to depend necessarily on preceding warfare or a declared state of war. The act specifies that the emergency shall terminate upon the issuance of a presidential proclamation or the passage by Congress of a concurrent resolution to this effect.

During the existence of a civil defense emergency, the president may take a great variety of measures, including the speedy acquisition of materials and facilities, the assumption of obligations on behalf of the United States, provision for financial assistance to the states, and direction of all relief activities. Regularly, these powers may be exercised without regard to the limitations of any existing laws. Among other emergency actions, the president may direct any federal department or agency to provide their personnel, materials and facilities for the aid of states and to furnish emergency shelters and other protective devices for the preservation of life and property. For purposes of civil defense, the president may sell, lease, lend, transfer or deliver materials or perform services without regard to statutory limitations; he may also reimburse the states and their political subdivisions for the expenses of personnel employed or materials used in rendering aid outside the state. In addition, the president is authorized to grant financial assistance for the temporary relief of civilians injured or in want as the result of attack, and to employ additional personnel without regard to civil service laws or regulations. As the act stipulates, the federal government shall not be liable for any property damage or for any death or personal injury occurring directly or indirectly as a result of the exercise of or the failure to exercise, any function or duty by federal agencies or government employees in carrying out the emergency provisions of the act.

The section of the title dealing with acquisition of property goes far beyond the procurement authority in nonemergency situations. The act empowers the president to exercise this authority without regard to the limitation of any existing law, which means obviously that the procuring officer does not have to follow general statutory provisions regulating the taking of property. Thus, during a civil defense emergency, the act grants the president a broad power of seizure as one possible form of government acquisition of property. As it appears, a good case can be made for the proposition that this general procurement authority, including the power of seizure, applies also to real property since the proviso excluding realty is not repeated in the emergency section.[48] During congressional hearings and debates, the question was raised whether the language of the act exempting the procurement power from the "limitation of any existing law" excluded also the payment of just compensation in violation of constitutional principles. As a result of this inquiry, another section was added which specifies that, except in cases where property is taken in conformity with statutory provisions or through condemnation proceedings, the procuring officer must promptly determine the amount of compensation to be paid for the property. Concerning the final disposition of property, the act provides that, upon determining that any realty is no longer required for civil defense purposes, the president shall return the property to the owner if the latter desires such return and is willing to pay the fair value of the property. In cases of personal property, the president may make such dispositions as he deems appropriate but, to the extent feasible, shall give the former owner an opportunity to reacquire the property.

3. MILITARY VERSUS CIVILIAN CONTROL
AND THE QUESTION OF MARTIAL LAW

The described statutes provide ample authority for the president and his subordinates to act in emergency situations; however, congressional acts can hardly be expected to anticipate all necessary courses of action in case of nuclear attack or threat of attack. In the event of actual or impending catastrophe, the president may decide to invoke additional prerogatives of an independent or

[48] Compare Val Peterson, "Civil Defense and Law," *Nebraska L. Rev.*, 35: 427 (1956).

nonstatutory character, prerogatives which are supposedly derived from his war powers and from the aggregate of constitutional clauses dealing with the presidency. One of these prerogatives is the power to proclaim martial law or to institute some other form of military rule. Even while the Federal Civil Defense Act was considered in Congress, some congressmen voiced the opinion that much of the proposed legislation was of doubtful value since, in time of emergency, the military would probably assume control, possibly under a proclamation of martial law. In the words of Representative Kilday: "I do not think we have to worry too much about the emergency because under the general powers of the military in the event of an attack upon the United States they could move in and take anything they wanted. They would not hesitate to take anything and everything." At another point, the same congressman observed:

His duties must be set out and his powers and his authority when you come to what he can do in the emergency period or after an attack . . . that he will then have very broad powers, and in the very nature of things he should have, although we do not need to worry too much about it, because in the event of a serious attack upon the United States justifying the exercise of those powers, even under this bill or without it, quite likely you would have a situation of martial law prevailing with all of the powers which are called for in that situation, so that after the bomb drops it is an entirely different thing.[49]

Obviously, what the president may or may not do in case of emergency is a matter of speculation. In any event, the imposition of martial law or some other form of military rule can only be viewed as an ultimate remedy after all other means of maintaining regular civil government have been explored, even in our atomic or missile age. Martial or military rule by necessity implies a drastic curtailment of civil rights and liberties. Moreover, there is the danger that martial rule, once established, becomes easily self-perpetuating and difficult to abolish. In the United States, martial law has never actually been used on a national scale and it is to be hoped that it never will. The instances where martial law was invoked occurred either on the state level or in the theatre of

[49] See *LH 1950*, pp. 280, 263.

military operations during war.[50] These past examples offer little
guidance for the evaluation of military rule during a civil defense
emergency in the atomic age. Prior to World War I, martial law
was imposed primarily during labor disputes or in cases of
domestic violence and its use left much to be desired. After the
entrance of the United States into World War I, a bill was introduced in the Senate whose objective was to punish spies and
which permitted the possible use of martial law on a national
scale. Due to the stern opposition of President Wilson, however,
Senator Chamberlain, the author of the bill, withdrew the measure
and the matter was dropped.

The second World War brought a more serious preoccupation
with the problem of martial law and military rule. The preoccupation was caused primarily by the danger or fear of an invasion
of Hawaii and of the Pacific Coast. On the Pacific Coast, the possible impact of such invasion on Japanese aliens and citizens of
Japanese ancestry living in the area created considerable apprehension among government leaders and in the high military
command. Among other suggested methods of handling the situation, martial law was proposed and given support in some quarters;[51] however, this approach clearly would have imposed great
hardship on the entire population in the area, not only the
Japanese. On February 19, 1942, President Roosevelt issued an
executive order which empowered the Secretary of War and military commanders designated by him to establish "military areas"
from which persons might be excluded in order to prevent espionage and sabotage. Another executive order authorized the
creation of the War Relocation Authority to handle the "relocation," maintenance, and supervision of those persons designated

[50] For a comprehensive treatment of the problem see Charles Fairman,
The Law of Martial Rule (2d ed., Chicago, 1943); Louis W. Koenig, *The
Presidency and the Crisis* (New York, 1944); Benneth M. Rich, *The Presi-
dent and Civil Disorder* (Washington, 1941); Robert S. Rankin, *When Civil
Law Fails* (Durham, 1939).

[51] Compare Robert Bendiner, "Cool Heads or Martial Law," *Nation*, 154:
183 (February 14, 1942); Earl Warren, "Wartime Martial Rule in California," *California State Bar J.*, 17: 185 (1942); W.A. Graham, "Martial Law
in California," *California L.Rev.*, 31: 6 (1942). Martial rule was actually imposed in the Japanese relocation center at Tule Lake, California, from November 13, 1943 to January 15, 1944; see Dorothy S. Thomas and Richard S.
Nishimoto, *The Spoilage* (Berkeley and Los Angeles, 1946), pp. 147-183.

by military orders. An act of Congress of March 21, 1942, ratified the presidential action and provided penalties. On the basis of the presidential action and the congressional legislation, a series of orders and proclamations were issued by the West Coast military commander relating to curfew provisions and to removal and detention procedures for Japanese aliens and citizens of Japanese ancestry. The Supreme Court generally upheld these regulations arguing that the orders were not beyond the war powers of Congress or the military authority of the president and that, to prevent espionage and sabotage, the restriction of civil liberties of the Japanese was permissible in an area threatened by Japanese attack.[52]

Drastic limitations on the entire population were imposed in Hawaii following the Japanese attack on Pearl Harbor of December 7, 1941. Within a few hours on the same day, Governor Poindexter proclaimed martial law, suspended the writ of habeas corpus, ordered the local courts closed and transferred the powers of government to General Short, the commanding general of the United States Army in Hawaii. The action of the governor was approved by the president. General Short immediately announced the assumption of the responsibility and proclaimed that the territorial courts were closed, a declaration which was seconded by the chief justice of the supreme court of Hawaii. At the same time, the commanding general issued an order stating that all major offenses were to be referred to military commissions and lesser offenses to provost courts; he also advised the population that punishments would be commensurate with the offense and that the death penalty would be applied in appropriate cases. During subsequent months, minor relaxations of martial rule were gradually instituted; nevertheless, the military remained basically in control of Hawaii until October 24, 1944. As the danger of Japanese attack decreased, there were growing demands that martial rule be lifted. In August, 1942, a stockbroker in Hawaii was sentenced by a provost court to five years imprisonment for embezzling stock

[52] In *Hirabayashi* v. *U.S.*, 320 U.S. 81 (1943), the curfew orders were upheld; *Korematsu* v. *U.S.*, 323 U.S. 214 (1944), upheld an order excluding all persons of Japanese ancestry from designated West Coast military areas. However, in *Ex parte Endo*, 323 U.S. 283 (1944), the Court refused to sanction the involuntary detention of a citizen of Japanese ancestry whose loyalty was conceded.

in violation of Hawaiian law. In February, 1944, a civilian ship-fitter employed by the Navy was convicted of assault by a military tribunal for engaging in a brawl with two marine sentries. Both prisoners brought habeas corpus proceedings to test the validity of the convictions and the Supreme Court finally decided to inter-vene. Upholding the actions of the petitioners, the Court ruled that, while martial law might have been proper at the time of the Pearl Harbor disaster, its continued use and drastic application was a violation of the Hawaiian Organic Act and of constitution-ally protected liberties.[53] The Hawaiian experience is a good illustration of the self-perpetuating tendency of martial rule and does not recommend itself for future imitation.

Postwar Anxiety

Even during World War II, the danger of an attack on the American homeland, apart from certain areas such as Hawaii, was only a distant and unlikely possibility. In the immediate post-war years, the expectation of a lasting peace encouraged for a short period a feeling of security. With the development of the cold war and the loss of nuclear monopoly, a danger of unprece-dented magnitude suddenly faced the country—and with this threat the problem of military rule made its reappearance. The extent of the nuclear danger was only gradually realized and, to the degree of this realization, was prone to produce a curious response. The very magnitude of the potential destruction fostered a feeling of frustration and a tendency to repress the problem while, on the surface, an attempt was made to carry on life as usual. This psychological response was reflected in the planning and policies of governmental agencies and civic groups. On the rational level, efforts were concentrated on the formulation of plans which, through strengthened civil defense programs and other means, would insure the maintenance of civil government even in the face of catastrophe; however, the underlying anxiety manifested itself in the frequently voiced expectation that, in case

---

[53] *Duncan* v. *Kahanamoku,* 327 U.S. 304 (1946). Compare *e.g.,* J.G. Anthony, "Hawaiian Martial Law in the Supreme Court," *Yale L.J.,* 57: 27 (1947); John P. Frank, "Ex parte Milligan v. The Five Companies: Martial Law in Hawaii," *Columbia L.Rev.,* 44: 639 (1944).

of disaster or threatened disaster, the military would soon take over and martial law would be invoked. The situation was further complicated by the ambiguous position of military authorities. The prevailing attitude of the military was that the basic task of the armed forces was military defense and that other problems should preferably be handled by the institutions of civil government. At the same time, however, the assumption was sometimes expressed that civil defense and civil government could not be counted upon in case of disaster and that military rule might be inevitable. The confusion was compounded by the fact that there was little contact or coordination between civilian and military planning efforts. Thus, at least during the first postwar decade, the problem of military versus civilian rule was caught in an entangled web of frequently contradictory or unrelated policies and expectations.

In the immediate postwar years, civil defense planning was carried on primarily by the military establishment. The Civil Defense Board created by the War Department gave serious attention to the problem of the allocation of civil defense functions to civil and military authorities. The Bull Report emphasized that civil defense is basically a civilian responsibility and recommended a coordination of functions between federal and state levels of government and between civil and military agencies. However, in the absence of a better alternative and pending final decision on civil defense responsibilities, the board urged that the agency best suited to initiate coordinated planning was the War or Defense Department. The Office of Civil Defense Planning established by the Secretary of Defense in 1948 made another thorough study of civil defense needs and experiences. The Hopley Report described civil defense as the missing link in the defense structure. In recommending the establishment of a national civil defense office, the Hopley group explored again the problem of the proper allocation of civil and military responsibilities. The report concluded that the national office should best be located in the Defense Department since a large part of the civil defense program required "continuous coordination with all agencies responsible to the Secretary of Defense." [54]

[54] U.S. Office of Civil Defense Planning, *Civil Defense for National Security* (Washington, D.C., October, 1948), p. 2.

The Hopley Report was favorably received by the great majority of civic leaders and newspaper editors. However, in some quarters, the report was vehemently attacked as an infringement of civil liberties and as a "military conspiracy to supersede the Bill of Rights." The attack was prompted in part by the proposed location of the civil defense agency in the Defense Department. To a considerable degree, however, the criticism was provoked by a section in the Hopley Report which stated that, in the event of grave calamity such as atomic bombing, martial law would probably be declared in the afflicted area. The inclusion of the martial law problem in the Hopley study of over-all civil defense planning was defended by several observers as a realistic and reasonable approach. As Clinton Rossiter commented at the time:

We must be on our guard against every needless or capricious invasion of our valued liberties, but where a temporary, calculated intrusion is necessary to save the whole structure of our freedom, we must permit the intrusion and concentrate our efforts upon making it as temporary and carefully-guarded as possible. The Hopley proposals are open to criticism, and they should indeed be scrutinized by Congress and the people with excessive care before they are set in motion, but not in a spirit of arrant frivolity.[55]

While accepting the need of considerable executive emergency power and possibly of military intervention in case of catastrophe, Rossiter suggested that a means of reducing the danger of a "capricious invasion" of civil liberties was the speedy establishment of "a nationwide organization for civil defense" and the initiation of "an exacting training program for all citizens willing to serve in it," adding that "the more tasks that the civilian population can do, the less the military will have to do."

The proposal of the Hopley Report with respect to the incorporation of the civil defense office in the Defense Department was not followed by President Truman who, in March, 1949, transferred major civil defense responsibilities to the National Security Resources Board. The master plan or "Blue Book" which the board submitted to the president in September, 1950, envisaged the creation of an independent civil defense agency in the execu-

[55] See Clinton L. Rossiter, "Constitutional Dictatorship in the Atomic Age," *The Review of Politics,* 11: 395, 416, 417 (1949).

tive branch of government. At the same time, the plan reviewed the role which the armed forces should play in a national civil defense program. According to the board's recommendations, the armed forces were to give guidance and information to the federal civil defense agency as to geographic areas most likely to be attacked and as to anticipated forms of attack and possible means of defense. In addition, the military was to establish a warning system, make decisions concerning passive defense measures required by military necessity and, upon request, give assistance wherever possible to civil authorities in the event of war-caused disasters. The "Blue Book" also proposed a general coordination and cooperation of military authorities and state and local governments in the development of civil defense programs. "Military installations distributed throughout the United States," the report stated,

often have common problems of defense and protection with adjacent communities under civil government. The military commanders of these installations are responsible for coordinating defense problems with the civil authorities of adjacent communities.[56]

Thus, the report of the National Security Resources Board ascribed to the military primarily a supporting role in aid of civil authorities, while the imposition of martial law was relegated to the realm of "last resort" remedies. However, although the recommendations of the report became the general planning assumption of the Federal Civil Defense Administration established in 1950, the specter of martial law was not removed from public thinking and deliberation. It has already been mentioned that, even during consideration of the Federal Civil Defense Act of 1950, the statements of some congressmen reflected an anticipation of military rule in case of disaster; but this anticipation was more widespread and certainly not limited to Congress. As Project East River and other study projects disclosed, many people continued to think that "when the 'real thing' comes the Army will have to 'take over,'" and that a "dictator, backed by martial law, would be the

[56] U.S. National Security Resources Board, *United States Civil Defense,* NSRB Doc. 128 (Washington, D.C., 1950), ch. 4. See Brewer, *op. cit.,* pp. 41-42.

only solution." [57] Reflecting on the impact of atomic attack on civil government and the administration of justice, a member of the bar stated in 1951: "Immediately following an atomic bombing, where the civil authorities are unable to act, comes martial law." The writer of this comment was not pleased with the prospect of military rule but cautioned that, unless there was a definite effort to strengthen civil defense plans and to limit the need for martial law, military authorities could not be expected to display special restraint in emergency situations.

Martial law . . . is at best but a necessary and temporary expedient and should not be declared for a territorial area greater than the absolute necessity requires . . . but unless there is a strong public opinion to confine the martial law rule to the area immediately affected there is altogether too much temptation to enlarge the military jurisdiction beyond all reasonable need. The placing of an area under martial law does of necessity alter materially the ordinary relations of business and personal life. Under the conditions resulting from an A-bombing, . . . the current of ordinary life cannot flow at all, and surely no military commander can be held to the circumspection that is proper and necessary in other cases.[58]

While civilian thinking thus manifested considerable bewilderment, military authorities did not contribute greatly to a clarification of the situation. As it appears, there was a strong tendency in the Defense Department and in the military high command to side-step the issue of civil defense and to remain as noncommittal as possible. In its report of 1952, Project East River pointed out that much of the ambiguity and confusion in civil-military relationships was due to "the reticence of military forces to accredit civil defense as a partner along with the Army, Navy, and Air Force in the national security team." Among the reasons for this reticence, the report mentioned the apprehension that greater military involvement in civil defense matters might reduce the chances for receiving congressional appropriations and might be interpreted as an admission of military weakness or of an inability to deter attack through military force alone. General Otto

---

[57] Compare Charles Fairman, *Government Under Law in Time of Crisis* (Harvard Law School, Cambridge, 1955), pp. 108, 110.

[58] Homer D. Crotty, "The Administration of Justice and the A-Bomb: What Follows Disaster?" *American Bar Association J.*, 37: 893, 895 (1951).

Nelson, the chairman of the project, later testified that, because of the military reticence toward civil defense, "it will be very difficult to get the Defense Department to express itself very clearly in this field." [59]

Despite the reluctance of military authorities to become actively involved in civil defense matters, attempts were made on a modest scale by the Defense Department to maintain liaison with civil defense agencies and to specify the role of the armed forces in civil defense emergencies. At the top level, the Assistant Secretary of Defense for Manpower, Personnel, and Reserve was made responsible for all civil-military relations in the field of civil defense. Within the office of the Assistant Secretary, a small Civil Defense Division was created whose staff director was to maintain contact and liaison with the Federal Civil Defense Administration and other agencies and whose functions were mainly of a coordinating rather than operating character. With regard to the role of the armed forces, a Department of Defense Directive of January, 1952 outlined the functions of the three military departments by making the Army responsible for planning emergency support of civil defense operations in case of enemy attack and for coordinating Navy and Air Force participation in such emergency support. Army regulations of July of the same year further specified the conditions for the employment of Army resources in civil defense emergencies. As manifested in these directives and regulations, official military planning contemplated primarily a supporting role of the armed forces in aid of civil authorities, rather than the imposition of military rule or martial law. However, the weakness of existing civilian preparations made it likely that, in the event of emergency, there would be no authority for the armed forces to support or assist, and military planning was not oblivious of this fact. As Charles Fairman commented, the Army felt that they had enough to do as it is and "do not like to take on these responsibilities," but in the absence of civilian preparedness "they cannot escape being forced to act. . . . The failure of Congress and the people to understand the danger . . . is incomprehensible." [60]

Preoccupation with the possibility of martial law was displayed

[59] *Investigative Hearings,* p. 668; see also *Subcommittee Report,* p. 60.
[60] Fairman, *op. cit.* (*supra*, n. 57), p. 111.

in a study written by an army colonel in 1954 which attempted to distinguish between various forms of military intervention in domestic affairs. The study can hardly be considered as representative of top level planning although it probably reflected the thinking of many high ranking officers. In the opinion of the writer, martial rule was likely to emerge at least on the local or state level in case of nuclear disaster. "A future world conflagration," he stated,

carries with it the strong possibility that the United States proper will be subject to mass bombings with horribly destructive weapons. Actual invasion is not beyond the realm of possibility. It appears to me that, with respect to the mass bombings, we shall have a reemergence of the states and the imposition of martial law, if temporarily necessary from those sovereigns. . . . Should there be an actual invasion, I think it is apparent that the active area of operations would, of necessity, require martial rule.

The writer added that "it should be remembered that few military commanders relish the idea of the additional burdens which befall them when martial law is imposed;" he also observed that "when dictated by necessity, and only then, can we expect to relinquish the rights which must be sacrificed upon civil administration's being deposed." Martial law proper was sharply contrasted in the study with military aid to civil authorities. "The vast distinction between the two concepts," the colonel observed,

is that martial law replaces the former civil law whereas military aid furnishes no body of law whatsoever but merely the force of arms to ensure that the civil law will remain supreme and not degenerate into military rule. Thus, military forces exercise no legal jurisdiction over offenses committed by civilians or over their persons. . . . Because there is no general criminal jurisdiction over civilians vested in the military under military aid to civil authority, punitive detention is not possible and preventive detention is recognized only to the extent necessary to turn the offenders over to civil authorities.[61]

The problem of military versus civilian control in emergency situations was reexamined and reevaluated in early 1955 by the National Planning Association. The report of the study group

[61] Edward L. Farrell, Jr., "Civil Functions of the Military and Implications of Martial Law," *University of Kansas City L.Rev.*, 22: 157, 159, 165 (1954).

emphasized that, despite the necessity of executive discretion in time of emergency, the maintenance of civil government and regular judicial process was of paramount importance and had always been viewed as a "touchstone of liberty" in this country. However, the study observed that the danger of military rule or martial law continued to exist as long as civilian preparations were basically inadequate and inefficient. "There is good reason to fear," the report cautioned,

that if adequate preparations are not made in advance, an attack disaster would perforce bring military administration in its wake. If the agencies of civil administration buckle under the burden of an attack, a cry would go up for the President and the state governors to declare martial law.

If martial law were imposed—the report continued—"the only channel of communication between the stricken country and its directing centers would be lines of Army command. It would mean that the Department of the Army would have the responsibility for directing the activity of the entire populace in addition to its suddenly expanded responsibilities for military operations." In the opinion of the study group, such an arrangement "would not only be a huge burden for the Army, but a basic error of the first magnitude," since "the nation would then be at war on a false pattern, from which it later could withdraw only with extreme difficulty." The only way to avoid the evil of martial law, the report concluded,

is to take steps now to determine how our civil institutions can best be prepared to withstand the blow, and then to proceed, promptly but calmly, to make the needed preparations. The critical requirement is for advance planning and testing, to discover effective civil administration procedures and working relationships.[62]

Operation Alert 1955 and Aftermath

As can be seen, both civilian and military thinking in the first postwar decade was characterized by a mixture of hope that civil

[62] National Planning Association, "A Program for the Nonmilitary Defense of the United States," reproduced in *Senate Hearings,* Exhibit 11, pp. 814, 815.

government could somehow survive, of fear that under real emergency conditions the military would probably take over and of a realization that military rule would be undesirable even if inevitable. These assumptions and expectations were not always consciously stated or formulated; in large measure they remained inarticulate and unrelated. There was little hope of clarification unless public attention was somehow alerted or brought to focus on the problem of military versus civilian control. The opportunity for such reassessment presented itself unexpectedly in 1955 in the form of a startling but otherwise unfortunate episode of that year's civil defense exercise. The so-called Operation Alert 1955 was the second national civil defense exercise since the establishment of the Federal Civil Defense Administration. However, while the first test in 1954 had passed calmly and without producing noticeable effects, Operation Alert of 1955 aroused considerable public attention and concern primarily because of one incident: the president's proclamation of limited martial law on a nationwide scale.

The test exercise which was held from June 15 to 17 was planned well in advance. Already at the beginning of March, the standards and planning assumptions were issued by the Federal Civil Defense Administration. According to these instructions, nine days of actual operations were to be condensed into twenty-six hours. Over fifty critical target cities were singled out for attack and the size of bombs and type of burst was specified, except for the fact that some cities were to be prepared for whatever was disclosed later. Target areas were given assumptions as to the total number of persons killed and injured supposing no evacuation. The major emphasis of the exercise was clearly upon relocation and evacuation. On June 15, the described planning assumptions went into effect together with some other, previously undisclosed estimates. The beginning of the exercise saw a large-scale evacuation of government officials and employees in many parts of the country. The top of the national executive—including the president, the cabinet, the Joint Chiefs of Staff, the director of the Office of Defense Mobilization and the head of the Federal Civil Defense Administration—went to an emergency capital outside of Washington. Immediately casualty and damage reports from all over the country poured in at this emergency capital.

The reports were gruesome beyond description. Some sixty cities were struck by sixty-one bombs and of these cities, fifty-three were located in the continental United States. The bombs ranged from twenty kilotons to five megatons and were delivered by air or through guided missiles launched from submarines. Over eight million people were dead from blast and other causes on the first day; another eight million died in the following weeks with almost four million of all deaths being due to radioactive fallout. An estimated eight million required varying degrees of medical care, while some six million dwelling units were rendered uninhabitable and some twenty-five million persons homeless.[63]

An exercise conducted on such a large scale was bound to produce difficulties and problems of considerable magnitude. In assessing the performance of the alert, one reporter was prompted to write that "everything was simulated but the confusion." [64] The most surprising and unsettling event of the exercise was certainly the declaration of martial law by the president. The measure had not been included in the preparations and planning assumptions for the test and was clearly the result of an on the spot decision. The proclamation was issued by the chief executive in his capacity "as President of the United States and Commander-in-Chief of the Armed Forces" and was based on the effects of an atomic attack resulting in "unprecedented destruction of life and property, the breakdown of civil authority, the need for the restoration of authority and the reduction to a minimum of interference with the military effort." [65] In his proclamation, the president declared martial law to be in effect "throughout the United States, its territories and possessions;" he also suspended the privilege of the writ of habeas corpus. Termination of martial law was to occur by successive declarations of the president or Congress covering particular areas. Although the proclamation envisaged a minimum of interference with the primary mission of the armed

[63] For these estimated results and other test assumptions see Federal Civil Defense Administration, *Annual Report 1955* (Washington, D.C., 1956), pp. 32-33; Charles Fairman, *Government Under Law in the Shadow of a Nuclear War,* Industrial College of the Armed Forces, No. L 56-127 (Washington, D.C., 1955-1956), p. 32; *Subcommittee Report,* p. 11.

[64] Ralph E. Lapp, "A Confused Alert—But Even a Good One May Be Obsolete," *Life,* 38: 48 (June 27, 1955).

[65] For the text of the martial law proclamation see *Investigative Hearings,* pp. 279-280.

forces, the Secretary of Defense and subordinate military commanders of the respective Army areas were directed to enforce law and order and, at the same time, to carry out decisions and regulations of federal agencies in civil defense and other fields. The imposition of martial law was limited primarily by the fact that the writ of habeas corpus was suspended only with respect to federal offenses—a limitation which hardly made sense—and by the statement that no authority granted in the proclamation was to affect the conduct of elections and the functioning of regular civil courts to the extent that they did not obstruct the war effort.

With regard to the legal or constitutional basis of the proclamation, a very pertinent preliminary question was raised by Representative Holifield in the course of subsequent subcommittee hearings. Addressing himself to Governor Peterson, head of the Federal Civil Defense Administration, the congressman inquired whether the president's action was founded on statutory authority, such as the emergency title of the Federal Civil Defense Act, or on the "inherent" powers of the chief executive. The Civil Defense Administrator who had been present at the emergency capital during the exercise was obviously not very eager to discuss the manner in which the presidential decision was reached. Nevertheless, after some prodding, he indicated that the president at first had invoked the powers under the emergency title of the Federal Civil Defense Act; however, after "protracted debate" the initial decision was changed and martial law was proclaimed by the president.[66] Referring to the emergency title of the Civil Defense Act in the light of the martial law declaration, Chairman Holifield commented: "It would appear to me that this section was not used." The congressman apparently would have preferred presidential reliance on the statutory authority for he continued that, in his estimate, this section

would give the President all the power he needs to declare an emergency condition and operate under it, according to this statute. It provides a method of termination by the Congress or by the President, which I think is desirable. As to what can be done under this emergency authority, I am not quite sure. . . . What really confuses me is what can be done under the declaration of martial law that could not

[66] *Ibid.*, p. 1421.

be done under this emergency authority that would be necessary to be done.[67]

As a hastily drafted document, the martial law declaration of 1955 was obviously not a model of clarity and left open many doubts with respect to the precise role of the military authorities. In the proclamation, the Army was directed to enforce law and order; but at the same time, it was instructed to carry out orders of federal agencies.[68] During congressional hearings conducted by the Senate civil defense subcommittee and the Holifield subcommittee in the House, some witnesses actually took the position that, in their view, the proclamation simply contemplated the use of the armed forces in a supporting role in aid of civil authorities. "The military's mission," Governor Peterson argued,

is to fight the enemy and under martial law we would have to utilize all of our existing agencies to the full. Martial law would simply mean that these agencies would have the support of the military of the United States in maintaining law and order and in carrying out these activities which are vital to the survival of America in case support of that type is needed. . . . For instance, in civil defense I would anticipate that we would carry on our responsibilities just exactly as we do now but we would have this additional support.[69]

Director Flemming of the Office of Defense Mobilization commented: "We did not presuppose in connection with Operation Alert 1955 the complete breakdown of civilian government. What we were after was maximum military aid to the civilian government." When asked why, under such conditions, martial law was declared, Dr. Flemming merely replied: "That is debatable back and forth." [70]

Clearly, this interpretation was in conflict with common ter-

[67] *Ibid.*

[68] As Charles G. Stevenson, state judge advocate of the New York National Guard, pointed out in a critical analysis submitted to the Holifield subcommittee: "But, the main thing wrong with the 1955 proclamation was that it mixed 'limited martial rule' with 'military aid to the civil authorities' without making clear the extent of each. The proclamation said that the Army should enforce law and order (limited martial rule) and 'carry out decisions of Federal agencies' (military aid to civil authorities)." *Ibid.* p. 1863.

[69] *Senate Hearings,* p. 734. Compare also his testimony in *Investigative Hearings,* p. 1421.

[70] *Ibid.,* pp. 1071-1072.

minology. If the president's action merely intended to give maximum military support to civil authorities, a declaration of martial law was both undesirable and unnecessary. Moreover, the conception did not accord with the language of the presidential order which directed the military to enforce law and order— rather than assist in the enforcement of law and order—and which in large measure suspended the privilege of the writ of habeas corpus. The great majority of observers took the declaration to mean what it said, namely, the imposition of some form of military rule over domestic territory. This view, in any event, was adopted by the Defense Department during the exercise. In a memorandum prepared by Secretary of Defense Wilson at the emergency capital and addressed to the Secretary of the Army, the Chief of Staff was ordered to prepare to "carry out, with military authority, whatever actions are required (a) to restore and maintain law and order; (b) to initiate recovery and rehabilitation from the effects of enemy action." The meaning of this order was specified in the memorandum in this manner:

For the purpose of the problem play all agencies are to assume that civilian agencies in the civil defense and mobilization areas are to continue to function under authoritative leadership and enforcement by the military.[71]

The memorandum thus contemplated a military administration of the country in the sense that civilian agencies were to function under military control.

With the exception of those who viewed the action merely as a form of military assistance to civil authorities, the proclamation of martial law was deplored and criticized by most observers and witnesses. The most vocal and articulate opponent of the declaration was Charles Fairman, then professor at Harvard Law School. When testifying before the Holifield subcommittee, Professor Fairman called the use of martial law "a great mistake" and expressed the opinion that the proclamation was "hashed up" at the spur of the moment, that it was "an unstudied work and that it falls apart on examination." In addition to challenging the imposition of martial rule, he also questioned the president's authority to suspend the writ of habeas corpus under the circumstances. As he

[71] *Senate Hearings,* p. 749.

pointed out, it might be argued that, in passing the Emergency Detention Act of 1950, Congress had pre-empted the field and precluded the president from exercising this kind of emergency power, in analogy with the Supreme Court decision in the steel seizure case of 1952. In Professor Fairman's opinion, the martial law declaration in 1955 was due mainly to inadequate legislation and to the lack of a coordinated and unified civil defense program. In order to reduce the likelihood of a repetition of the experience, he urged a strengthening of nonmilitary defense preparations and a stepped-up program to insure the maintenance of civil government in case of disaster.

The great objective is to preserve the civil institutions of the states, to preserve the United States Government, and to preserve the American people, and to do this by developing the system of civil government to the point where it will be adequate to this challenge. The end is necessary, the means are indispensable.[72]

With the development of an improved civil defense system, the military forces could more easily be maintained in a supporting role in aid of civil authorities.

Despite his disapproval of the president's action in 1955, Professor Fairman did not entirely reject the idea that the chief executive might be entitled to proclaim martial law in case of catastrophe. His testimony on this point is particularly valuable as it restated and reformulated some of the basic principles governing the use of martial law in this country. His observations made it clear that martial law is not an extra-constitutional device whereby the chief executive somehow rises above the constitutional framework; rather, it constitutes an activation of latent constitutional powers of the executive in case of public necessity. However, as Professor Fairman pointed out, resort to martial law must be reserved to extreme emergencies and has to be viewed as an ultimate remedy and rare exception. "I would say," he testified,

that, being utterly unprepared when the blow fell, a military administration might be the best in the worst extremity; but I would not make

[72] *Investigative Hearings*, pp. 282, 283.

the best we could do in the worst extremity become the standard operation procedure.[73]

Moreover, justification for the use of martial law—if there is such
justification—can only be found in the actual necessity and not
merely in the paper proclamation. The determination of the
emergency character of the situation is regularly made by the
chief executive. However, in order to prevent abuse of power and
an arbitrary infringement of civil liberties, the finding of necessity
must be subject to judicial review which examines the proclamation in the light of existing factual conditions. "Our constitutional
system," Fairman concluded,

has no mysterious booster charge which, when released by a proclamation, enables the executive to soar above the limits of the Constitution.
Or, to change the figure of speech, the executive cannot add a single
cubit to its stature by pronouncing the words "martial law." A proclamation of "martial law" makes nothing lawful that would have otherwise been unlawful. Where, as in an invasion upon the territory of the
United States, or where invasion is immediately threatened, it becomes
necessary then and there to carry on some or all of the functions of
government by military administration, it is appropriate to issue a
proclamation announcing such martial rule; but it is the actual necessity, not the paper proclamation, that justifies such extraordinary
action.[74]

The use of martial law in 1955 was not only deplored by civilian
witnesses, but also by spokesmen of the Defense Department and
of the military high command. Although these spokesmen obviously would not criticize the president's decision as such, they
uniformly expressed the view that the primary task of the armed
forces was military defense and that it was undesirable to augment this task by the burden of military rule in civil defense
emergencies. As Admiral Radford, Chairman of the Joint Chiefs
of Staff, pointed out,

The primary mission of our Armed Forces is to fight and defeat the
enemy by offensive action anywhere and at any time under any circum-

---

[73] *Ibid.*, p. 287. When asked whether martial law could or should be completely outlawed by Congress, he replied: "In all candor, I would not want
that to be done; because it never seems to me, Mr. Fascell, you ought to
close the very last door; if you and I found this was the only way to pull ourselves out, we would do it." *Ibid.*, p. 299.

[74] *Ibid.*, p. 309.

stances. The mission is so comprehensive and vitally important as to make wholly undesirable the assignment of any additional diversionary functions and responsibilities such as civilian defense to the Department of Defense.

General Taylor observed in a similar vein that "the Armed Forces should not be placed in the position of running civilian communities except as a final emergency." The Joint Chiefs of Staff and spokesmen of the Defense Department were agreed that primary responsibility for civil defense should rest in the hands of civil authorities and that the military should regularly be employed only in a supporting role. To quote General Taylor again:

You cannot depend upon the Army to perform the civil defense of the United States. It is neither organized, trained, nor equipped, nor directed to do that sort of thing. We are here to supplement the civilian defense.

While objecting to additional civil defense burdens and to the imposition of military rule as a regular device, the Joint Chiefs of Staff admitted that the armed forces would not hesitate to implement martial law if used as a final resort. In the words of Admiral Radford, "we have to be prepared to go further in case we are directed to." General Taylor affirmed that "the Army is always prepared to execute martial law if so directed by the Commander in Chief. We have very little enthusiasm for doing that. We do it only because we are told by responsible civilian leaders." [75]

Although the use of martial law in 1955 was generally deplored, it had the advantage of bringing the issue more clearly into the open and of encouraging a re-examination of the problem of military versus civilian control. Already in his news conference of July 6, 1955, the president announced that he had asked the attorney general to review the national experience with martial law and to evaluate the significance of this experience for civil defense emergencies. Admiral Radford testified before the Holifield subcommittee that the Army had been directed soon after the incident to make a special study of the martial law problem and of the appropriate role of the military in emergency situations.[76]

[75] *Ibid.*, pp. 343, 352, 444, 445, 449.
[76] *Ibid.*, p. 352.

In August of 1955, the Secretary of Defense instructed the Joint Chiefs of Staff to place greater emphasis on support operations of the armed forces in civil defense activities. In accordance with this instruction, the Joint Chiefs directed the services to prepare plans for military assistance to civil authorities. On General Taylor's orders, additional hours of training in the Army's role during civil emergencies were incorporated in officer candidate courses and other training programs; also, instruction of duty and warrant officers in martial law was started by the six Army commands. In January of 1956, directions were sent to the Continental Army Command to amplify civil defense planning as a part of the overall military strategy.[77]

The first public illustration of the results of this re-examination came in the form of the third national civil defense exercise, Operation Alert 1956. In this exercise [78] which lasted from July 20 to 25 martial law on a national scale was avoided and military-civil relations were improved although a certain ambiguity persisted with respect to final control. There was also an effort to keep the operation more clearly within statutory confines. The proclamation issued by the president in 1956 obviously intended to place the armed forces in a supporting role. The Defense Department was directed to assist the Federal Civil Defense Administrator for a period of sixty days in the exercise of his duties under the emergency title of the Federal Civil Defense Act. However, assistance was specified to mean that any military personnel, facilities or resources made available would remain under military command. At the same time, the proclamation authorized the Secretary of Defense to establish military areas and institute martial rule if and where necessary for the performance of any military mission. Thus, the proclamation made the exercise of emergency functions in the first instance a responsibility of the civil defense organization. Nevertheless, as the Holifield subcommittee observed, the exercise did not completely eliminate martial rule, but rather left it "to the military authorities to determine how much of the United States must be brought under such rule for the purpose of carrying out their missions, and how much

[77] *Ibid.*, pp. 432, 433, 464, 465.

[78] Some 125 atomic and hydrogen bombs were presumed to have fallen from Hawaii to New England and from Alaska to Puerto Rico; the president proclaimed an "unlimited national emergency and state of war." See "Ducking for Cover," *Newsweek*, 48: 28 (July 30, 1956).

assistance they would give to civil defense for a sixty-day period." In addition to the imposition of martial law in specified military areas, the proclamation also raised the problem of military rule in connection with the supporting role of the armed forces.

If reliance is placed upon military troops and other military personnel for the performance of major emergency duties, the problem of martial rule still remains—the military would maintain their own channels of command and control.

In the evaluation of the Holifield subcommittee, the proclamation was basically "a compromise between complete military control implicit in a declaration of nationwide martial law and the more limited civilian control" by the Federal Civil Defense Administrator stipulated in the emergency section of the Federal Civil Defense Act.[79]

In its report which was issued a few days after the civil defense exercise of 1956, the Holifield subcommittee made several proposals designed to clarify and improve further civil-military relations in civil defense emergencies. One of these proposals was that the Secretary of Defense, in consultation with the top civil defense official, should establish or expand a program of instructing active and reserve military personnel in civil defense duties as a part of regular military training. The report also urged that the role of military forces in civil defense should be clearly defined and that state and local officials should be "fully informed as to the terms and conditions under which military assistance to civil-defense authorities will be rendered in the event of wide-spread disaster and the breakdown of civil government." The Holifield group finally recommended that the studies of martial law conducted by the attorney general, the Department of the Army, and other federal agencies should be made public promptly upon completion.[80] The American Bar Association during the same year estab-

[79] *Subcommittee Report*, p. 72.

[80] Attorney General Brownell declined to appear before the subcommittee and stated that the martial law study of his office had not been completed; see *ibid.*, p. 70; also *Investigative Hearings*, p. 3139. As the writers have been informed by the Justice Department, a martial law report was subsequently prepared by an attorney on the staff of the Internal Security Division of the Department; however, the manuscript was intended only for staff use and has not been released to the public.

lished a Special Committee on the Impact of Attack on Legal and Administrative Processes. In January of 1957, this committee issued a statement of objectives which formulated the relation of civilian to military authority as follows:

Civilian authority should be prepared to govern the country in the event of atomic attack. It is no task for the Armed Forces, who in war must give priority to their military missions and should not be compelled to divert manpower and organization to the vast complex operations needed to keep our shattered economy and government functioning. Nor is martial law a solution. It is, at best, a form of authority and organization that can rapidly be invoked if we as a country have not adequately prepared for civilian defense but permit ourselves to be surprised by what, instead, we should anticipate and prepare for.[81]

In April, 1957, Professor Fairman considered it a valid generalization to say that

It is our national policy, in the event of a nuclear attack, to maintain effective civil government throughout the entire country; that we will constantly endeavor to strengthen the institutions of civil government against the nuclear danger; and that if they were overcome by an attack it would be our national purpose to restore them as rapidly as possible.[82]

As it appears, the general assessment of Professor Fairman was based at least in part on testimony received by the Holifield sub-committee in preparation of and during its hearings on new civil defense legislation in February and March, 1957. Already in August, 1956, the subcommittee had requested the Defense Department to submit observations on, and make available plans for, implementing the recommendations contained in the Holifield report of July, 1956. Later in August, Carter L. Burgess, Assistant Secretary of Defense for Manpower, Personnel and Reserve, had informed the subcommittee of several changes and new measures which had been instituted by the military in the past year.[83] In October, the Assistant Secretary of Defense had transmitted to

[81] *Statement of Objectives* (mimeographed; January 14, 1957), p. 2. The statement was approved by the House of Delegates of the American Bar Association in February, 1957.

[82] Charles Fairman, *The Problem of Maintaining Governmental Authority Under Conditions of Nuclear Attack,* Industrial College of the Armed Forces, No. L 57-146 (Washington, D. C., 1956-1957), p. 2.

[83] *Legislative Hearings,* p. 160.

the subcommittee a memorandum containing the comments of an emergency planning group of the Defense Department and a special statement on martial law and military rule. The latter statement was the outcome of the martial law study conducted by the Army Department which had evolved into a Department of Defense position. The statement started from the premise that basic responsibility for civil relief should be vested in the civil defense authorities "subject to overriding control by military authority when military necessity and circumstances dictate" and that the primary mission of the armed forces was military defense. However, the statement continued that Defense Department resources not required for military operations would be used to provide all possible emergency support for civil relief in the event that other resources proved inadequate. Regarding military support, considerable emphasis was placed upon the principle that "military commanders should receive orders and instructions relating to civil relief and control through the established chain of command." [84]

The imposition of martial rule was viewed in the statement as an ultimate remedy "to preserve order and insure the public safety in domestic territory in time of emergency when civil agencies are unable to function or when their functioning would itself threaten the public safety." In the opinion of the Defense Department, martial law could be declared either in the country as a whole or in specified geographic areas, but authority for its use derived always from inherent emergency powers of the chief executive.

Martial law may be proclaimed, as far as the country as a whole is concerned, only by the President, by virtue of his inherent power as Chief Executive. The right to declare, apply and to exercise martial law is inherent in the concept of sovereignty, and is as essential to the existence of a state as is the right to carry on war. When he acts at the expressed command of the President, a local military commander may enforce martial law in a particular area. In the absence of a martial law proclamation, a military commander will assume control in a civil emergency only when it is necessary because civil authority is unable to perform its normal function, and will, at the earliest opportunity, request authority to proclaim martial law in the affected area. [85]

[84] *Ibid.*, p. 173.
[85] *Ibid.*, p. 174.

As the statement observed, there was no conflict between the concept of martial law and the authority granted in the emergency title of the Federal Civil Defense Act since, under martial rule, the emergency authority would be subject to overriding military considerations in the same manner as other statutory powers. In case martial law was invoked, the enforcement of existing civil and criminal laws might be suspended by the military commander to the extent that military necessity required such suspension. Also, according to the Defense Department, martial law would authorize the use of military tribunals for the trial of civilians if civil courts were unable to function and if the situation required this procedure. Nevertheless, the Defense position recognized that the operation of military tribunals would be subject to judicial review by regular courts, a review extending to the necessity of the court-martial procedure. The statement finally asserted that, as an incident to his martial law power, the president might suspend the writ of habeas corpus in declared military zones or areas without distinction between federal and non-federal offenses.

In its report of July, 1957, the Holifield subcommittee commented that the position of the Defense Department coincided in many respects with legislative proposals sponsored by the subcommittee, although there remained certain differences in emphasis or detail. As will be recalled, the Holifield bill recommended the establishment of a cabinet-level civil defense department and the creation of a Military Liaison Committee to serve as a bridge between civil defense and military authorities. The bill also proposed a revision of the emergency section of the Federal Civil Defense Act. The revised section was to carry a declaration of policy making it clear that Congress intended to retain strong civilian direction of civil defense in any emergency. The implementation of this policy, the subcommittee report stated, required a realization "that a strong national civilian organization, adequately equipped and in command of the resources of the Federal government, is essential if military rule is to be avoided in time of a civil-defense emergency." Under the revised section, the Secretary of Civil Defense was to direct civil defense operations while being relieved from certain legal restrictions on procurement and employment of personnel; the Secretary was also authorized to requisition supplies, to coordinate and direct the activities of federal departments and agencies, and if necessary to assume control of state and local civil defense operations. The purpose of such emergency authority, according to the report, was "to create a civilian government substitute for military rule and martial law." [86]

The Holifield report did not ignore the fact that, in certain instances, military participation or intervention might become necessary. The subcommittee emphasized, however, that, as a rule, the role of the armed forces was to be conceived as one of "cooperation and assistance to civil authorities consistent with military missions." In respect to the performance of military assistance, the report noted a divergence of opinion between the Defense Department position and the proposed legislation. While the Defense Department maintained that military commanders rendering assistance in civil defense emergencies should be subject to the military channel of command, the Holifield bill provided for the employment of military resources and personnel under the general supervision and direction of civil defense authorities. Greater uniformity of opinion existed with regard to the use of martial law as ultimate remedy. The bill admitted that "in the event of enemy attack military rule may be necessary in certain areas and under exceptional circumstances" but declared that "such rule shall be strictly limited in time and place and instituted only to serve urgent and immediate military requirements." The subcommittee apparently accepted the Defense Department observations on martial rule, including the provision for strong military control of all operations under a martial law declaration: "In view of the broad sweep of powers inherent in martial law as defined by the Department of Defense, civilian control of civil defense operations in any case would depend upon the avoidance of a declaration of martial law." [87] As a means for overcoming and resolving some of the remaining differences of opinion, the Holifield report pointed to the Military Liaison Committee contemplated in the proposed legislation.

---

[86] *Status of CDL*, pp. 20, 7. The report added that the arrangements of the revised emergency section were "patterned on the Presidential proclamations for exercise of Federal authority issued during Operation Alert 1956."

[87] *Ibid.*, pp. 20, 21.

The bill sponsored by the Holifield subcommittee was not passed by Congress. Nevertheless, civil defense programs were improved in 1958 through the consolidation of previously separate agencies in the new Office of Civil and Defense Mobilization. As it appears, subsequent planning of this office with respect to military-civilian relations was based on the assumption of a strengthened civil defense organization permitting the retention of civilian control in most situations and, on the military side, on the described directives and policy statements of the Defense Department. The National Plan of October, 1958 made the local government the basic institution responsible for the emergency maintenance of law and order, with the state government performing primary supporting functions. However, the plan specified that, upon request of the state government or where the state government was unable to act, the federal government would assume and exercise all necessary government functions during an emergency in areas where local authorities were incapable of performing vital functions. Under the same heading of federal responsibilities, the principle was announced that, upon request, the Secretary of Defense would "provide emergency military aid to the civil authority to assist in the maintenance of law and order, to the extent that such commitment will not interfere with the conduct of primary military missions." [88]

The various forms and differing degrees of military involvement in civil defense emergencies were set forth in greater detail in one of the annexes of the National Plan. The explanation started from the premise that civil defense is essentially a civilian function while the primary mission of the armed forces is military defense; consequently military assistance was to be rendered in a manner which would interfere as little as possible with regular duties. The major limitation imposed on the concept of military aid was that military resources would be made temporarily available to civil authorities to the degree that "such support does not interfere with the essential military mission" and with the further proviso that "resources thus committed will be responsive to military command and remain under military control . . . and will be subject to recall to meet the operations requirements of the mili-

[88] *National Plan*, p. 12; compare also Annex 4: "Authorities for Civil Defense and Defense Mobilization" (August, 1959), p. 18.

tary mission." Concerning military support, the annex also stated that planning and operational liaison had been established between the zone of the Interior Army Commanders and the regional directors of the Office of Civil and Defense Mobilization, while the maintenance of similar contacts was contemplated between local military commanders and local civil defense officials. Although efforts were to be continued to avoid the necessity of military rule, the annex envisaged the possibility of martial law as a final resort.

Martial law will not be imposed except when the agencies of the civil law have been paralyzed, overthrown, or overpowered and are unable to operate and function adequately. Martial law cannot be imposed without specific executive authorization. Priority will be given to support civil authorities in maintaining law and order.

As in the case of military assistance, military commanders acting under a declaration of martial law or in a specified military area were to receive orders relating to civil relief and control through the established chain of military command. The annex concluded that in areas where martial law has been declared by the president, "the military authorities may perform all acts reasonably necessary for the restoration and maintenance of public order, until such time as it is determined by the President that the appropriate civil authorities are able to operate and function adequately." [89]

The functioning and implementation of the National Plan was part of the object under inquiry during the civil defense hearings conducted by the Holifield subcommittee in March, 1960. Testifying at these hearings, the director of the Office of Civil and Defense Mobilization reiterated the view that the maintenance of civil government at all levels was a primary objective in civil defense planning and that, wherever possible, military forces would be deployed in support of, rather than as substitute for civil authority. As Governor Hoegh pointed out, an arrangement had been worked out between the Army and the civil defense authorities according to which the armed forces and particularly the Army would be committed in support of the civilian agencies if the primary mission of the military permitted such assistance.

[89] *National Plan*, Annex 7: "Role of the Military" (August, 1959), pp. 3, 5.

The civil defense director also indicated that his office had made an arrangement with the Defense Department whereby most of the National Guard forces would be available to the states and under the control of the state governors for deployment in support of postattack recovery operations. When not needed in their home state—Governor Hoegh observed—the national guard units could be employed in interstate assistance either with the consent of their governors or under orders federalizing the units. With regard to the use of military reservists, the federal director expressed support of the Department of Defense position that reserves should be concerned primarily with military missions, but observed that negotiations were in progress between his office and the Defense Department on the future training of reservists for civil defense emergencies. While stressing the supporting role of military forces, Governor Hoegh acknowledged that it might not always be possible to avoid substituting martial law for civil authority; he added, however, that military rule should remain an ultimate remedy.[90] The Holifield subcommittee appeared basically satisfied with the development of military-civilian relations disclosed in the testimony, although its report expressed a desire for greater reliance on military reserve units in support of civil defense operations.

A New Type of Martial Law?

Since the establishment of the Federal Civil Defense Administration in 1950, civilian and military planning had been basically separated and conducted in two different channels of the executive branch. While, under changing names, the federal civil defense and mobilization agencies had directed civilian programs, the Department of Defense and the military services had made preparations for military support and assistance in case of emergency. Coordination and liaison between the two channels was frequently a difficult matter, although considerable improvements were made after the test exercises of 1955 and 1956. The reorganization of 1961 inaugurated a completely new form of civilian-military relationship. The major planning and operational functions in the field of civil defense were transferred to the

[90] *CD Hearings 1960*, pp. 92, 119-120.

Defense Department, while only limited supervising or advisory functions were assigned to the Office of Emergency Planning. In his Civil Defense Message of May 25, the president emphasized that civil defense should remain "civilian in nature and leadership" and that this feature would "not be changed." The Secretary of Defense, in his statement of July 20, endorsed the view that the civil defense effort "must remain under civilian control," and he predicted that it would be "organized within the Department of Defense as a civilian function, drawing where necessary on the military departments for available support." However, despite this insistence on a separate civilian function, the Secretary observed that "in the age of thermonuclear war," civil defense must be closely "integrated with all aspects of military defense against thermonuclear attack" and must "not be permitted to downgrade the military capabilities of our armed forces." [91]

For all practical purposes, the reorganization of 1961 signified a consolidation of military and nonmilitary defense planning within the department which previously had been concerned only with military preparations. It is debatable whether this arrangement amounted to a clarification or to a further confusion of responsibilities and functions. In any event, the consolidation injected a note of ambiguity into the traditional concept of military assistance and support to civil defense agencies. While previously the concept was based on two separate lines of command and involved primarily the problem of the degree of military subordination to or coordination with civilian defense authorities, the new arrangement encouraged doubts as to whether the notions of "support" and "subordination" were still exact or meaningful. Although, in a technical sense, the military services and the new civil defense office were constituted as separate branches within the Defense Department, the basic authority for both branches was obviously vested in one head, the Secretary of Defense. Under these circumstances, it became possible to ask the legitimate—albeit somewhat facetious and almost metaphysical—question whether, in regard to the supporting role of the military, the Defense Department intended to support itself and to subordinate its military to its civilian "personality." At the same time, the consolidation effected in 1961 tended to modify the

[91] See *CD Hearings 1961*, App. 1A, p. 375; App. 3D, p. 383.

previous understanding of martial law as an extraneous military intrusion into civilian affairs and to suggest a more intimate fusion of military and civilian aspects under martial rule than had previously been considered possible or perhaps desirable.

The potential implications of the 1961 reorganization for civilian-military relations were first noticed—apparently without causing any significant apprehension or concern—by the Holifield subcommittee and its chairman. Already on previous occasions, Congressman Holifield had expressed himself in favor of a closer coordination and integration of military commitments and civil defense programs. In July, 1961, while the reorganization was still in progress, the congressman, speaking on the floor of the House, welcomed the prospect of increased federal leadership and direction in civil defense matters; he also envisaged the possibility of a new type or new concept of martial law on the basis of the projected reorganization. To be sure, the congressman in his remarks did not abandon his previously expressed distaste for military rule or his insistence on the importance of civilian planning. "If we make no comprehensive plans," he stated,

if we do not prepare ourselves for the blow—which we hope never comes—then we can be certain that the military will take complete command in an emergency. Bayonets will condition our responses, and the harsh discipline of military organization will regulate our work and welfare. . . . Pre-emergency planning . . . would safeguard our traditional Federal-state constitutional structure and insure that post-attack recovery operations would proceed in a governmental environment compatible with our constitutional democratic society.[92]

The remarks also emphasized that the continuity of civil government should be preserved wherever possible so that the civil defense effort might be "directed to the best national advantage and so that we do not subject ourselves to more military dictatorship than absolutely necessary."

While thus reiterating his previously stated sentiments, the congressman did not fail to perceive the modification of civil-military relations implicit in the transfer of civil defense functions to the Defense Department. Although, in earlier reports, his subcommittee had repeatedly voiced reservations with regard to such

[92] 107 Cong. Rec. 12719-12720, 87th Cong., 1st Sess. (July 17, 1961).

transfer, Representative Holifield now refused to be swayed by timid apprehensions. The proposed allocation of functions to the Defense Department, he observed,

has created concern in some quarters whether we are about to witness a military takeover in the civil defense field. Let me say immediately that we should not be carried away by slogans. I hope and trust that we shall not get into an argument about who will do the task of civil defense when we have not yet found firm agreement on what the tasks are, or the level of national effort required. I am not interested in bureaucratic maneuvering and empire-building. I am interested in an effective civil defense for the people of the United States. As far as I am concerned, the Department of Defense has large resources to contribute to a civil defense program, and these resources should be employed to the fullest possible extent.

Rather than being impressed by "slogans" of a military takeover, the congressman expressed the expectation that the reorganization might contribute to a more intimate coordination of military and civilian authorities and to the development of a new and more appropriate type of martial law in case of extreme emergency. "Martial law in its more primitive sense," he argued,

—where civil institutions are unable or not permitted to function, and military sovereignty is supreme—is no longer an adequate concept for our times. We need to devise new forms of control in which all the resources of the Nation, all institutions—military and civil alike—are utilized for the common overriding purposes of survival, recuperation, and recovery after a nuclear attack. . . . If we plan wisely, I foresee a civilian type of martial law which would permit the exercise of full emergency authority by the President and would embrace all civilian as well as military resources of the nation. Unlike martial law in the traditional sense, the system I envision, would utilize—rather than suspend—all civilian institutions surviving the enemies' attack, including the civil courts and elected officials of government.[93]

The conviction that the new combination of civilian and military forces would not deteriorate into an "old-type" military rule was based in the congressman's remarks on the authority and leadership of the president in whose "constitutional person" civil and military powers are combined.

It is at least doubtful whether it is possible or even advisable

[93] *Ibid.*

to use the term "martial law" to designate a situation in which civil courts and other civil institutions are functioning—unless, of course, the envisaged combination of military and civil authority serves merely as a disguise for an "old-type" martial rule. In subsequent hearings and committee reports, Congressman Holifield reasserted the basic tenor of his remarks although he did not greatly expand on the idea of a new category of martial law; his additional statements and other testimony were not completely able, however, to allay some of the mentioned doubts. In the course of the civil defense hearings of August, 1961, Chairman Holifield stressed again the importance of pre-planning as a means to reduce the need for an "old-type" martial law and to decrease the dangers inherent in the transfer of civil defense functions to the Defense Department. "The concept of martial law as we have had it in the past, it seems to me," he stated,

is not only alarming to a great many people, but I think the effect which has been obtained in the past by summary martial law can be obtained by preplanning of the utilization of civilian organization under their respective civilian superiors, such as the Governors of the various states. . . . I believe the alarm that is in the minds of a great many people about the transfer of civil defense to the Department of Defense can be allayed if they know in advance the extent of authority which the Defense Department intends to take over in an emergency. . . . I think that in a society that is dedicated to the predominance of civilian authority, the necessary preliminary planning can obviate the necessity of the rigid, harsh continuous type of martial law which has obtained in other countries.

While emphasizing the need for civil defense preparations to strengthen the capabilities of civilian authorities, Chairman Holifield admitted the possibility of martial law in extreme emergencies; in this context, he returned to his conception of a new form of martial rule. "I recognize," he said,

that there will be martial law almost inevitably. The thing that I am recommending is preplanning to soften the effect of martial law insofar as it is possible through the Governors and other state officials which ordinarily would perform the function instead of having men with bayonets come in to do the job of policing and fire protection and sanitation, and that sort of thing, where it is possible to utilize civilians. . . . I am thinking something along that line, and hoping that a real

new study and a new concept will be given, so that when martial law
is declared in those areas where it is necessary to declare it, that it
will be declared in such a way that its implementation will take full
advantage of all of our civilian resources and maintain to that extent
possible our civilian organizations and our civilian lines of authority and
functions, meanwhile recognizing that they must report possibly to a
military command.[94]

The testimony of witnesses, and especially of the Secretary of
Defense and of the Joint Chiefs of Staff, did not disclose a particular appreciation or understanding of the conception expounded
by Chairman Holifield. A review of this testimony suggests that
the thinking of most witnesses moved along more traditional
lines, with an element of confusion injected by the reallocation
of civil defense functions. In his opening statement, Secretary
McNamara repeated the principles which he had first announced
at the time of the reorganization order: that "the civil defense
effort must remain under civilian direction and control," that "in
the age of thermonuclear war, civil defense must be integrated
with all aspects of military defense," and that "the civil defense
functions of the Department must not be permitted to downgrade
the military capabilities of our Armed Forces." Elaborating on
these principles, the secretary explained somewhat vaguely that,
under the new arrangement, civil defense would not degrade the
military function and the military function would not impair civil
defense. The secretary admitted that "many people, including
previous Defense officials, have been apprehensive about the consequences of bringing civil defense under what has been described as 'military control.'" However, when asked whether the
assignment of civil defense functions to his Department would
dilute or jeopardize civilian authority and finally subject it to
military command, the secretary simply replied: "I do not believe
it will." With regard to the specific implications of the "integration" of civil and military defense functions, Secretary McNamara
and other witnesses adhered to the customary concepts of military
assistance and martial rule. Although military operations were
described as the primary mission of military forces, the secretary
stated that, in certain contingencies, military personnel might be
available to assist in providing emergency services; as he indi-

[94] *CD Hearings 1961*, pp. 36, 37-38.

cated, standby reserve and retired reserve forces would normally be used in this supporting function. Concerning martial rule, the staff administrator of the subcommittee queried whether, in the event of emergency and in specified areas, martial law would be invoked "in the conventional or traditional sense." On this point, the Chairman of the Joint Chiefs of Staff, General Lemnitzer, observed:

Well, that would depend entirely upon the ability of other branches of the Government to function. It is generally regarded that the need for martial law arises only when all civil authority has ceased to function and there is no other means of exercising control.

When asked whether there was any new conception or new military policy in this field, the general answered: "None that I know of." [95]

On the basis of these and similar statements, it seems fair to conclude that the 1961 hearings did not produce a real meeting of minds on the issues of civil-military relations and martial law. Perhaps, it was partly due to this fact that the subcommittee report of September, 1961, omitted any reference to the martial law problem and concentrated its attention entirely on the customary aspect of military support and assistance in postattack emergency situations. In this context the report noted a gradually changing emphasis in Army and Defense Department regulations. While in the early postwar period Army regulations stipulated that civil defense assistance would be given only "with minimum practical diversion" from the Army's primary mission and while Defense Department directives of 1956 described civil defense as an "emergency task" of military forces, the support role was termed in 1960 as a "responsibility within the mission" of military units "second only to combat operations." The notion that the reorganization of 1961 might becloud and seriously jeopardize the concept of military support was not pondered by the committee; the report merely stated that "with the vesting of civil defense responsibilities in the Secretary of Defense, new adjustments will have to be made." The subcommittee welcomed the announcement of Secretary McNamara that standby and retired reserves

[95] *Ibid.*, pp. 5, 10, 23, 37.

might be available for civil defense programs, although its report added that "in view of the rather complex legislative and administrative problems relating to the use of Reserve forces," the secretary should submit new proposals "if necessary, for legislative action." [96] As it appears, the subcommittee assumed that, with minor legislative revisions, civil-military relations would develop smoothly and that the new arrangements were no significant cause for alarm. The same optimistic attitude was displayed in the hearings and report of 1962 dealing with shelter policy. The report of May, 1962, observed that, with the exception of three military officers, the personnel of the new Office of Civil Defense were "all civilians," although "close liaison and coordination" were maintained between the office and other branches of the Defense Department.[97]

In view of the critical and aggressive attitude of the subcommittee in earlier reports, it seems surprising that the modification of civil-military relations implicit in the 1961 reorganization should have been accepted with such grace and optimism. It is true that civil defense programs had languished for a long time due to organizational weaknesses; however, the question remains to which degree normal civil procedures and constitutional safeguards may be sacrificed to the requirements of efficiency. Although the transfer of civil defense functions to the Defense Department may be the only remedy in catastrophic emergencies, one may still wonder whether this transfer is advisable as a permanent organizational arrangement. As previously noted, the

[96] *New CD Program,* pp. 62-63, 64.

[97] *National Fallout Shelter Program,* p.7. The relationship between civil and military rule in civil defense emergencies was also discussed during hearings held by a subcommittee of the House Armed Services Committee in May and July of 1963. The preponderant view of the testimony was that the military would normally be employed in a supporting role and that only in case of extreme disaster would martial law—in the traditional sense of the term—replace civilian control. One member of the subcommittee, Alexander Pirnie of New York, actually argued in favor of broader military power and of a more ready resort to an old-type martial law in emergencies. See U. S. Congress, House, Hearings before Subcommittee No. 3, Committee on Armed Services, *Civil Defense—Fallout Shelter Program* (hereinafter cited as *CD 1963*), 88th Cong., 1st Sess. (May and July, 1963), pt. II, vol. 1, pp. 3654, 3663, 4478; pt. II, vol. 2, pp. 4972, 5365-5371, 5489-5510. Compare also H. Rep. 715, 88th Cong., 1st Sess. (August 27, 1963); and 109 Cong. Rec. 16359-16360 (September 17, 1963).

concept of military support to civil defense authorities is rendered ambiguous under the new arrangement since it resolves itself into the assistance of one branch of the Defense Department to another. The "integration" or partnership of military and civilian authorities under a "new" type of martial law also raises many difficult problems. As Charles Fairman observed some time ago: "'Partnership' has a beguiling sound: everybody ought to pitch in and work for the common good. 'Partnership' tends to produce obscurity of thought in a matter where rigorous analysis is desperately needed." [98] It is not sufficient to say that all forces and agencies should cooperate; the question is exactly who is going to command and direct the operations. If under the "new" conception the civil authorities are supposed to retain control, it appears hardly justified or advisable to designate the situation as martial law. If, on the other hand, the military authorities are expected to exercise ultimate control, then the new conception resembles very closely the "old-fashioned" or traditional type of military rule. There is reason to believe that the latter alternative would probably prevail, especially with the present concentration of civil and military defense functions in the Defense Department.

As long as the present arrangement exists, one should at least insist on the maintenance of constant watchfulness on the part of civil authorities and the public in general to insure that civil functions remain civilian in nature wherever possible. Other, more concrete plans and preparations can be made by competent agencies to obviate the necessity of military intervention in case of emergency. A prominent part of these plans and preparations is the so-called "continuity of government" program, a program designed to preserve civil institutions in the event of nuclear attack. The major elements of the program are the establishment of adequate lines of succession for key personnel, the building of relocation sites for government emergency operations, and the preservation of essential records and documents.

Under the terms of the 1961 reorganization, planning in this area is one of the functions expressly assigned to the Office of Emergency Planning.[99] Nevertheless, the program is not of recent

[98] Fairman, *op. cit.* (*supra*, n. 82), p. 5.
[99] Exec. Order No. 10952, 26 Fed. Reg. 6577 (July 20, 1961), Sec. 2(b) (c).

origin and dates back over at least ten years. Efforts in the described direction were initiated by lawyers or legal experts [100] and by the Federal Civil Defense Administration. Following the establishment of the Office of Civil Defense Mobilization in 1958, the continuity of government program became an essential part of the "National Plan" for civil defense and defense mobilization. In July, 1960, the Holifield subcommittee attested that the Office had made "commendable progress in assuring the continuity of government at the Federal level." By June, 1961, it was reported that, in addition to the twelve levels of succession to the presidency, adequate lines of succession had been established for other key officials in departments and agencies of the executive branch of the federal government. While legislation was found to exist to fill vacancies in the Senate and the federal judiciary, a constitutional amendment was considered necessary to assure the operation of the House of Representatives under nuclear attack conditions. It was also disclosed that all federal agencies had selected relocation sites for their headquarters operations as well as a great number of sites for field operations and that the federal civil defense agency had planned construction of protected underground control centers for each of its eight regional offices. At the same time, federal departments and agencies continued to maintain essential records at protected emergency facilities.[101]

4. STATE POWERS AND FUNCTIONS

In the preceding pages, attention has been focused primarily on emergency powers of the federal government and of the president. It is obvious, however, that no civil defense and mobilization program could function effectively without the active

[100] For an excellent treatment of the problems involved in the preservation of civil institutions and civil law see David F. Cavers, "Legal Planning Against the Risk of Atomic Attack," *Columbia L.Rev.*, 55: 128 (1955). Compare also Homer D. Crotty, "The Administration of Justice and the A-Bomb: What Follows Disaster?" *American Bar Association J.*, 37: 893 (1951); Martin Granirer, "The 'H' and 'A' Bombs—Serious Challenges to Civil Process and Civilian Life," *New York State Bar Bulletin*, 30: 362 (1958).

[101] Executive Office of the President, Office of Civil and Defense Mobilization, *Annual Report 1961* (through June 30, 1961), reproduced in S.Rep. 1124, *11th Annual Report of the Activities of the Joint Committee on Defense Production*, 87th Cong., 2d Sess. (January 23, 1962), pp. 105-106.

cooperation of state and local government authorities. The co-ordination and integration of federal and state activities in this field presents many novel and difficult problems; in fact, the unresolved question of federal-state relations accounted to some degree for the invocation of martial law in the civil defense exercise of 1955. The concept that state and local government bodies must play a vital part in nonmilitary preparations has been a fixed assumption in civil defense planning during the postwar period. Likewise, the principle has been widely accepted that, on the state level, the governor is the final authority in civil defense and mobilization programs. In this capacity, the chief executive of the state is endowed by statutes or state constitutions with vast emergency powers which, in some measure, resemble the emergency prerogatives of the president. As the director of the former Office of Civil and Defense Mobilization observed during congressional hearings in March, 1960:

The Governor has the responsibility for civil defense and for the protection of people. The Governor has a chief of staff for nonmilitary defense just like the President does. He is the civil defense director of that state. . . . The Governor is the overall commander, just like the President is.[102]

Although emphasis on the necessity of state participation has been a constant feature in postwar planning, the exact place which state governments and their chief executives should occupy in over-all nonmilitary defense preparations has not been entirely free from controversy or change. While the immediate postwar years witnessed a concentration of primary responsibility on the state and local level, the development of the hydrogen bomb and of intercontinental missiles led to increased reliance on federal leadership and to a more equitable distribution of functions between the federal and state governments. In the same measure, the role of the governor changed from a position of preeminence to one of partnership. During the second World War, civil defense efforts centered very strongly around the state as the primary unit in the over-all program. The Bull Report of 1948 affirmed that self help constituted the basic principle of civil defense and that primary responsibility should be vested in state and local service units. The study of the Office of Civil Defense

[102] *CD Hearings 1960*, p. 93.

Planning followed a similar approach, although it was more explicit on the organization of state functions. Among other things, the Hopley Report designated the governor as the final authority of the state program and proposed that the governor appoint a director of civil defense and an advisory civil defense council composed of outstanding citizens and representatives from the legislative and judicial branches of the state government. The National Security Resources Board which was in charge of civil defense and mobilization planning from 1949 to 1950 also relied on the state as the key operating unit. The Blue Book of September, 1950, placed operational control of the civil defense system unequivocally in the hands of the state governments; it also proposed organizational arrangements of state functions, including the appointment by the governor of a state civil defense director with cabinet rank.[103]

Mainly on the basis of the described studies and recommendations, the Federal Civil Defense Act of 1950 vested primary responsibility for civil defense "in the several states and their political subdivisions." The adequacy of this arrangement was subjected in subsequent years to growing criticism, both on the part of private study groups and of the Holifield subcommittee. The review committee of Project East River affirmed in 1955 the need for greater federal leadership, while the National Planning Association proposed the "coordination and direction under centralized responsibility of the nonmilitary defense program within the federal government." In its report of 1956, the Holifield subcommittee recommended the strengthening of federal control, a recommendation which was incorporated in legislation sponsored by the subcommittee. The Holifield bill of 1957 made civil defense "a direct responsibility of the Federal Government" while assigning to the states and local communities "an important supporting role." The legislative proposal of the subcommittee was not enacted; however, in 1958, Congress passed an act which changed the policy declaration of the Federal Civil Defense Act by stating that "the responsibility for civil defense shall be vested jointly in the Federal Government and the several states and their political subdivisions." The National Plan of the same year declared the federal government "responsible for direction and coordination of the total national effort," while the government

---

[103] Brewer, *op. cit.*, p. 27.

of each state was held "responsible for the direction and coordination of the civil defense and defense mobilization activities of the state and its political subdivisions." The document also specified that

The chief executives of state and local governments direct the civil defense and defense mobilization activities within their jurisdiction. With the assistance of their civil defense staffs, the chief executives will direct the performance of emergency functions within the regularly constituted government structure, augmenting it where needed.[104]

The reorganization of 1961 produced a further coordination and integration of federal and state efforts.[105]

Legislative Authority

The powers of the governor and other state officials in the field of civil defense and defense mobilization are in large measure determined by statutes. All states today have legislative enactments concerning civil defense; in many states there is also specific statutory authority for the conduct of activities associated with defense mobilization. Most of the emergency statutes in this area are a product of the postwar period. At the end of World War II, wartime legislation relating to civil defense and disaster preparedness existed and continued in effect in only a few states. The beginning of the cold war soon focused the attention of state legislatures on civil defense problems. By early 1949, civil defense and preparedness laws were in effect in at least seventeen states. At the same time, the drafting committee of state officials of the Council of State Governments, in collaboration with the Office of Civil Defense Planning, had developed a Model State Civil Defense Act, a draft law which was included in the suggested state legislative program for 1949.[106] The model act was endorsed in its major provisions by the National Security Resources Board in its report of 1950; subsequent amendments were proposed and

[104] *National Plan*, pp. 3, 5.

[105] The Defense Department was directed to give emergency assistance to state and local governments in a postattack period and to develop programs for making financial contributions to the states, while the Office of Emergency Planning was to coordinate federal civil defense activities with state activities.

[106] Council of State Governments, *Suggested State Legislation Program for 1949* (Chicago, November, 1948).

incorporated in the act by the drafting committee of the Council of State Governments. Between 1949 and 1951, some forty-three states acted to provide basic civil defense legislation. Much of the pertinent state legislation was passed after the adoption of the Federal Civil Defense Act and many laws followed closely the model state civil defense act sponsored by the Council of State Governments and the National Security Resources Board.

The powers granted to the governor in the model state civil defense act are patterned to a large extent after presidential prerogatives stipulated in federal civil defense legislation.[107] Concerning administrative organization, the model act authorizes the governor to appoint a civil defense director who, subject to the governor's direction and control, acts as the executive head of the state's civil defense agency and is responsible to the governor for carrying out the civil defense program of the state. The governor is also entitled to create a civil defense advisory council whose purpose it is to advise the governor and the director on all matters pertaining to civil defense. Like the federal civil defense act, the model statute distinguishes between regular "civil defense powers" and "emergency powers" of the chief executive. Under the section dealing with regular civil defense authority, the governor is given general direction and control of the civil defense agency; he is also vested with the responsibility for implementing the provisions of the act and, in the event of disaster beyond local control, with the authority to assume direct operational control over all or any part of the civil defense functions within his state. In exercising his general civil defense responsibilities, the governor is empowered, with due consideration of the plans of the federal government, to make, amend and rescind necessary rules and regulations, to prepare a comprehensive civil defense program for his state, to procure supplies and equipment in accordance with such programs, and "to take all other preparatory steps including the partial or full mobilization of civil defense organizations in advance of actual disaster, to insure the furnishing of

[107] For an up-to-date text of the model act and a comparison of the act with legislation enacted by the various states see Executive Office of the President, Office of Civil and Defense Mobilization, *Comparison of State Civil Defense Legislation* (hereinafter cited as *Comparison of State CDL;* Washington, D.C., March, 1960). Compare also Barry J. Galt, "Constitutional Law: Emergency Powers of the Governor in the Event of Enemy Attack," *Oklahoma L. Rev.*, 12:528 (1959).

adequately trained and equipped forces of civil defense personnel in time of need."

The section of the act dealing with "emergency powers" specifies that the provisions contained in the section shall become
operative only during the existence of a state of civil defense
emergency. The existence of such an emergency may be proclaimed by the governor or by resolution of the legislature

if the governor in such proclamation, or the legislature in such resolution, finds that an attack upon the United States has occurred or is
anticipated in the immediate future, or that a natural disaster of major
proportions has actually occurred within this state, and that the safety
and welfare of the inhabitants of this state require an invocation of the
provisions of this section.

The state of emergency may be terminated by a proclamation of
the governor or a resolution of the legislature. During the existence of the civil defense emergency, the governor is entitled to
exercise a vast range of powers, in some instances without regard
to statutory limitations. Among other things, the act empowers
the chief executive of the state to enforce all laws, rules, and
regulations relating to civil defense and to assume direct operational control of civil defense forces in the state; to sell, lend,
lease, transfer, or deliver materials and perform services for civil
defense purposes on conditions prescribed by the governor and
without regard to statutory provisions; and to compel the evacuation of all or part of the population from a stricken or threatened
area. A broad procurement power is granted in the provision
which authorizes the governor to "procure, by purchase, condemnation, seizure, or other means, construct, lease, transport,
stock, maintain, renovate or distribute materials and facilities for
civil defense without regard to the limitations of any existing law
provided he shall make compensation for the property so seized,
taken, or condemned." The act contains additional clauses relative to the fixing of the amount of compensation by the governor.
In parenthesis, state authorities are admonished to check pertinent provisions of the state constitution in order to insure the
constitutional validity of contemplated seizure or condemnation
proceedings.

As stated previously, all states have at present legislation covering, more or less adequately, the field of nonmilitary defense. In many states, legislative enactments follow rather closely the provisions of the model act, although there are considerable variations in detail. There is no need in the present context to examine all these statutory differences and variations. Suffice it to say that in almost all states the governor is charged with the over-all responsibility of preparing and administering civil defense programs. Also, in nearly all the states, the civil defense director is appointed by the governor, while in more than two-thirds of the states a similar provision is made for the appointment of an advisory council whose membership usually includes a broad representation of interest groups. In implementing state civil defense programs, governors are regularly authorized to make, amend and repeal necessary rules and regulations, to receive and distribute supplies and equipment, to make studies and surveys of available or needed state facilities, and to direct state evacuation activities. In addition, state chief executives are commonly granted extraordinary emergency authority in the event of war or in case of catastrophic disaster. Obviously, many of the executive civil defense powers would be offensive in normal peacetime; some of the powers are expressly limited to times of extreme emergency. Nevertheless, even if viewed within the context of cold war exigencies, statutory provisions relating to nonmilitary defense frequently give rise to grave questions of constitutional validity. A good illustration of such constitutional problems can be found in the development of emergency measures in New York, one of the most active and resolute states in the area of nonmilitary defense.

A civil defense measure of comparatively modest proportions was enacted by the legislature of the State of New York in 1950. However, as a result of federal civil defense legislation passed in the same year and in view of growing cold war tensions manifested especially in the Korean crisis, Governor Dewey of New York recommended a broad revision of the 1950 statute and a strengthening of the nonmilitary defense programs of the state. In his legislative message proposing the change, the governor stressed the need for new legislation in these terms:

The one thing of which we can be sure is that the devastation caused by any modern atomic bomb will require advance preparation of a kind never before undertaken any place in the world. . . . only by spelling out in advance the things which would have to be done and the powers and duties of your State Government, could martial law be avoided in the terrible event of such destruction of life and property.[108]

Early in 1951, the state legislature passed the new statute, called the New York State Defense Emergency Act.[109] The law stated in its declaration of policy that

in view of the professed determination of the government of the United States to resist further communist aggression, and because of the likelihood of resort to atomic and radiological weapons in the event of further conflict between this nation and communist aggressors, the peril to the people of this state is sufficiently great that the precautions embodied in this act must be taken.

The policy statement also declared it to be the general purpose of the legislation "to meet these dangers and problems with the least possible interference with the existing division of the powers of the government and the least possible infringement of the liberties of the people, including the freedom of speech, press, and assembly."

The New York statute of 1951 contemplated a broad program of nonmilitary preparedness including both civil defense and defense mobilization activities. For the implementation of the larger objectives of this program, the act created a State Defense Council whose membership comprises the governor, a number of ex-officio members, and twelve additional persons appointed by the governor. The chief executive of the state is designated as the chairman of the defense council. In the more limited field of civil defense planning, the statute establishes a special Civil Defense Commission whose responsibilities include the adoption of a comprehensive plan for the civil defense of the state, the execution of mutual defense pacts with other states, and the coordination and direction of local government activities. The commission is composed of specified ex-officio members and of members ap-

[108] See Note, "New York State Defense Emergency Act of 1951," *St. John's L. Rev.*, 26: 175 (1951).

[109] The major provisions of the act are reproduced in *Comparison of State CDL*, pp. 32.1 to 32.49.

pointed by the governor. In the performance of their respective functions, both the council and the commission are endowed with a vast range of powers. Like other civil defense statutes, the New York act distinguishes in this context between regular powers which may be exercised in pre-attack situations and emergency powers which become operative in case of attack or extreme catastrophe. However, due to the fact that "attack" is defined to include imminent danger, many emergency powers would seem to be available to state authorities even in the absence of direct military operations. Despite the allocation of major responsibilities to the council and the commission, the statute makes it clear that "no provision of this act shall be construed or interpreted as expressing a limitation . . . of the power of the governor . . . to effectuate any or all of the purposes of this act" and that, to the extent necessary for the performance of his duties, "the governor may execute . . . any of the powers, granted in this act to any agency or officer, in such manner as he deems necessary or proper." The recognition of this broad gubernatorial authority is not limited to situations of attack or imminent threat of attack.

Under the provisions of the act, the state defense council—and alternately the governor—is directed to encourage maximum production and, for this purpose, may establish orders of priorities for construction work by the state or political subdivisions and may authorize the conduct of business or manufacture of goods on Sundays and legal holidays. Also in the interest of maximum productivity, the Industrial Commissioner, or the governor in his place, is authorized to grant employees engaged in defense work dispensation from state labor laws where, under existing labor conditions, the employer would be unable to maintain efficient production. In order to insure an adequate supply of food, clothing, fuel and other essential materials during an emergency, the defense council is empowered to "adopt and make effective rationing, freezing, price-fixing, allocation or other orders or regulations imposed by the authority of the federal government in aid of the defense effort." In the event of attack, the council or alternately the governor may provide for the protection and preservation of public and private property by the owner or person in control of the property. In addition, private property rights are subjected by the act to a drastic power of eminent domain. In case of attack, the civil defense commission or the governor is entitled to "take, use, or destroy any and all real or personal property, or any interest therein, necessary or proper for the purposes of civil defense." The statute specifies, however, that any taking of private property must be accompanied or followed by the payment of adequate compensation. Severe limitations of personal liberty are contemplated in sections of the act providing for conscription and impressment into public service. On a temporary basis, local authorities may impress into service any person necessary for the destruction of property or clearance of debris in the aftermath of an attack. Moreover, when authorized by the council or the governor, each county or city may conscript persons to perform the statutory duties imposed upon the localities, a measure which is possible in case of declared war, attack or impending attack.

The described provisions clearly imply a considerable curtailment of constitutional rights, a curtailment which is all the more serious in view of the fact that many of the statutory powers may be exercised in the absence of direct attack or military operations. Questions of constitutional validity arise primarily with regard to the taking of private property and conscription procedures. Although the statute provides for the payment of compensation in case of property seizure, the assignment of procurement powers to the state and local government bodies imposes upon the property owner the task of ascertaining which authority is required to make the payment; moreover, there is no sufficient insurance that compensation is paid in case of unauthorized seizure. The power of conscription may conceivably be exercised in pre-attack situations. In the light of this possibility, it is important to notice that the conscription section of the act does not make provision for any notice or hearing, procedures which are considered basic requirements of regular due process. The section also raises doubts under the constitutional prohibition of involuntary servitude. Although, when dictated by public necessity, impressment into public service regularly does not violate this prohibition, the statute does not properly delimit the service which may be exacted of citizens of the state without compensation. Moreover, there is the problem of the delegation of legislative authority to the defense council or the governor. As one observer pointed out:

It is submitted that the conscription provision as it now stands, considered from all its facets—the possibility that it may be exercised today; its omission of provisions for notice and hearing; the broad and sweeping delegation of legislative authority without sufficient criteria as to length of service, distinction between sexes, and duties which may be imposed; its omission of provision for compensation or sustenance when the duty to serve may prevent the right to earn a living —raises grave questions of constitutionality.[110]

In July of 1959, Governor Rockefeller of New York established a Committee on Fallout Protection which was charged with developing a program for protecting citizens of the state against radioactive fallout in the event of nuclear attack. On February 15, 1960, the committee submitted its report to the governor, together with a suggested outline of legislation required to implement the committee's findings.[111] The suggested legislation which was strongly endorsed by Governor Rockefeller was submitted during the same month to the state defense council and the state legislature. The main feature of the legislative proposal was a mandatory shelter program which required home owners and landlords of commercial premises to provide minimum fallout shelter facilities on their property. The plan was unfavorably received by the state legislature and was criticized by many government leaders. From the perspective of constitutional validity, the major problem raised by the program was whether the requirement of shelter construction constituted a proper exercise of the state's police power. Unless covered by the police power concept, the requirement was likely to amount to a deprivation of property without due process of law. Mandatory action on the part of private citizens has customarily been compelled under the state's police power if such action was designed to promote the public health, safety, and welfare and if individual compliance was beneficial to the community. In the case of home shelter construction, however, the required action is of benefit to the home owner and not immediately to his neighbors. These considerations led one student of the problem to the conclusion that,

since the proposed New York fallout shelter program represents an expansion of the police power into an area of compelling positive

[110] See *St. John's L.Rev.*, 26: 175, 187 (1951).
[111] See *CD Shelter Policy*, pp. 21-23.

action beneficial only to those complying with the statute, and since to uphold such a program would open a vertitable Pandora's box of social legislation considered oppressive and inappropriate to our form of democratic government, the courts should feel constrained to reject the plan as not properly within the police power and therefore violative of due process of law.[112]

On March 23, 1960, Governor Rockefeller formally withdrew his shelter program and endorsed instead a plan for voluntary shelter construction with state tax inducements and other incentives for public participation. After having been submitted to and adopted by the state defense council in October of 1961, the shelter incentive plan was enacted by a special session of the New York legislature in November of the same year.

Military Powers

Despite their comprehensive character, the use of the described statutory powers may not always be sufficient to combat and overcome widespread disaster in a state. In such instances, the governor may decide to call out the military forces of the state. The employment of the state militia by the governor in civil defense emergencies is sometimes, but not always specified by state legislation. In the case of New York, the state's defense emergency act stipulates expressly that no provision of the statute is to be construed as expressing a limitation of the power of the governor "or of the military forces of the state to effectuate any or all of the purposes of this act or to execute the powers and duties otherwise vested in either of them." The model state civil defense act, in its section dealing with emergency powers, authorizes the governor to "enforce all laws, rules and regulations relating to civil defense and to assume direct operational control of any or all civil defense forces and helpers in the state" and to "perform and exercise such other functions, powers, and duties as are necessary to promote and secure the safety and protection of the civilian popula-

[112] Kenneth W. Mateer, "Nuclear Survival Versus Due Process," *Intramural L. Rev. of New York University*, 16: 79, 90 (1961). The writer suggested, however, that it might be possible to require "owners of multiple residences and business establishments to provide shelters for those persons to whom these owners offer their buildings for purposes of living, working, or participating in some public activity."

tion." The language of these provisions would seem to include the use of state troops. The National Plan expresses the general policy that state personnel and forces should "support local police serv- ices in emergency as the situation allows." [113] In the absence of legislative authority, the governor's control over the state militia derives from the provisions of state constitutions which designate the governor as commander-in-chief of the state's forces and em- power him to use the militia in case of invasion, insurrection or other serious emergency.

Obviously, the governor's authority over the state militia would be of little value if, in case of a national or civil defense emer- gency, state units were immediately called into active federal military service. In view of this possibility of federal use of militia units, Congress in 1955 passed a law which permitted the states to organize special state defense forces for the purpose of disaster relief, forces which would be supported by state appropriations and would not be subject to federal call. The establishment of such forces was strongly endorsed at the time by the Defense Department and the Joint Chiefs of Staff. As Admiral Radford observed in the course of hearings before the Holifield sub- committee:

Trained in survival techniques and composed of individuals not eligible for service in the Armed Forces, state defense forces can well mean the difference between organized recovery and chaos in coping with mass panic, dislocation, and serious refugee problems.[114]

However, mainly because of the expenses involved in the arrange- ment, most states failed to take advantage of the congressional act. Since 1958, efforts have been made to keep militia forces as far as possible subject to state control during emergencies. Ac- cording to the National Plan, national guard forces which are not in the active federal service are "available to the state governors for support of civil defense operations, and remain under state control, until ordered or called into active Federal Military serv- ice." In subsequent consultation between federal civil defense authorities and the Defense Department, a temporary agreement was reached according to which only six of the twenty-seven

[113] *National Plan*, p. 12.
[114] *Investigative Hearings*, p. 342; see also *ibid.*, pp. 438, 443, 451, 566.

National Guard divisions were given military mobilization assignments while the great majority was made available, at least in immediate postattack situations, to the command of the state governors. The reason for this arrangement was clearly to enable the governors to cope more promptly with disasters in their respective states. In the words of Governor Hoegh:

> The Governor is the overall commander, just like the President is, and he has these forces, initially. . . . He can commit them as he can commit all the personnel of the state government, and the resources and facilities therein. . . . I am a strong advocate that the Governor needs an additional force, in uniform, capable of rendering assistance to people immediately, to augment the many services within the local governments and the state governments, to go in and cope with this crisis.[115]

If militia forces are available to state governors in civil defense contingencies, they should regularly be used in a supporting role in aid of civil authorities. However, in extreme emergencies, guard units might conceivably be employed by some governors to enforce a declaration of martial law. States have a long and not always very fortunate experience with martial law proclamations, and there is no insurance that the same device would not be used in nuclear disasters. During Operation Alert of 1955, the imposition of martial rule was seriously considered by some state governors, but no uniform action was taken. The proclamation of nationwide martial law by President Eisenhower stated as one of its reasons the fact that military rule had not been uniformly imposed by the governors of the several states. If this statement implied that a declaration of martial law should be regular procedure on the state level in civil defense emergencies, the implication would hardly seem acceptable. As in the case of military rule on the federal level, state martial law can only be tolerated as the very last remedy and in the severest of catastrophes, with the finding of necessity remaining subject to judicial review.

There are many methods through which the need for martial law in the states may be reduced if not eliminated. Among these

---

[115] *CD Hearings 1960*, pp. 93-94. The arrangement concerning limited mobilization assignments has apparently been abandoned and all national guard units are now potentially subject to federal call; see *CD 1963*, pt. II, vol. 1, p. 3658.

methods are the enactment of adequate civil defense legislation and the strengthening of civil defense organizations. In his message to the New York legislature in January of 1951, Governor Dewey put considerable emphasis on the aspect that the recommended legislation would make resort to military rule less compelling. Another means to the same end may be found in constitutional or legislative provisions designed to insure the continuity of state and local governments in the event of disaster. In this respect, the past decade has witnessed determined efforts on the state level to revise existing procedures in the light of cold war dangers.[116] All state constitutions provide for succession to the office of the governor, while statutory rules in many states establish lines of succession to other state offices. More elaborate lines of succession to legislative, executive and judicial offices at the state and local levels were proposed by the Council of State Governments in its suggested legislative program for 1959. By June of 1961, it was reported that forty-five states had adopted at least some of the measures contained in this proposed legislation. At the same time, constitutional amendments dealing with continuity of government had been approved by thirty-one state legislatures and ratified by the electorates of eighteen states. With regard to relocation sites, seven states had protected emergency operating centers for their executive branches, seven states had such facilities under development, and the remaining states had designated unprotected relocation areas. Legislation for records management and preservation had been proposed in fourteen states and passed in at least four states.[117]

---

[116] See Crotty, *op. cit.*, pp. 894-895; Note, "Can Government and Justice Survive the H-Bomb?" *Los Angeles Bar Bulletin*, 32: 163 ff. (1957); James W. Beebe, "Local Government and the H-Bomb: A New California Statute Prepares for Attack," *American Bar Association J.*, 44: 149 (1958).

[117] Executive Office of the President, Office of Civil and Defense Mobilization, *Annual Report 1961* (through June 30, 1961), reproduced in S.Rep. 1124, *11th Annual Report of the Activities of the Joint Committee on Defense Production*, 87th Cong., 2d Sess. (January 23, 1962), pp. 105-106.

3

Labor Disputes

IT IS DIFFICULT to conceive of any other area of executive activity which today is more deeply immersed in popular excitement and emotional charges and countercharges than the field of industrial relations. The memorable collision between President Kennedy and the steel industry in April, 1962, over the issue of price increases produced nationwide concern over the growing power of government in the nation's economy and led to heated charges of "tyranny," "despotism" and "police state" methods. In a statement of April 19, 1962, the Republican congressional leadership accused President Kennedy of having resorted to "a display of naked political power never seen before in this nation," and identified the fundamental issue before the country in these terms: "Should a president of the United States use the enormous powers of the federal government to blackjack any segment of our free society into line with his personal judgment without regard to law?" According to the Republican statement, the president in his reaction to the price increase

directed or supported a series of governmental actions that imperiled basic American rights, went far beyond the law and were more characteristic of a police state than a free government.[1]

This is clearly not the place to enter into partisan controversy or to attach exaggerated significance to political accusations in a congressional election year. Nor does the steel conflict in itself present any significant constitutional or legal problems. As a

[1] *Milwaukee Journal* (April 20, 1962), p. 3, col. 2. On the entire steel crisis see Grant McConnell, *Steel and the Presidency, 1962* (New York, 1963).

political maneuver the action of the president was certainly not based on any specific statutory provision; but at the same time the action was not prohibited by a clear constitutional or congressional limitation. The Republican charge that the president acted "without regard to law" by disregarding certain principles of competitive bidding seemed to overlook the fact that there is no vested right in a government contract and that, by boosting the steel prices, the companies had boosted themselves out of the lowest price bracket within which government contracts tend to be negotiated. In this manner the government—by announcing to channel its steel purchases through firms which maintained the lower price line—simply relied on the force of competitive free enterprise which the companies claimed to defend against government intervention. Nevertheless, one does not have to endorse the charges of the opposition party in order to agree that the president's action in the steel conflict was merely the catalyst in a mounting controversy, a catalyst which served to bring into focus a question of considerable magnitude: the proper role of the executive in industrial relations and the proper goal of national policy in regard to labor and management.

The problem of executive power in the economic field is not of recent origin; it is at least as old as the debates on tariff policy during the early years of the nation. Under the federal constitution, the major power in economic and industrial matters is obviously vested in Congress under the "commerce clause." However, the executive branch of government has always played a large role in this area either through legislative delegation of power or through the exercise of "inherent" or emergency powers in times of national crisis. The two world wars of our century vastly increased executive authority. Both wars were fought as much on the production front as on the military, with the result that the traditional war powers of the president were progressively intermingled with emergency powers in industrial relations and wage-price developments. Some of the latter powers were abandoned or revoked at the end of military hostilities; others were continued in force and were temporarily or periodically extended.

International and domestic developments after the second World War presented the problem of executive power in a new perspective. The abandonment of isolation involved the United

States increasingly in international commitments of both a military and economic character, thereby strengthening and modifying the traditional authority of the president in international relations. The development of the cold war posed the baffling question of the extent to which presidential war powers and powers in war-like emergencies were applicable to a struggle fraught with all the strains of belligerence except direct military action. In addition, the gradual shift of cold war emphasis from military to economic competition tended to confuse even further the lines between war powers, authority in international relations, and economic emergency powers. Congress, it is true, has discouraged such a confusion and has maintained "peacetime" standards by insisting on congressional regulation of commerce and industry even to the extent of specifying emergency procedures which the president is to use in case of economic crisis or critical labor disputes. However, the legislative delegation of emergency powers frequently leaves to the president considerable discretion in the exercise and application of the delegated authority. Moreover, a slight "warming-up" of the cold war, or simply an intensification of international economic competition, is bound to bring forth assertions of nonstatutory emergency powers of the executive branch. One should also keep in mind that the described international developments coincide with far-reaching domestic changes in industrial relations such as automation and dislocation of manpower.

1. THE RECONVERSION PERIOD

The reconversion period following World War II witnessed one of the severest crises in labor-management relations in the country's history. The reasons for this crisis were manifold. More than any previous military conflict, the second World War had been an industrial war. The huge extent of the military establishment had entailed an unprecedented mobilization of industry and a vast utilization of civilian manpower. With the end of the war, more than 10 million service men and women were demobilized while at the same time workers in industries were faced with the abrupt curtailment of innumerable items of military production.[2] As a

[2] See "Postwar Work Stoppages Caused by Labor-Management Disputes," *Monthly Labor Rev.*, 63: 872 (December, 1946).

result, many factories had to reduce the work week or to shut down temporarily or permanently. These changes were further aggravated by the wage and price developments of the period. During the war, production of civilian goods was limited in many respects while full employment and a swollen money supply intensified the competition for available goods thereby raising the cost of living. With the gradual abandonment of stabilization controls, the unbalanced character of the wage-price relationship became increasingly manifest. The discontent of wage earners over high prices was intensified by the loss of overtime premiums received at war plants, by lay-offs, and by the reclassification of many workers to lower-paying peacetime jobs.[3]

The conflict of economic interests during this period was also influenced by a new attitude of labor and management and by a changed power relationship between the two parties. During the war, the National War Labor Board had controlled, or at least influenced, industrial relations to a significant degree. Moreover, a few days after the attack on Pearl Harbor, the labor unions had issued a voluntary "no strike" pledge which imposed a considerable self-restraint on union leaders and on collective bargaining in general although it did not prevent stoppages in all instances. The end of military operations terminated labor's no strike pledge. Also, on August 16, 1945, President Truman announced that the War Labor Board would be liquidated as soon as possible. Both labor and management were anxious to escape wartime controls and to match their forces at the bargaining table, or if necessary, in a test of strength. This contest assumed entirely new proportions in view of the growth of labor unions and the almost complete unionization of mass production industries. The decade after the passage of the Wagner Act had witnessed a steady increase of the union movement with the result that by 1945 some fifteen million workers were organized in labor unions. Bolstered by this numerical strength, labor during the reconversion period was able to pressure steadily for wage increases and other benefits, while—faced with forecasts of an early postwar recession—many employers were unwilling to meet these wage demands.

In the year following VJ-Day, the country experienced no less than 4,630 work stoppages involving some five million workers

[3] Compare Ludwig Teller, "What Should Be Done About Emergency Strikes?" *Labor L.J.*, 1: 263-264 (1950).

and resulting in almost 120 million man-days of idleness. The strike wave reached its peak during January and February of 1946 when over 1,125,000 workers participated in stoppages in steel, automobile, electrical and other industries.[4] In the spring of 1946, the number of workers involved in strikes and the loss in man-days decreased somewhat; however, the frequency of stoppages and in some instances the vehemence of conflicts increased. Between spring and winter, bitter and complicated disputes plagued such important branches of the economy as bituminous-coal mines and transportation facilities. In the bituminous-coal controversy, President Truman on May 21 ordered government seizure of the mines and their operation under the direction of the Secretary of the Interior. A contract agreement between the Secretary, Julius A. Krug, and the president of the United Mine Workers, John L. Lewis, was subsequently denounced by the union, an action which provoked another stoppage. Due to their failure to comply with a restraining order, the union and its president were fined for contempt of court and the decision was upheld by the Supreme Court.[5] Strong methods of government intervention were also occasioned by the railroad dispute of the same year. On May 17, the president ordered seizure of the railroads and their operation under the direction of the Office of Defense Transportation. Nevertheless, refusal of the unions to accept a compromise proposal resulted in a nationwide stoppage of rail transportation beginning May 23. On May 25, in an address to a joint session of Congress, the president urged the passage of drastic legislation which, among other things, would have permitted him to draft the railway strikers into the Army.

The unprecedented strike activity of the reconversion period provoked a number of immediate responses on the part of the government and a great variety of proposals and other efforts designed to prevent critical disputes of nationwide proportions.

[4] Joseph P. Goldberg and Bernard Yabroff, "Analysis of Strikes, 1927-49," *Monthly Labor Rev.,* 72: 1, 5 (January, 1951).

[5] *United States* v. *United Mine Workers,* 70 F.Supp. 42 (D.D.C. 1946), *aff'd,* 330 U.S. 258 (1947). The use of the injunctive procedure against the strike gave rise to the charge of a revival of the anti-labor injunction; see Charles O. Gregory, "Government by Injunction Again," *University of Chicago L.Rev.,* 14: 364 (1947); Richard F. Watt, "The Divine Right of Government by Judiciary," *ibid.,* p. 410 (1947).

The immediate methods used by the government to combat re-conversion unrest included primarily the appointment of fact-finding boards and government operation of industries through seizure. The numerous fact-finding boards created by the president were nonstatutory in character and were based on the general powers of the executive branch of government.[6] On the other hand, the presidential seizure orders were issued under the provision of wartime emergency legislation, especially the War Labor Disputes Act of 1943. The various forms of government intervention demonstrate that the original policy of relinquishing wartime controls was not very successful and was supplanted by an increasingly active participation of the government in the settlement of labor-management unrest.

2. COLLECTIVE BARGAINING AND EMERGENCY POWERS: THE TAFT-HARTLEY STORY

The disturbing experiences with industrial unrest during the reconversion period were among the major issues in the mid-term campaign of 1946 which returned Republican majorities in both houses of Congress for the first time since 1930. The new Congress which met in January of 1947 produced immediately a prodigious quantity of legislative proposals. Over two hundred bills dealing with labor relations were introduced during the first week of the new session.[7] One of these bills, introduced by Senator Ball of Minnesota, proposed to curtail industry-wide or multiple-employer bargaining by an amendment of the Wagner Act making it an unfair labor practice for an employer to bargain collectively with a labor union, or for a labor union to act as representative of employees unless the principal places of employment of the members represented were "located within the same labor market." Other bills aimed at the introduction of compulsory arbitration or similar limitations of collective bargaining al-

[6] For an examination and a tabulation of these boards see U. S. Department of Labor, *Work Stoppages, Federal Fact-Finding Boards and Boards of Inquiry, 1945-1951*, Series 5, No. 1 (Washington, D.C., July, 1952), pp. 1-2, 5-17. For background material on some of the bills filed during the 79th and 80th Congresses between 1945 and 1947 compare Harry A. Millis and Emily C. Brown, *From Wagner Act to Taft-Hartley Act* (Chicago, 1950).

[7] See Gerard D. Reilly, "The Legislative History of the Taft-Hartley Act," *George Washington L.Rev.*, 29: 285, 289 (1960).

though few proposals went to the extreme of suggesting the application of antitrust laws to labor unions.

As can be seen, Congress was faced at the time with a bewildering choice of possible courses of action; but the central issue was clearly how to strike a balance between freedom of collective bargaining—a principle firmly established since the passage of the Wagner Act in 1935—and the necessity of protecting the public interest in labor emergencies. A major consideration which impelled prompt action on the part of Congress was the impending expiration of the War Labor Disputes or Smith-Connally Act on June 30, 1947. In addition, congressional attitude was influenced already at this time by the growing shadow of the international cold war and by the challenge of foreign systems to the economy of the United States. As Congressman Holifield observed during debates on the Taft-Hartley bill in April of 1947:

We are in a dramatic period of history. Part of the world is Communist. Great Britain is no longer a free enterprise nation in our sense of the term. Our system is competing in the world market of ideas and things with the other great systems. We should be made sober by our historic responsibility—the responsibility of making strong and stable, for the future, all of our institutions, including our industrial relations.[8]

The mentioned reasons and considerations, combined with the propitious advent of a safe Republican majority in Congress, finally led to the enactment of new emergency procedures for the handling of critical labor disputes endangering the nation's health or safety.

The emergency provisions of the Labor-Management Relations or Taft-Hartley Act of 1947 [9] are described in all texts on industrial relations and do not require great elaboration here. Very briefly, these procedures are the following: whenever in the opinion of the President of the United States an actual or threatened strike or lockout affecting an entire industry or a substantial part thereof would, if permitted to occur or to continue, imperil the national health or safety, the president "may" appoint a board of inquiry with authority to study the issues in the dispute and to

[8] 93 Cong. Rec. 3564 (April 15, 1947). The congressman voiced strong objections, however, to the emergency provisions of the proposed Taft-Hartley bill.
[9] 61 Stat. 155 (1947), 29 U.S.C. 176-180 (1958).

report to him, but without the power to make recommendations. Upon receiving a report from this board, the president may then direct the attorney general to seek an injunction against the strike or lockout in a federal district court. If the court finds that the strike or lockout fulfills the described conditions of an emergency dispute, it issues an order enjoining the strike or its continuation.

During the ensuing "cooling off" period, labor and management are required to continue or resume negotiations and to seek a settlement, possibly with the help of the Federal Mediation and Conciliation Service. In the meantime the board of inquiry is reconvened by the president for the purpose of reporting to him on the position of the parties at the end of sixty days. The president makes the latter report public and, during the following fifteen days, the National Labor Relations Board conducts a secret poll of the employees on the "last offer" of each employer involved in the dispute. Within five days thereafter, the Board certifies the results of the poll to the attorney general who, regardless of the outcome of the ballot, asks the court to discharge the injunction, with the entire injunctive process to be completed in eighty days. Finally, the president—with or without recommendations for legislative action—submits a record of the entire proceedings to Congress.

Emergency Procedures — Pro and Con

The passage of the Taft-Hartley Act in 1947 by a Republican dominated Congress has fostered the growth of a popular conception or legend according to which the act constitutes one of the great divides between the two American parties. Although the immediate circumstances surrounding the enactment of the law lend credence to this belief, the subsequent operation of the act and especially the fact that the emergency procedures were used without strong reluctance by both Republican and Democratic administrations, justify scepticism. In the light of the Democratic performance since 1947, one may ask whether the original opposition to the act was based on substantive or procedural grounds, or in other words, whether the opposition was directed against the grant of executive emergency powers—especially powers of a discretionary character—or simply against the machinery pre-

scribed for the exercise of such powers. The legislative history of
the act seems to point to the second alternative.

Limitations of space prevent a detailed analysis of the act's
legislative journey in the present context. Nevertheless, objections
raised by Democratic representatives in committee and on the
floor of the House may serve as an illustration of the general tenor
of the debates. These objections reveal a curious blending of
heterogeneous arguments. On several occasions, attacks were
leveled against the ill-defined and discretionary character of
executive authority. As the House Minority Report stated:

There is no rule, or yardstick, provided for the President to guide him
in his determination as to whether or not a "substantial curtailment" of
interstate or foreign commerce has occurred or is about to occur.
Neither is there any guide to determine whether this "substantial curtailment" refers to any particular plant, or any particular group of plants
or the industry as a whole. The broad scope of these words and phrases
would undoubtedly add to the heat of controversies growing out of a
decision by the President to act, or not to act, in any given case.[10]

While thus denouncing the dangers of ill-defined power, opposition members frequently criticized the slow and intricate operation of the proposed emergency procedures—although it would
seem that the latter aspect should be a welcome relief for any
person seriously objecting to discretionary authority, since removal of statutory complications would increase the danger of
governmental intervention. As Congressman Madden observed on
the floor of the House, "the procedure which would be established
under this bill is heavy and cumbersome. It is unnecessarily complicated. It is surrounded by legal intricacies." In view of these
conflicting objections, it is a fair inference that the real target of
the opposition was a third feature of the bill, namely, its one-
sided and inequitable treatment of labor. Again in the words of
Congressman Madden: "This bill would give to the employers
engaged in these fields an inordinate power over the employees
with whom they deal. The threat of injunction would constantly
be held over the unions." [11]

[10] See U.S. Govt. Printing Office, *Legislative History of the Labor Management Relations Act, 1947* (hereinafter cited as *LH 1947;* Washington,
D.C., 1948), p. 393.
[11] *Ibid.*, pp. 807-808.

A similar blending of arguments can also be found in the veto message of President Truman of June, 1947. In this message, the president objected strongly both to the inefficiency and to the discriminatory character of the emergency procedures. "A fundamental inequity runs through these provisions," he observed.

The bill provides for injunctions to prohibit workers from striking, even against terms dictated by employers after contracts have expired. There is no provision assuring the protection of the rights of the employees during the period they are deprived of the right to protect themselves by economic action. In summary, I find that the so-called "emergency procedure" would be ineffective. It would provide for clumsy and cumbersome government intervention; it would authorize inequitable injunctions; and it would probably culminate in a public confession of failure. I cannot conceive that this procedure would aid in the settlement of disputes.[12]

It is a fair conclusion from these statements that the president was not basically adverse to the idea of executive emergency power provided that its exercise was conditioned by less cumbersome procedures and offered a better protection for labor. The ambiguity of the president's remarks—the fact that they could be interpreted either as an attack on additional governmental power or as an objection to an inefficient and unfair method of intervention—was reflected in Senator Taft's comments when he pointed out that

perhaps the most extraordinary provision of the message is the President's attack on the section permitting an injunction against a nationwide strike affecting the national health and safety. It was through such a procedure that he secured an injunction against John L. Lewis last fall. Last year when faced by a nation-wide strike, it was the President himself who recommended government seizure and the drafting of all the strikers into the United States Army. Because Congress now gives him a carefully drafted authority to delay such a strike, to attempt mediation and finally to conduct a strike vote when other remedies have been exhausted, he says the procedure will do more harm than good.[13]

[12] *Ibid.*, p. 919. See also H.Doc. 334, 80th Cong., 1st Sess. (1947), p. 8.
[13] *LH 1947*, p. 1626. Senator Taft's sponsorship of the bill was based on the assumption that the bill attempted to abolish the existing "inequity" of one-sided union power and to redress the balance between management and labor; *ibid.*, p. 1627.

The Labor-Management Relations Act, as finally passed by both houses over the veto of the president, constituted in many ways a compromise solution. Its procedures for handling emergency disputes were not likely to please the extremists on either side of Congress. The moderate, middle-of-the-road character of these provisions—the effort to circumscribe but not to eliminate free collective bargaining—has frequently been described as the basic achievement of the act.[14] Some members of Congress would have desired a stronger curtailment of collective bargaining, either by means of a prohibition of strikes in essential industries or through the establishment of compulsory arbitration or through seizure provisions. On the other hand, some members felt that no new authority was needed in this area and that at least in the majority of cases, the processes of free collective bargaining could be relied upon as a sufficient instrument for achieving industrial peace. The intermediary solution adopted in the act was defended by Senator Taft in these often quoted terms:

We did not feel that we should put into the law, as a part of the collective bargaining machinery, an ultimate resort to compulsory arbitration, or to seizure, or to any other action. We feel that it would interfere with the whole process of collective bargaining. If such a remedy is available as a routine remedy, there will always be a pressure to resort to it by whichever party thinks it will receive better treatment through such a process than it would receive in collective bargaining, and it will back out of collective bargaining. . . . Eighty days will provide plenty of time within which to consider the possibility of what should be done; and we believe very strongly that there should not be anything in this law which prohibits finally the right to strike.[15]

The moderate character of the solution, however, can hardly be considered as the central aspect of the emergency provisions. This aspect of moderation does not account for the excitement and intense hostility evoked by the passage of the act; it also does not explain the controversy in Congress and the arguments used by the two parties of the dispute. As it seems, the central feature resides not so much in the character and extent of the emergency powers, but rather in the potential use which can be made of

[14] *E.g.*, Thomas J. McDermott, "Ten Years of the National Emergency Procedure," *Labor L.J.*, 9: 228 (1958).
[15] *LH 1947*, p. 1008.

these powers. The sponsors of the act, it is true, advocated a circumscribed though vaguely formulated emergency authority of the president and a limited interference in the process of collective bargaining; but they endorsed for this purpose the procedure of injunction—a device extremely distasteful to labor since it could be used against striking unions without any adequate protection of union interests and without a similarly strong interference in the activities of management. The opponents of the bill, on the other hand, relied for their attack primarily on three arguments. As has been shown, some members of the opposition criticized the broadly formulated, discretionary character of the emergency authority. At the same time, however, they objected to the cumbersome, complicated and inefficient procedures stipulated for the exercise of the authority. Obviously, a discretionary authority which is also cumbersome and inefficient does not constitute a serious danger; the two arguments practically cancel each other. The chief objection of the opposition, thus, did not consist in the broad, discretionary authority of the president as such, but rather in the third argument: the inequitable use of the authority against the unions, and against labor in general.

Should Taft-Hartley be Amended?

The fact that the party struggle in 1947 was not really or not in the first place a struggle about the existence and extent of presidential emergency power was demonstrated clearly in the subsequent congressional history of the Taft-Hartley Act. When in 1948 the Democratic Party was able to win the presidential election and to gain a majority in both houses of Congress, one of the foremost aims of the administration became the repeal or at least drastic revision of the act and of its provisions concerning emergency disputes.[16] Among the many bills introduced for this purpose in the Senate or the House of Representatives, special attention must be given in the present context to the Thomas-Lesinski bill of 1949, and to the more ambitious Morse bill of 1952. It is common knowledge, of course, that these and similar bills were ultimately unsuccessful.

[16] See Lloyd G. Reynold, *Labor Economics and Labor Relations*, 2d ed. (New York, 1954), p. 294.

The Thomas-Lesinski bill of 1949 is significant here primarily by virtue of the fact that it rekindled the age-old controversy concerning the "inherent" powers of the president. It also deserves consideration for the reason that policy proposals recently submitted to the Kennedy administration revive some of the features of the 1949 act. The companion bills whose provisions were for all practical purposes identical were sponsored by Senator Thomas of Utah and by Representative Lesinski of Michigan, one of the signers of the House Minority Report in 1947. The existing emergency provisions of the Taft-Hartley Act were described by the Senate Report as entirely "too elaborate and too inflexible"; but the major criticism was leveled against the injunction procedure which was termed "neither a necessary nor desirable method" of preventing or settling emergency strikes.[17] In contrast to these provisions, the new bill completely eliminated the injunctive procedure from the emergency provisions. Upon a presidential finding that a national emergency existed or was threatened by a labor dispute in a vital industry affecting the public interest, the president could issue a proclamation to that effect and appoint an emergency board to investigate the dispute and to make recommendations for its settlement. The issuance of the presidential proclamation was to be followed by a thirty day cooling-off period during which the parties were to continue or resume work and operations, normally under existing conditions of employment.

During Senate hearings and subsequent congressional debates on the bill, one of the primary controversies centered around the problem of enforcing the cooling-off period. In contrast to the belief expressed by Secretary of Labor Tobin, that the only enforcement would be public opinion, Attorney General Clark was convinced that the government could enjoin a violation of the cooling-off provisions since "the inherent power of the President to deal with emergencies that affect the health, safety and welfare of the entire nation is exceedingly great."[18] Relying for his purpose primarily on a 1939 opinion of Attorney General Murphy and on a Supreme Court decision of 1947,[19] Clark pointed out

[17] S.Rep. 99, 81st Cong., 1st Sess. (March 8, 1948), pp. 35, 36.
[18] U.S. Congress, Hearings before the Senate Committee on Labor and Public Welfare on S. 249, 81st Cong., 1st Sess. (1949), pp. 37, 232.
[19] 39 Ops. Att'y Gen. 344, 347 (October 4, 1939); *United States* v. *United Mine Workers*, 330 U.S. 258 (1947).

that, should the parties refuse to obey the pertinent sections of the bill and should this refusal result in a national crisis, "it is my belief that in appropriate circumstances the United States would have access to the courts to protect the national health, safety and welfare." The opinion of his attorney general was strongly supported by President Truman himself. Reminiscing that some of his predecessors, especially Washington, Jackson, and Lincoln, had repeatedly utilized inherent executive powers, Truman stated that his authority was a combination of powers as president and commander-in-chief and that, in time of emergency, this combination gave him immense power to do what was right for the country.[20]

These and similar statements by members of the administration turned the attempted revision of the Taft-Hartley Act into a struggle between the famous "stewardship" theory of Theodore Roosevelt and the strict constructionist view of the presidency as propounded by William Howard Taft. Members of the opposition to the new bill in Congress were quick in denouncing the unexpected revival of the "inherent powers" theory. As the Minority Report submitted to the House of Representatives pointed out:

The Republican members regard this theory of inherent powers of the President as an extremely dangerous one. We believe that if it is the intention of Congress that there be an adequate and effective remedy for such national emergencies, the remedy should be specifically provided in the law, and not left to the future determination of a controversy as to the inherent powers which the President may or may not have. In all fairness to employees, employers and the public, if Congress does not intend that an injunction shall issue if the parties do not voluntarily resume or continue work, then the legislation should say that clearly and specifically.[21]

The Minority Report on the Senate bill, as submitted by Senator Taft, was even more pointed and uncompromising on the issue of presidential emergency powers. "Several witnesses who testified against an injunction provision," the report said, "implied that there was some inherent power in the President to obtain an injunction whether or not the authority was spelled out in the law. Their objection to retaining such a provision in the law in view

[20] *The New York Times* (February 4, 1949), p. 1, col. 4.
[21] H.Rep. 317, 81st Cong., 1st Sess. (March 28, 1949), pt. 2, p. 11.

of such belief was not clear. We deny the existence of this power." [22]

The controversy provoked by the emergency provisions of the Thomas-Lesinski bill was ably pursued and elucidated by legal commentators and experts in the field of labor law. The prevalent feeling among these observers was that, while the blunt denial of the existence of inherent presidential emergency powers by the opponents of the bill was perhaps too restrictive and inflexible, any affirmation of such powers had to be phrased in much more careful terms than was done in the majority statements, at least in the absence of congressional authorization. It was comparatively easy to point out that the doctrine of "inherent" powers of the president had traditionally been applied to the areas of war powers and foreign affairs and that its application to a domestic work stoppage in peacetime raised considerable problems unless, of course, the aspect of the cold war was accepted as constituting a valid intrusion of military and international considerations into internal peacetime labor disputes. In any event, the two authorities cited by Attorney General Clark in support of his position were of little aid in peacetime disputes, nor were they as yet influenced by the cold war situation. The 1939 opinion of Attorney General Murphy was entirely directed toward the war emergency and consisted simply of a brief, undocumented assertion of inherent power of the president. In the 1947 decision cited by Clark, the Supreme Court upheld an injunction where the government, again in a wartime emergency, had seized coal mines under the authority of a statute prohibiting strikes in certain industries and where the government was consequently in the position of an employer. In the absence of such circumstances one competent observer, Ludwig Teller, expressed the cautious opinion

that the President does possess inherent executive powers to deal with emergency strikes, but that it is desirable for him to withhold its use until specifically authorized by Congress in each case of emergency.[23]

Reflecting on the impact of the anti-injunction provision of the Norris-La Guardia Act on the government's power to seek injunctive relief, another observer reached the following conclusion:

[22] S.Rep. 99, 81st Cong., 1st Sess. (May 4, 1949), pt. 2, p. 56.
[23] Teller, *op. cit.*, p. 271.

The President's assertion that he would be able to cope with national emergency strikes without statutory authorization is highly questionable. Under "orthodox" principles of constitutional law, it appears that the Federal Government does not have the right to obtain strike injunctions until Congress acts to create the right. . . . On the other hand, if a national emergency arises from the work stoppage, and the situation becomes critical enough, it is safe to say that the courts will probably find that the Government is entitled to an injunction. . . . Neither an apparent lack of authority nor a statutory bar is likely to keep the courts from doing what they feel is absolutely necessary for the protection of the health and safety of the nation.[24]

One of the most ambitious subsequent attempts to revise or improve the emergency provisions of the Taft-Hartley Act was the proposed "National Emergency Labor Disputes Act" of 1952. This bill, which was sponsored primarily by Senators Morse and Humphrey, was at least partially influenced by the experiences of the Korean crisis and the president's seizure of the steel mills. The bill was no longer designed to supplant or repeal the Taft-Hartley Act, with a concomitant reliance on "inherent" executive powers, but to supplement existing legislation and to make the power of the government more comprehensive and equitable. The sponsors of the bill were cognizant of one of the basic objections which had been leveled periodically against the existence of emergency powers in labor disputes: the argument that after the recovery from economic dislocations of the immediate post-war period, few if any labor disputes ever reached the proportions of a national emergency. Consequently, the Senate Report on the bill pointed out that strikes confined to a few cities or a single region, or strikes of a short duration, would usually not be of an emergency character and that "few industrial stoppages, even if in basic industries and of substantial length, have a profound effect upon national stability or well-being." [25] At the same time, however, the report—apparently under the impact of cold war developments and the Korean crisis—admitted that "war, the threat of war, and conversion from a war economy create national emergencies," and

[24] See "National Emergencies and the President's Inherent Powers," *Stanford L.Rev.*, 2: 319-320 (1950). This conclusion should perhaps be modified in the light of the subsequent steel seizure case of 1952 where the Supreme Court denied the president's right to seize the steel mills in the face of conflicting statutory provisions.
[25] S.Rep. 2073, 82d Cong., 2d Sess. (July 2, 1952), p. 3.

that such crisis situations might convert a labor dispute in a major industry into a national emergency dispute. While admitting the necessity of emergency powers in such situations, the report emphasized that any powers granted to the government would have to be devised in such a manner as to maintain, as far as possible, the procedures of free collective bargaining.

The draft bill rejected proposals of compulsory arbitration, prohibition of industry-wide bargaining, and application of anti-trust laws to labor unions; however, it did provide the government with a variety of important powers. Upon a presidential finding that an actual or threatened strike or lockout in a vital industry created a national emergency, the president was authorized to issue a proclamation to that effect, call upon the parties to continue or resume work, and appoint an emergency board to investigate the dispute and to recommend terms of settlement. After issuing the proclamation, the president was required to submit a full statement of the case to Congress, with his recommendations. At any stage of the dispute, the bill granted to the president the power of seizure—admittedly "an extreme remedy" —whose exercise could be vetoed by Congress within ten days and which was to terminate within sixty days unless continued by concurrent resolution of Congress. During the period of government operation, the president could request the issuance of an injunction to prevent or terminate a work stoppage. Also during this period the government was entitled to change wages, hours and working conditions within the limits of recommendations of the emergency board. In order to induce the employer to bargain and settle the dispute, the government after the first thirty days of seizure could impound and hold the income of the seized company and was to be reimbursed for its operating expenses. At the same time, the owners of the enterprise were entitled to just compensation, with consideration being given, among other things, to the fact that possession was taken when operations were disrupted or about to be disrupted by a work stoppage.

The proposed bill of 1952 did not directly touch on the problem of "inherent" presidential powers; but it indicated a change in the attitude of some of the former opponents of the Taft-Hartley Act and their greater willingness to specify broad emergency powers in statutory form. At the same time, the bill made national emergency powers more definitely a shared responsibility of both the president and Congress, and thus applied to this area some of the principles and developments characterizing in recent decades the domain of war powers. While the draft act was still debated in committee, the problem of statutory versus "inherent" executive power received a full-scale treatment in the Supreme Court decision of June 2, 1952, invalidating President Truman's seizure of the steel mills at the height of the Korean crisis. Although the decision resulted in a nationwide steel strike which lasted from June 2 until the middle of August, the political melee of the presidential election campaign prevented the enactment of new emergency legislation by Congress.

With the advent of the Republican administration in 1953, the assault on Taft-Hartley procedures began to lose impetus and appeal.[26] In fact, the two terms of the Eisenhower administration witnessed few serious efforts to devise a new national machinery for the handling of emergency disputes. Among the more significant proposals of the period were two very similar bills introduced by Senator Ives of New York in early 1953. The objective of these bills was apparently to extend a modified version of the voluntary settlement procedures of the Railway Labor Act [27] to critical industries. In both bills, the president, upon finding that a labor dispute had an adverse effect on the national interest, was entitled to establish an "emergency board" with authority to mediate the dispute and offer recommendations. Together with the activation

[26] In the 1952 presidential campaign, the Democrats had pledged themselves to repeal of the act, while the Republican platform had promised revision. Extensive congressional hearings were held and numerous bills were introduced during 1953, but Congress adjourned without taking action on them. See Reynolds, *op. cit.*, pp. 294-295; Sumner H. Slichter, "Revision of the Taft-Hartley Act," *Quarterly J. of Economics*, 67: 149 (1953).

[27] The Railway Labor Act of 1926 provides for the presidential appointment of "emergency boards" and for a 60-day suspension of critical disputes on the nation's railroads and airlines, but without specifying how the suspension can be legally enforced. Despite the barriers of the Norris-LaGuardia anti-injunction act of 1932, federal courts in recent years have been somewhat liberal in granting injunctive relief in disputes covered by the act; compare *Brotherhood of RR. Trainmen* v. *Chicago River and Indiana RR.*, 353 U.S. 30 (1957); also John McGuinn, "Injunctive Powers of the Federal Courts in Cases Involving Disputes under the Railway Labor Act," *Georgetown L.J.*, 50: 46 (1961). However, for a more rigid observance of Norris-LaGuardia with respect to the Taft-Hartley Act see *Sinclair Refining Co.* v. *Atkinson*, 370 U.S. 195 (1962).

of the emergency board, a period of strike suspension was to go into effect. Both bills were very vague on the question of the voluntary or mandatory character of the suspension. According to the first bill, the president was merely to "call upon the parties ... to refrain from a stoppage of work," with no time limit being placed on this request. The second bill used a slightly stronger language by providing that the parties "shall refrain" from work stoppage for sixty days.[28] The only sanction which apparently was envisaged by the two bills was contained in the provision which required the president to refer the dispute to Congress if a strike occurred at any time after the described procedures had been initiated.

The bills sponsored by the Republican Senator were much less ambitious than the Morse bill of 1952 and resembled more closely the Democratic proposals contained in the Thomas-Lesinski bill of 1949. Both the Thomas-Lesinski and the Ives bills omitted any reference to a court injunction. In both instances, the establishment of an emergency board was followed by a strike suspension of varying duration. The only significant difference between the two legislative proposals consisted in the fact that the Ives bills made it mandatory for the president to refer a violation of the strike suspension order to Congress, while the 1949 bill left this appeal to Congress optional with the president. The efforts to amend or replace the emergency procedures of the Taft-Hartley Act were resumed with new vigor after the steel strike of 1959 and with the advent of a Democratic administration in 1961. In the course of the ensuing reappraisal of the act, some of the mentioned proposals of the Thomas-Lesinski and Ives bills experienced a dramatic revival, especially in a report issued by President Kennedy's advisory committee on labor-management relations in May, 1962. However, in order to place the recent proposals in their proper historical perspective, a brief review of the past operation of the Taft-Hartley procedures and of their application to individual emergency disputes appears indicated. The review illustrates the evolution of such ingredients of the Taft-Hartley machinery as boards of inquiry and judicial verification of emergency situations, and in a broader perspective the

---

[28] On both bills see Donald E. Cullen, "The Taft-Hartley Act in National Emergency Disputes," *Industrial and Labor Relations Rev.*, 7: 21 (1953).

interrelation between domestic labor disputes and international cold war developments.

National Emergency Disputes

The operation of the emergency provisions of the Taft-Hartley Act has been the subject of numerous studies displaying attitudes ranging from benevolent appraisal to scathing denunciation. This is not the place to discuss in detail the criticisms leveled against the functioning of the emergency procedures and the performance of public authorities involved in these procedures. For present purposes, two issues seem to stand out in the discussions of Taft-Hartley procedures: first, the question of whether intervention by the president is a suitable method of bringing the weight of the public interest to bear on a dispute or whether other procedures would be more effective; and second, the question of whether a finding by the president is an adequate determination of the existence of a national emergency dispute.

In regard to the first question, the sentiment was sometimes expressed that the emergency procedures of the act did not sufficiently insure the manifestation of the public interest, primarily in view of the fact that the president was not entirely immune to partisan considerations and that due to the necessity of haste and the absence of recommendations the reports of the boards of inquiry usually failed to stimulate public concern and arouse the pressure of public opinion.[29] In order to remedy the situation, many proposals have been advanced, some of them of a truly spectacular nature. Apart from the suggestion that the boards of inquiry should be able to submit recommendations and play a larger role in the bargaining process, some observers have urged the creation of an administrative agency authorized to investigate and disseminate the facts of a dispute and to exercise sanctions for curbing abuse of power by the parties and promoting the public interest, or a return to the procedures of World War II, that is, the institution of tripartite emergency boards composed in equal numbers of representatives of the employer, the employees,

---

[29] Charles M. Rehmus, "The Operation of the National Emergency Provisions of the Labor Management Relations Act of 1947." *Yale L.J.* 62: 1047, 1055 (1953).

and the "public." [30] More recently, Professor Herbert Rothenberg
has stepped forward with the idea that the settlement of emergency disputes should be entrusted to a popular referendum
which would decide whether or not the public wishes the strike
to continue, "with the expense of the poll to be borne in part by
the public and the remainder in prescribed proportions according
to the outcome of the poll." [31]

The question of the adequate implementation of the popular
will is closely linked with the other question of the appropriate
method of determining the existence of a national emergency.
Experience with the invocation of emergency procedures on the
basis of presidential findings has given rise to the charge that such
invocation was frequently spurious and unwarranted and that a
better method of determining emergencies should and could be
found. Reviewing the experience with emergency procedures in
bituminous-coal strikes since World War II, some observers have
pointed out that "the public and members of Congress have in the
past tended to overestimate the national emergency character of
coal strikes" and that excess capacity, stockpiling and pressures for
settlement prior to the crisis stage prevented any of the reviewed
disputes from developing into real national emergencies. In contrast to the "rule of thumb of government intervention" or the
"pragmatic test of a decision by President or Congress," these observers proposed more definite, factual criteria according to which
a strike, in order to constitute a national emergency, had to produce actual rather than potential effects; also, it had to impose
hardship rather than inconvenience and to involve national rather
than strictly local repercussions.[32] Similarly, the examination of
major work stoppages during a period of thirty-six years has led
another observer to the general conclusion that "while there has
been much discussion of strikes which might 'imperil national

[30] Frank E. Cooper, "Protecting the Public Interest in Labor Disputes,"
Michigan L.Rev., 58: 873 ff. (1960).
[31] I. Herbert Rothenberg, "National Emergency Disputes: A Proposed
Solution," *Dickinson L.Rev.*, 65: 5 (1960); also reproduced in *Labor L.J.*, 12:
112 (1961). For a critical evaluation of this proposal see Richard A. Givens,
"Professor Rothenberg's Proposed Solution for National Emergency Disputes:
A Reply," *Dickinson L.Rev.*, 65: 201 (1961).
[32] Irving Bernstein and Hugh G. Lovell, "Are Coal Strikes National
Emergencies?" *Industrial and Labor Relations Rev.*, 6: 352, 353, 367
(1953).

health or safety,' there have been few such situations in history."
This general assessment suggested to the observer the need—at
least for peacetime purposes—of a closely circumscribed definition of a national emergency strike as "one which has resulted in
a dangerous curtailment of supplies of necessary goods or services
where substitutes are not available." [33]

As it appears, arguments of this kind ignore, or at least under-
estimate, the subjective element in any determination of a national
emergency. It is comparatively easy to point out that a finding
that past strikes have usually not entailed national emergencies
may be attributed just as well to the availability of governmental
emergency procedures and, thus, be used both as an argument
for continued government intervention and as proof that no intervention is needed. Moreover, there is no complete agreement
among experts concerning the proper definition of a national
emergency and the application of such a definition to specific
instances. Even on the basis of a commonly accepted, elaborately
circumscribed definition, considerable disagreement may arise
on the question of whether a particular dispute meets the criteria
of a national emergency. In such a situation, a decision has to be
reached, and the President of the United States is certainly no less
qualified to reach this decision than any other public authority,
especially if the president's determination is substantiated by the
findings of a board of inquiry and subject to judicial scrutiny prior
to the issuance of an injunction. Judicial review of a determination
of emergency has perhaps not been used to the fullest possible
extent in Taft-Hartley proceedings, but the act does not seem to
preclude its broad application. With respect to the boards of
inquiry, it should be pointed out that at least in some of the
disputes in which Taft-Hartley procedures have been invoked,
the reports submitted by these boards contained discussions of
and evidence on the emergency character of the situation.

Whatever the theoretical solution to the definition and ascer-
tainment of a national emergency may be, presidents as a rule
have not displayed great reluctance to utilize the powers attributed to them in the provisions of the Taft-Hartley Act. This
attitude does not seem to have been influenced greatly by the

[33] Edgar L. Warren, "Thirty-Six Years of 'National Emergency' Strikes,"
Industrial and Labor Relations Rev., 5: 12, 13 (1951).

party affiliation of the president or even by a previously stated rejection of the Taft-Hartley Act in general. Despite his vehement veto message and the attempts of his administration to amend or repeal the act, President Truman invoked the emergency authority on ten occasions and, in some instances, was even criticized for agreeing much too readily to intervene in labor disputes. President Eisenhower seemed anxious at the beginning of his administration to depart from the practice of his predecessor and, apparently under the influence of a prominent director of the Federal Mediation and Conciliation Service, announced a policy of nonintervention.[34] Nevertheless, labor disputes during the period of the Republican administration gave rise to seven invocations of the Taft-Hartley procedures. President Kennedy, although one of the original opponents of the passage of the act, has demonstrated very rapidly that he is not adverse to utilizing the powers granted to him in case of critical labor disputes. The experience with governmental intervention under the Truman and Eisenhower administrations has led one experienced labor reporter to this observation:

The net result appears to be the same—intense White House pressure on labor and management to accept a voluntary peace formula on pain of wage-price legislation that neither side will like. The chief difference is that the Democratic pattern involved the application of the Government whip without waiting until the country approached the point of economic strangulation.[35]

The emergency procedures of the Taft-Hartley Act have been used in many different areas: in disputes involving bituminous-coal mines, atomic energy, nonferrous metals, shipping, aviation, meat packing, locomotive and telephone companies. In the present context, it may suffice to discuss briefly those disputes which had a particularly close relationship to cold war developments or which indicated the extent to which the application of emergency provisions is subject to court action and judicial review. One area which certainly has a definite impact on the cold war struggle is the field of atomic energy. Actually, the first controversy in which

[34] Compare R. W. Fleming, "Emergency Strikes and National Policy," *Labor L.J.*, 11: 270 (1960).

[35] A. H. Raskin, *The New York Times* (October 16, 1959), p. 22, col. 2.

Taft-Hartley procedures were used was the atomic energy dispute of March, 1948. In this instance, the critical impact of the plant's operation on the atomic energy program convinced the president that, irrespective of the reasonable attitude of the unions, a national emergency was imminent, and this conclusion was supported, or at least not contradicted, by the board of inquiry and implemented by the court issuing the injunction. However, the fact that the emergency was finally averted and settlement achieved must be attributed primarily to voluntary bargaining and a sober awareness that the public interest did not permit strike action.[36]

The spring and summer of 1948 witnessed disputes in the meat-packing industry and in long-lines telephone communications; however, although boards of inquiry were appointed, both disputes were settled without the use of the injunction. More complicated and important were two disputes which occurred during the same year in the bituminous-coal mining industry. The development of these disputes was observed with considerable interest since the adoption of the emergency procedures of the Taft-Hartley Act had been occasioned at least in part by previous work stoppages in the same industry. The disputes in 1948 were closely interrelated, in the sense that the settlement of the second conflict depended to a large degree on the outcome of the first. In the first case, noncompliance of the union with a court injunction led to dramatic contempt proceedings in which the court found John L. Lewis and the United Mine Workers guilty of civil and criminal contempt.[37] In neither instance can settlement really be ascribed to the Taft-Hartley provisions; rather, the termination of the disputes was due, in the one instance, to a court decision on a disputed pension fund and in the other, a contempt citation and the intervention by a member of Congress.

The most serious and protracted disputes in 1948 occurred in the shipping industry. In fact, contrary to the expectations of the

[36] Compare Oscar S. Smith, "The Effect of the Public Interest on the Right to Strike and to Bargain Collectively," *North Carolina L.Rev.*, 27: 204 (1949).

[37] *United States* v. *United Mine Workers*, 77 F.Supp. 563 (D.D.C. 1948), aff'd, 177 F.2d 29 (D.C.Cir. 1949), *cert.denied*, 338 U.S. 871 (1949). See Howard T. Rosen, "Effectiveness of the Judiciary in National Emergency Labor Disputes," *Rutgers L.Rev.*, 6: 409 (1952).

framers of the Taft-Hartley provisions, longshore disputes ever since 1948 have constituted the most frequent sources of the invocation of emergency controls, overshadowing in impact and length of duration the bituminous-coal controversies of the same period. The complicated and critical character of the two longshore disputes of 1948 can be gauged from the fact that, in both cases, strikes erupted or were resumed after the dissolution of the statutory injunction and that the eighty day period served as a "warming up" rather than a "cooling off" period. The first longshore dispute had the proportions of a far-reaching controversy which involved shipping companies on the Atlantic, Pacific and Gulf ports and on the Great Lakes, and the members of at least seven unions, most of whom were affiliated with the CIO.[38] The second dispute occurred on the Atlantic Coast and originated in demands of the International Longshoremen's Association, AFL, for wage increases, a welfare and pension plan, improved vacation benefits, and the payment of overtime rates.

In the fall and winter of 1949-1950, another bituminous-coal dispute developed—the last one, so far, in which the national emergency procedures were applied. In this case, the union seemed to have learned the lesson of previous contempt proceedings. The case is noteworthy also for the reason that it illustrates the length to which the government at that time was willing to go in the face of an open defiance and breakdown of the Taft-Hartley procedures. Prior to invoking the provisions of the act, President Truman intervened and proposed a nonstatutory fact-finding board to investigate the situation and make recommendations, a proposal which was accepted by the operators but rejected by the union. The president then appointed a board of inquiry on February 6, the date of the strike deadline. The board set itself to task with considerable dedication, departing from its usual fact-finding function and engaging in a deliberate, although unsuccessful, effort of mediation and conciliation. On February 11, the government secured an injunction restraining the continuance of the strike and ordering the union to take appropriate action to terminate the work stoppage. Apparently due to previous experi-

---

[38] See *United States* v. *International Longshoremen's and Warehousemen's Union*, 78 F.Supp. 710 (N.D.Cal. 1948); the court argued that the injunction did not violate freedom of speech, due process, or constitute involuntary servitude since it was directed at the union and not at individual workers.

ences, the union's president, John L. Lewis, wired his district and local leaders to go back to work; however, the miners refused to comply either with the court injunction or the order of their union officer. In subsequent contempt proceedings, the federal district court on March 2 found the union and its president not guilty of contempt on the grounds that Lewis, in urging his locals to return to work, had done everything that could have been expected of him and that the government had failed to produce sufficient evidence to show that "appropriate action" under the terms of the injunction included the revocation of the charters of recalcitrant locals by the union.[39] On the following day, President Truman asked Congress for special legislation to permit the government to seize and operate the mines with a portion of the profits to go to the government. Faced with this threat, the parties finally reached an agreement on March 5, before any emergency legislation was enacted by Congress.

Much less dramatic, but also more promising and reassuring from the viewpoint of the Taft-Hartley provisions, was the dispute in the nonferrous metals industry in 1951. The issuance of the injunction in this case was at least partially responsible for the fact that negotiations were resumed in a serious manner and that most of the disputes with the various employers were settled during the eighty day period. For present purposes, one should also note that the controversy marked the beginning of broadened efforts on the part of the board of inquiry to examine the critical character of the controversy in support of, or in addition to, the presidential finding of a national labor emergency. A similarly beneficial or effective contribution of the Taft-Hartley procedures toward the settlement of a controversy can be found in the American locomotive dispute of late 1952 and early 1953. The operation of the emergency procedures, however, was influenced and conditioned in this case by the fact that atomic energy facilities were involved and that the Taft-Hartley provisions were applied only to one plant of the company, thus permitting the union to use the strike weapon in other plants. The case witnessed again a considerable effort on the part of the board of inquiry to determine the emergency character of the strike. A particularly significant

[39] *United States* v. *United Mine Workers,* 89 F.Supp. 179 (D.D.C. 1950), *dismissed as moot,* 190 F.2d 865 (D.C.Cir. 1951); compare also H.Doc. 492, 81st Cong., 2d Sess. (1950).

aspect of the case consisted in the fact that the findings of the board were subsequently accepted in evidence by the federal courts when the union challenged the issuance of the injunction and when, for the first time, the courts had thus to examine the constitutionality of the emergency provisions in their application to a particular plant or company. Rejecting the union's contention that only nationwide or industry-wide strikes were subject to emergency injunctions, the Court of Appeals for the Second Circuit ruled that the test of applicability was not the quantitative extent of the strike within a given industry but rather the qualitative extent of the effect of a strike upon an industry and upon national health and safety.[40] The decision has been criticized for finding an implied congressional intent where such an intent is not at all apparent. However, it is a fair assumption that the Court was at least partially influenced in its ruling by the peculiar implications of the case with respect to atomic energy programs and the nation's posture in cold-war developments.

An awareness of such implications was even more directly present in the two atomic energy disputes of 1954 at Oak Ridge, Tennessee, and Paducah, Kentucky. In these instances considerations of national interest greatly mollified the attitude of labor and its willingness to resort to the strike weapon, thereby increasing the chances of a peaceful settlement. The application of national emergency procedures was preceded by the use of a special atomic energy labor-management relations panel and by a voluntary no-strike pledge during the operation of this panel. An extremely complicated and protracted dispute occurred in the East Coast shipping industry in late 1953 and early 1954. In this case, the government had to resort twice to the Taft-Hartley Act and a work stoppage erupted after the dismissal of the first and in defiance of the second restraining order. The controversy in this case was deepened by the union's demand for a contract to cover all major ports in the East, by the waterfront crime disclosures of the New York State Crime Commission, by the expulsion of the union from the AFL, and by the creation of a new longshoremen's association affiliated with the AFL. Issues of a similar character were at the basis of another longshore dispute which

[40] *United States* v. *United Steelworkers of America*, 202 F.2d 132 (2d Cir. 1953), *cert. denied before judgment,* 344 U.S. 915 (1953). Note, *Harvard L.Rev.,* 66: 1531 (1953); also *Michigan L.Rev.,* 51: 1092 (1953).

occurred in late 1956 and early 1957. The dispute involved a demand by the union for a master agreement intended to cover the entire East and Gulf Coasts. The summer of 1957 brought a new atomic energy dispute, this time at the Portsmouth plant of the Atomic Energy Commission near Waverly, Ohio, a plant operated by the Goodyear Atomic Corporation.

Apart from the atomic energy controversies and the two longshore disputes on the Atlantic and Gulf Coasts, the first four or five years of the Eisenhower administration had witnessed a certain relaxation of the struggle between labor and management. The government had less reason, or was less willing to interfere in national labor disputes, with the result that public concern over the impact of labor controversies on the national welfare and safety was less pronounced than it had been during the Truman administration. However, the industrial "peace" was more apparent than real and was due rather to temporary exhaustion of the parties than to any increased mutual sympathy. This fact was demonstrated very clearly during the latter part of the second Eisenhower term when labor-management hostilities erupted again with unexpected vigor.

The reasons for the resumption of industrial warfare, or for the deterioration of labor-management relations were numerous. Prominent among these reasons were such factors as technological improvements in industry, automation, and the entire set of economic, sociological and cultural changes commonly identified with the "second industrial revolution." Technological improvements enabled management to attack wasteful work practices, "featherbedding," and other encumbrances limiting the introduction of new processes in many industries. This attack was bolstered by the achievement of a certain economic prosperity, attended by high wages and high employment figures during the first Eisenhower administration and by public concern over the prospect of jeopardizing this prosperity and security through the infamous wage-price spiral or the inflationary impact of higher wages on higher prices. Fortified by this public attitude and by the timely disclosure of labor corruption dredged up by the McClellan Committee, management was encouraged to use the "featherbedding" charge as an opening wedge through which to launch a more general and ambitious campaign against the labor movement and against the prerogatives it had acquired during the decades since the New Deal. Needless to say, this challenge produced a vehement response on the part of labor and a sudden awareness of the magnitude of the issues at stake. As one observer described the situation: "In the long history of labor-management conflict, I think 1959 will go down as the year in which the boss fought to prove that he was still boss. . . . On this basis, every company and every union involved in a bargaining showdown tends to feel itself part of a larger struggle in which its manhood is being tested." [41]

Apart from technological changes and domestic economic developments, the deterioration of labor-management relations was certainly also influenced by the international situation and by the changing character of the cold-war struggle. Anxiety over the specter of foreign competition was aroused to a degree by the recovery of overseas, especially European, industries which had been crippled by the war but more directly by the entirely new atmosphere in East-West relations in the post-Stalinist period. During Stalin's time, the East-West conflict was dominated by the comparatively simple and straightforward dictates of a military power contest. The Soviet take-over of Eastern Europe, the Red victory in China, and the communist attacks in Korea and other parts of the world had produced in the West a powerful desire for military security, coupled with a strong appreciation of economic stability and industrial peace. In the United States, the communist "scare" of the early 1950's had fostered an anxious willingness on the part of the labor movement to rid itself of communist infiltration and to obviate charges of an attempt to "socialize" or "sovietize" the economic system. After Stalin's death and especially with the rise of Khrushchev to power, the Soviet bloc began to shift its attention from military attack to a much more subtle and pervasive challenge in the economic domain and to transfer the real battlegrounds from the arms race to the production front. Faced with this momentous challenge, management in many Western countries felt impelled to clamor for more rapid industrial changes and bolder technological improvements. At the same time, however, with the cold-war conflict turning increasingly into a competition for higher living standards and

[41] A. H. Raskin, "Labor-Management Tactics as Affected by the Steel Strike," *American Bar Association, Section of Labor Rel.L.*, 16, 18, 19 (1959).

improved working conditions of the masses, labor's role was bound to assume a new meaning and its struggle a new and far-reaching significance.

The interrelation between industrial tensions and cold-war developments was manifested in a curious and unexpected way in one of the major labor disputes of the second Eisenhower administration, the steel strike of 1959. The strike, which began in July, lasted no less than 116 days—the longest recorded strike period in a basic industry in the postwar period—and involved approximately 500,000 steel workers and over 350,000 workers in related industries. The public concern aroused by this controversy was highlighted by the fact that, for the first time in the history of the Taft-Hartley injunction, the Supreme Court of the United States decided to intervene and to review the constitutionality of the emergency procedures and of their application to the dispute at hand. In another historical "first" the steel strike coincided with the first visit of a head of the Soviet government to the United States: Khrushchev's visit of September 15 to 27, 1959. The coincidence of Khrushchev's visit with the national steel strike inspired a competent labor correspondent to write these comments:

The day Khrushchev arrives will mark the start of the third month of the national steel strike. At this moment the only thing that seems likely to end the strike before that is the possibility of a Taft-Hartley injunction, and the President indicates he will not move for such a back-to-work order until some time after Khrushchev's arrival. The prospect that our steel mills, the most productive in the world, will be in mothballs when the Soviet ruler gets here does not worry the President. . . . What makes the whole prospect so disheartening is that the steel strike is only one of a long list of items that point to an abrupt deterioration in the relations between employers and unions. The sum of these manifestations may convince Khrushchev that, far from exaggerating the extent of class warfare in this country, he actually minimized it.[42]

The intervention of the entire hierarchy of federal courts in this case [43] offers a particularly good illustration of the extent to which

[42] *Ibid.*, pp. 16, 17.

[43] For details of this steel dispute see U.S. Department of Labor, *National Emergency Disputes*, BLS Report No. 169 (Washington, D.C., February, 1961), pp. 20-21; compare also J. Malcolm Smith and Cornelius P. Cotter, *Powers of the President During Crises* (Washington, D.C., 1960), pp. 139-143.

the presidential determination of a national labor emergency and the decision to obtain injunctive relief against a strike are subject to judicial review. The original decision of the president to secure an injunction was bolstered by the findings of the board of inquiry. The Federal District Court for the Western District of Pennsylvania in which the relief was sought reviewed again the factual background of the petition and issued the injunction on the basis of findings that the strike would produce an irreparable time-lag in the nation's military and research programs and would adversely affect the nation's economic health because of the large number of lay-offs occasioned in related industries.[44] In addition to restraining the union from striking, the injunction required the steel companies to make their plants available for the resumption of production. The decision of the district court was appealed by the union on the grounds that the facts of the case did not warrant an injunction, that the district court did not have the right to issue an injunction in the absence of a "case" or "controversy," and that the issuance of the order constituted an exercise of legislative or executive rather than judicial power. The Court of Appeals for the Third Circuit rejected these contentions and upheld the injunction, with one dissenting judge expressing the view that the injunction should not issue unless the government made a positive showing that the order would facilitate a settlement of the dispute.[45]

On certiorari, the Supreme Court in a *per curiam* opinion affirmed the decision of the lower court, with Justices Frankfurter and Harlan concurring and Justice Douglas dissenting.[46] In a thorough review of the objections of the petitioner, the Court examined the constitutionality of the Taft-Hartley procedures and especially the objections that an injunction could not issue because

[44] *United States* v. *United Steelworkers of America,* 178 F.Supp. 297 (W.D.Pa. 1959). Arthur J. Goldberg, acting as counsel of the union, contested the petition for injunction on the grounds that the strike did not imperil the health or safety of the nation and that the emergency provisions of the Taft-Hartley Act were unconstitutional.

[45] *United Steelworkers of America* v. *United States,* 271 F.2d 676 (3d Cir. 1959).

[46] *United Steelworkers of America* v. *United States,* 361 U.S. 39 (1959). Compare James N. Adler (Note), *Michigan L.Rev.,* 58: 595 (1960); Robert J. Carson and Howard S. Chasanov (Note), *Maryland L.Rev.,* 20: 287 (1960).

of the absence of a "case" or "controversy" and that the exercise of such jurisdiction constituted a delegation of legislative or executive, that is, nonjudicial power. The contention of the union that there was no case or controversy was based on the argument that the union owed the United States no duty which could be enforced through injunction. Rejecting this contention, the Court found that the Taft-Hartley Act created, or at least implied a duty of the union, namely the duty to refrain at all times from endangering the national health or safety, and that this duty could properly be enforced by a restraining order although the latter was limited to an eighty-day period. The ruling on this point had an immediate bearing on the second contention which was predicated on the premise that in the absence of a preexisting duty, the issuance of an injunction amounted to the creation of a duty and thus to the exercise of a legislative and non-judicial function on the part of the district court. In this respect, the Court argued that the duty had been created by Congress itself; that Congress in the public interest had the right to prohibit certain types of strikes without violating constitutional clauses involving free speech, due process, and involuntary servitude; that even in the absence of statutory prohibition, strikes had sometimes been enjoined as public nuisances without judicial invasion of legislative prerogatives;[47] and that, in the instant case, the statutory provisions were sufficiently definite and certain to permit judicial enforcement.

Since the injunctive procedure of the Taft-Hartley Act was thus found to be constitutional, the question which remained to be determined was whether the injunction was properly applied to the steel controversy. As the extent of the strike—its impact on the entire steel industry—was conceded by both parties, one of the factual conditions for the issuance of the injunction was obviously met. The dispute thus centered on the issue of whether the strike imperiled the nation's health or safety. With respect to the term "national health" the petitioning union contended that the term should be interpreted in a narrow manner to denote only the tangible physical health of the nation, while the government urged the adoption of a broader conception embracing in more general terms the economic well-being and welfare of the country. With-

[47] *In re Debs*, 158 U.S. 564 (1895).

out resolving this issue, the Court was satisfied that the steel strike
had in any case imperiled the national safety. For this conclusion
the Court relied strongly upon the evidence of the strike's effect
on the nation's defense and space programs, and especially on the
military missile and manned satellite projects. This view of the
Court was endorsed and corroborated by the concurring opinion
of Justices Frankfurter and Harlan.

The mere determination that the district court was entitled to
issue an injunction did not, of course, by itself amount to a finding
that the issuance of an order restraining strikes in all steel industries was the only course open to the lower court. It was exactly
on this point that Justice Douglas departed from the majority view
and joined the union's objections to the injunction. In his dissent,
Justice Douglas did not contest the constitutionality of the restraining order but based himself on the consideration that less
than one percent of the nation's steel production was actually
needed for defense and thus for the maintenance of "national
safety." Consequently, he argued that a selective reopening of the
steel mills, that is, an injunction against strikes in selected plants
preserving the union's strike weapon in other facilities, would
have been a sufficient remedy in the hands of the district court.
Rejecting the validity of this reasoning, the majority of the Court
stated that the Taft-Hartley Act did not reveal a congressional
intent to make the issuance of the injunction depend on inquiries
into the availability of other remedies, the effect of the order on
the collective bargaining process, or the conduct of the parties
during negotiations. While not denying the possibility of something less than a blanket injunction, the Court could not find
anything in the statute which would require the government to
formulate a plan of selective reopening of plants or to demonstrate
the infeasibility of such a plan. For all practical purposes, therefore, the majority opinion made the issuance of the injunction a
mandatory duty of the district court once the factual conditions of
a national labor emergency have been established.

The steel strike was the most dramatic labor dispute in 1959,
but it was certainly not the only one. The same year witnessed the
longest strike in the rubber industry, a protracted strike in a
number of bituminous-coal mines, a six-months strike in the
copper industry, and a four-months strike in a segment of the

meatpacking industry; but none of these stoppages led to the use of the Taft-Hartley provisions. In addition, disputes in which settlements were reached without strikes occurred in the paper industry, the telephone industry, the men's cotton garment industry, the aluminum and can industries, the Pacific Coast lumber industry, major electronics companies and various other industries, with the controversy frequently centering on problems of work rules and automation. The only other occasion in which the Taft-Hartley procedures were used in 1959 was a longshoring dispute on the Atlantic and Gulf Coasts.

The strike wave of 1959 and especially the steel controversy occasioned considerable public excitement and a renewed preoccupation with the problem of the handling of national emergency disputes. Despite a flurry of new proposals, however, no concrete steps were taken at the time toward a revision of existing emergency procedures.[48] The Eisenhower administration soon indicated its desire to withdraw plans for the submission of new legislation. In some government circles the view was expressed that the alleged "hardening of attitudes" in labor-management relations was exaggerated and that there was perhaps a "better relationship between labor and management" than the public might have gathered from the steel strike and other disputes. At the same time, the Democratic leadership showed little enthusiasm to press the issue. Obviously this temporary relaxation of public concern was influenced by the political maneuvers of an election year. However, governmental inattention did not remove the persisting sources of labor unrest. The incoming Kennedy administration, from the very beginning, displayed a willingness to play a larger role in labor-management relations and to bring the weight of the public interest more fully to bear on industrial disputes. The attitude of the new administration was hampered, though not seriously limited, by previous statements of the president and his Secretary of Labor expressing an unfavorable opinion of the Taft-Hartley procedures and especially of their impact on labor unions. The policy of the administration, therefore, shifted to an effort to

---

[48] A bill introduced in 1960 by Senators Javits and Aiken proposed the use of seizure ("receivership") upon adequate compensation, an intervention which was to last until a settlement was reached; see Richard A. Givens, "Dealing with National Emergency Labor Disputes," *Temple L. Quarterly,* 34: 17, 34, n.65 (1960).

introduce the government as representative of the public interest at the bargaining table and to obviate, if possible, the necessity of injunctive relief. Nevertheless, in the absence of alternate methods, there was no hesitation to use existing emergency provisions as an ultimate remedy.

At the time of this writing, the Taft-Hartley procedures have been invoked by the Kennedy administration on at least six occasions: three times in reference to the maritime industry and three times in the aviation and aerospace industry. The first instance occurred in the summer of 1961, when a three-coast shipping strike threatened to idle the entire merchant fleet of the country. The dispute, which was occasioned by negotiations of new labor contracts, involved a great number of shipping companies represented by the American Merchant Marine Institute (AMMI) and five large seamen's unions. In this case, injunctive relief was obtained in July, 1961 on the basis of findings that the strike affected a substantial part of the maritime industry and that its continuance would impair the nation's overall defense position, disrupt the mutual security and foreign aid programs under the Mutual Security Act of 1954, slow down the government's food-for-peace program under the Agricultural Trade and Development Assistance Act of 1954, and endanger petroleum supplies throughout the nation as well as commerce between the states and territories of the United States. The second emergency dispute, which developed during the spring of 1962 in the West Coast shipping industry, originated in union demands for higher wages and increased benefits in the course of negotiations for new contracts between twelve shipping companies represented by the Pacific Maritime Association and three unions. The controversy led to a crippling strike and to the issuance of restraining orders on April 11, based on the strike's impact on maritime industry and especially on commerce with Hawaii; settlement of the major issues was reached on June 21, prior to end of the injunction period. Emergency procedures were also invoked in another protracted shipping dispute which led to a strike in the fall of 1962 on the Atlantic and Gulf Coasts. In this case, injunctive relief was granted on October 4; however, the strike was resumed on December 23 at the expiration of the "cooling off" period. In January of 1963, a special mediation panel was created by the president to assist the parties in reaching a settlement or to propose appropriate legislation if either party rejected the panel's recommendations. The stoppage ended later in the same month.

The first emergency conflict in the aviation industry during the Kennedy period occurred in spring and summer of 1962. The dispute involved the International Association of Machinists and the Farmingdale, Long Island, plant of Republic Aviation Corporation, manufacturer of supersonic F-105 bombers. Failure to reach agreement in contract negotiations and especially on the issue of job security led to a strike at the plant in early April. After the shutdown had lasted for eleven weeks despite government efforts of mediation, President Kennedy appointed a board of inquiry under the Taft-Hartley Act and on June 15 directed the attorney general to seek an injunction. The use of these measures was justified by the president on the grounds that the production shutdown of the nation's only modern supersonic, all-weather fighter-bomber imperiled the national safety. The finding was supported by the Secretary of Defense who declared that the F-105 was urgently needed at that time by American forces in Southeast Asia, especially in view of the crisis situation in Laos, South Vietnam and Thailand. On August 12 the dispute was settled with the signing of a new three-year contract.

More widespread conflicts in the aerospace industry developed during the summer of the same year over contract terms. Plans for work stoppages to begin on July 23 had been announced by United Auto Workers locals at Ryan Aeronautical Corporation and North American Aviation Company, and by the International Association of Machinists at General Dynamics Corporation and Lockheed Aircraft Corporation. The stoppages were postponed, however, due to a direct appeal of President Kennedy who emphasized that a strike in this industry "would substantially delay our vital missile and space programs and would be contrary to the national interest."[49] At the time of this appeal, a special three-member "aerospace board" was appointed by the president to aid the Federal Mediation and Conciliation Service in bringing

[49] See Note, *Monthly Labor Rev.*, 85:1034 (September, 1962). Compare also Loretto R. Nolan, "A Review of Work Stoppages During 1962," *ibid.*, vol. 86, pp. 796, 797 (July, 1963).

about contract settlements. In its report of September 11, the board recommended the adoption of full union shops and other wage and economic settlements, recommendations which were subsequently followed by all companies involved with the exception of Lockheed. As a result of Lockheed's refusal to accept the proposals of the presidential board, the International Association of Machinists struck two California plants of the corporation in late November. The president immediately invoked the emergency provisions of the Taft-Hartley Act and an injunction was issued on December 3. Before the expiration of the injunction period, an agreement was reached on January 27, 1963 which, in essence, continued existing maintenance-of-membership provisions. The issue of union security was also at the basis of a dispute between the machinists' union and Boeing Corporation which culminated in the threat of a strike scheduled to start on January 15, 1963. At the request of a special mediation board established by the president, the strike was temporarily postponed. However, when mediation efforts proved futile, President Kennedy on January 23 created a board of inquiry under the Taft-Hartley Act and restraining orders were issued a few days later. At the end of the cooling-off period in mid-April, a strike was averted through a presidential request of further negotiation and, on May 10, a new three-year contract was finally signed.

Recent Policy Proposals

In the mentioned disputes, the traditional emergency procedures were used in a modified and very flexible manner by the Kennedy administration. In the maritime cases of 1961 and spring, 1962, the government intervened at first through the Secretary of Labor and through the Federal Mediation and Conciliation Service in an effort to bring the parties back to the bargaining table and to reach a settlement without resort to Taft-Hartley procedures. In the three-coast shipping strike, the Secretary of Labor proposed a peace plan which envisaged the appointment by the president of a nonstatutory three-member mediation panel of top labor experts and a voluntary suspension of the strike for sixty days. In the West Coast dispute, a nonstatutory three-member team of federal mediators was actually appointed prior to the creation of a board of inquiry. The stoppage which erupted after the expiration of the injunction in the Atlantic and Gulf Coast dispute was again mediated through the use of a nonstatutory panel in January of 1963. The controversy in the aerospace industry in the summer of 1962 witnessed the personal intervention of the president and the activity of a special three-member "aerospace board," while the use of emergency procedures in the later Boeing Corporation dispute was preceded by the appointment of a nonstatutory mediation panel and followed by renewed presidential pressure after the removal of the injunction in April of 1963.

The same flexible approach was used by the new administration in other "emergency" situations where Taft-Hartley procedures were not directly involved. Automation and reduced need for manpower produced serious disputes on major airlines and on the nation's railroads which frequently required government intervention. While the airline disputes witnessed the operation of adjustment boards, presidential emergency boards and restraining orders issued by federal courts,[50] the controversy on the railroads resulted in the creation of nonstatutory mediation panels, presidential emergency boards and finally in the enactment of congressional legislation providing for procedures very similar to compulsory arbitration.[51] Other critical disputes de-

---

[50] The airline disputes which culminated in strikes or threatened strikes in the summer of 1962, revolved mainly around the proposed reduction of jet cockpit crews from three pilots and one engineer to a total of three men.

[51] The main issue in the railroad controversy was the abolition of firemen's jobs and the size of train crews. Already in November of 1959, the railroad carriers had served notice of impending changes in work rules and pay rates; although a presidential commission and the National Mediation Board mediated without success, the implementation of the changes was postponed. In July of 1962, the railroads announced again their intention to put into effect rules changes which had been endorsed by the presidential commission in February. In August, the unions sought an injunction in federal court to prevent the rules changes. While holding that the railroads could initiate the changes, the lower federal courts issued temporary restraining orders postponing such changes pending further appeal. On March 4, 1963, the Supreme Court ruled that, apart from the creation of a presidential emergency board, the parties had exhausted the procedures of the Railway Labor Act and that the railroads were consequently entitled to change work rules; *Locomotive Engineers* v. *Baltimore and Ohio Rr. Company*, 9 L.ed. 2d 759, 83 S.Ct. 691 (1963). On April 3, the president appointed an emergency board under the Railway Labor Act, thereby postponing a threatened strike for sixty days. At

veloped in missile and atomic energy facilities, disputes whose accumulated impact was able to produce serious consequences for the nation's defense posture. In 1961, the president, acting through his Secretary of Labor, at first enlisted support and a no-strike pledge from union and company representatives and subsequently appointed a special tripartite board for the review of existing disagreements.[52] A special "missile sites labor commission," created by the president, intervened in a stoppage which halted construction at the Marshall Space Flight Center in Huntsville, Alabama, in August of 1962. A strike of office workers against the Atomic Energy Commission's Nevada test site, Camp Mercury near Las Vegas, led to the intervention of an atomic energy labor-management relations panel in late January of 1963.

The handling of the described disputes, of course, is only a reflection of the ambitious, though somewhat inarticulate, role which the federal government under the Kennedy administration

---

the end of this period, the parties at the president's request agreed to negotiate for another month. However, at the beginning of July, the railroads announced their intention to put the changes into effect, while the unions retaliated with the threat of a nationwide strike. After obtaining the consent of the parties to another postponement of the changes and the strike, President Kennedy on July 22 sent to Congress his proposals for resolving the dispute, including the recommendation that Congress authorize the Interstate Commerce Commission to decide the extent of the rules changes for a span of two years during which time a strike or lockout would be illegal. While the proposals were examined by Congress, Labor Secretary W. Willard Wirtz made another unsuccessful effort to mediate the dispute. During congressional hearings and debates, several alternate solutions were advanced, including proposals for the nationalization or seizure of the railroads and for the application of Taft-Hartley procedures to railroads and airlines. On August 28, Congress enacted an emergency arbitration law which prohibited a strike for six months and authorized a seven-man board—with three public representatives and two representatives each from union and management—to dictate settlement terms of key issues within 90 days, terms which go into effect after two more months. This was the first congressional act in American history designed to effect compulsory arbitration of a specific peacetime dispute. See *Time*, 82:15-17 (July 19, 1963), pp. 13-16 (July 26, 1963), pp. 10-11 (August 2, 1963), p. 17 (August 30, 1963), pp. 16-17 (September 6, 1963).

[52] Stronger measures for dealing with such disputes were envisaged by the so-called McClellan bill of 1961 which proposed to outlaw strikes in missile bases and other strategic defense facilities. With regard to strikes on missile construction sites compare also J. R. Van de Water, "Growth of Third-Party Power in the Settlement of Industrial Disputes," *Labor L.J.*, 12:1135 (1961).

has assumed in labor-management relations in general. It is obvious today that President Kennedy has staked out an important place for the government as representative of the public interest at collective bargaining tables across the nation, especially in negotiations affecting wage and price developments. The government has discounted any desire to assume the power of fixing wages or prices. However, the policy which has emerged clearly implies that the national interest requires the government to keep a close eye on the impact of wage and price decisions on economic stability, and seems to be inspired by a feeling of the necessity of mutual cooperation at a time when the nation is faced with world-wide commitments and growing foreign competition. As President Kennedy said in a news conference of April 18, 1962:

We agree on the necessity of preserving the nation's confidence in free, private, collective bargaining and price decisions. . . . What we are attempting to do is to try to have them (*i.e.* union and management) consider the public interest which, after all, is their interest.[53]

Although this policy was more or less noticeable from the beginning of the Kennedy administration, it received nationwide attention and a somewhat tumultuous publicity only in April, 1962, during the steel price fracas.

The steel conflict illustrated the broad powers of the president and the federal government in the area of labor-management relations even without specific statutory authorization. At the same time, however, the uproar and excitement attending the conflict demonstrated the unsettling and disturbing consequences of haphazard government intervention in the absence of clearly formulated and publicized policy principles concerning the role of government and private parties in industrial and labor disputes. The need for the formulation of such principles has been recognized for some time. Already on February 16, 1961, President Kennedy by executive order established an Advisory Committee on Labor-Management Policy composed of recognized experts representing the business community, labor unions, as well as the government and the public. The assigned task of this committee

[53] *Milwaukee Journal* (April 20, 1962), p. 14, col. 1.

was to examine such problems as collective bargaining, wage-price stability, economic growth, automation and foreign competition, and to formulate or revise principles applicable to the solution of these problems. In addition, independent study groups were created by private organizations in an effort to take a fresh new look at national labor policy and labor-management relations.[54]

On May 1, 1962, the Advisory Committee on Labor-Management Policy submitted its recommendations to the president.[55] The committee which worked under the chairmanship of Secretary of Labor Goldberg and the vice-chairmanship of Secretary of Commerce Hodges, included five additional members representing the public and seven representatives each from industry and from labor. If adopted by the president and enacted by Congress, the proposals of the panel would signify a sharp revision of Taft-Hartley procedures for the handling of emergency disputes which imperil national health or safety, provisions which the majority of the panel considered outmoded and inadequate under present circumstances. Only one representative of management dissented from this view claiming that the act's procedures "have had remarkable success in fulfilling their intended purpose."[56] The starting point and guiding principle of the report was the maintenance of free collective bargaining which was described as "an essential element of economic democracy." At the same time, however, the committee emphasized that "at a time when world tensions underscore the need for democracy's institutions to work most effectively," collective bargaining had to be "responsive to the public, or common, interest." Consequently, it was felt that in emergency situations, broader governmental powers were needed for the protection of the public welfare.

[54] The first tangible result of these efforts was a report published in December, 1961, by a study group working under the auspices of the Committee for Economic Development (CED), a nonprofit research organization of business leaders. Some prominent members of the study group were also members of the president's labor-management committee; with respect to the handling of emergency disputes, the recommendations of the report were similar in many respects to the subsequent proposals of the president's committee. See Committee for Economic Development, *The Public Interest in National Labor Policy, by an Independent Study Group* (New York, 1961).

[55] Report to the President From Advisory Committee on Labor-Management Policy, *Free and Responsible Collective Bargaining and Industrial Peace* (Washington, D.C., May 1, 1962).

[56] Statement by Henry Ford II, *ibid.*, p. 6, footnote.

Inasmuch as the welfare of vast numbers of our citizens who are not directly concerned in these disputes is involved, and the economy of the country is often adversely affected, we conclude there is a clear need for more effective governmental action under existing circumstances.[57]

The report devoted attention first to the problem of improving collective bargaining in the absence of emergency disputes, proposing for this purpose the use of tripartite periodic conferences of labor, management and public officials, greater reliance on fact-finding procedures, voluntary arbitration, and private or governmental mediation. In approaching the problem of critical or emergency controversies, the panel rejected any methods which —like compulsory arbitration—would basically vitiate collective bargaining and impose settlement terms on the parties. Instead the committee opted in favor of a flexible range of procedures, or an "arsenal of weapons," to be used by the president, with restraint, in an effort to prevent or suspend emergency disputes and to bring the parties back to the bargaining table.

As the opening move in the proposed arsenal of procedures, the director of the Federal Mediation and Conciliation Service would be authorized to recommend to the president the appointment of boards of experts or "emergency dispute boards" to investigate any bargaining situation "in a major or critical industry which may develop into a dispute threatening the national health or safety." These boards—composed either entirely of public members or of labor, industry and public representatives—would have broad powers, including the authority to mediate strikes, to recommend procedures conducive to settlement and, with the approval of the president, to recommend settlement terms. After the appointment of such a board, the president could direct the panel to hold a hearing on the question of whether a strike or lockout threatened the national health or safety and, upon receiving the board's report, could determine the extent of the threat and, if necessary, declare the existence of a national emergency. This declaration would put into effect a cooling-off period of eighty days without the requirement of a court injunction,[58] dur-

---

[57] *Ibid.*, pp. 1, 6.

[58] Henry Ford II objected: "Orders to continue or resume operations should be issued through judicial process, as at present, rather than at the discretion of the President." *Ibid.*, p. 6, footnote.

ing which the parties would be expected to continue or resume operations. The report specified that the presidential stay-at-work order could be applied either to the entire industry involved in the dispute or to selective plants if the latter alternative was practicable. During the eighty-day period, the emergency dispute boards would continue to mediate between the parties and to make recommendations for settlement terms to the parties or to the public at the president's discretion; they would even be authorized to recommend interim changes in terms or conditions of employment on a concurrent or retroactive basis. The report eliminated the "last offer" ballot of the Taft-Hartley Act as ineffective and superfluous but retained the provision that, in case of an impending strike or lockout at the expiration of the eighty-day period, the president might refer the matter to Congress with his recommendations for settlement.

As it appears, the committee report resembles in many respects the previously described Thomas-Lesinski bill of 1949 and the Ives bills of 1953; to the degree of this resemblance, it leaves room for the same queries and doubts. The major question which the report does not entirely clarify concerns the elimination of the injunctive procedure and its replacement by a presidential declaration of emergency and back-to-work order. Some observers have welcomed this change as an adoption of the "long-time voluntary compliance procedures" contained in the Railway Labor Act.[59] However, it has long become an established opinion that the provisions of the Railway Labor Act, and especially its emergency procedures, are inadequate and in need of reform. Clearly, the advisory committee cannot have intended to "improve" existing Taft-Hartley procedures and to provide for "more effective governmental action" by adopting the even less satisfactory railway labor provisions. The goal of the committee cannot only have been "voluntary compliance" in a strict sense, but the possibility of legal enforcement of the presidential order even in the absence of a prior court injunction.

The report thus revives the complicated question of whether certain strikes constitute a "public nuisance" against the United States and whether the president can declare the existence of such a nuisance in a legally enforceable manner without statutory

[59] *Milwaukee Journal* (May 2, 1962), p. 1, col. 8.

authorization of a court injunction and in the face of the Norris-La Guardia anti-injunction act. The problem is not the presidential declaration of a national emergency, since this declaration would be supported by legislative delegation of power; rather it is the enforcement of the strike suspension. It is possible that the committee considered compliance as a part of the "arsenal of weapons" and, in the manner of the Ives bills, envisaged a presidential appeal to Congress in case of a violation of the strike suspension. Obviously, this interpretation would require repeated congressional intervention in every individual instance of non-compliance. On the other hand, if this interpretation is not correct, then the binding character of the strike suspension order hinges on the inherent power of the president to seek injunctive relief. Reliance on this power, however, exposes the report to the charge that the alleged revision of the Taft-Hartley procedures is more apparent than real, at least on this point.

Another criticism which has been levelled against the proposed change is much less justified. Some observers have felt that the elimination of the court injunction would remove the possibility of judicial review of a presidential declaration of emergency. As one writer put it:

What good would be accomplished by eliminating the need to obtain a court injunction as a step to the eighty day strike suspension is not clear. Congress should look carefully into such lodging of extra power in the executive and the elimination of a check on possible misuse of presidential power.[60]

The failure of a congressional statute to provide expressly for judicial intervention would hardly be able to prevent federal courts to review at any time the exercise of presidential emergency powers. The possibility of judicial review in such matters has become a fairly established principle of law. Moreover, the committee report makes explicit allowance for court intervention by stating: "The President's declaration of emergency should be subject to judicial review at the instance of any affected party." [61] The power of judicial review seems to apply to the exercise of both statutory and nonstatutory emergency authority by the

[60] *Ibid.* (May 4, 1962), p. 18, col. 1.
[61] *Free and Responsible Collective Bargaining and Industrial Peace*, p. 5.

president. The Taft-Hartley Act and its revised edition have the advantage of providing a statutory basis for a presidential declaration of emergency and of avoiding, at least to this degree, the complex problem of "inherent" powers. However, the legislative specification of procedures does not impair the right of a judicial verification of their exercise.

3. INDEPENDENT POWERS OF THE PRESIDENT

The steel seizure decision of 1952, which has been mentioned several times in preceding pages, has been interpreted as excluding the exercise of nonstatutory or "inherent" emergency powers by the president in the field of labor-management relations, especially the power of seizure. Stated in this sweeping manner, the interpretation appears exaggerated and in need of qualification. The ruling of the Supreme Court in 1952 was based to a considerable degree on a finding of congressional intent, manifested in the legislative history of the Taft-Hartley Act, to prevent the exercise of seizure power by the president. Some statements of the decision also permit the inference that, in the Court's opinion, the emergency situation was not grave enough to justify resort to "inherent" presidential authority. A prospective repeal or substantial revision of the Taft-Hartley law would remove some of the impediments to the exercise of presidential power derived from the legislative intent of the 1947 Congress. Moreover, a crisis situation of major proportions might well induce the Court either to overrule the earlier precedent or to distinguish between the two cases in the light of necessity and factual circumstances. These considerations justify a brief review of the president's "inherent" powers, including the power of seizure, in labor-management relations.

Political Influence and Mediation Boards

The methods through which a president may, without express statutory authority, intervene in labor disputes or other industrial situations are manifold and do not necessarily have to involve resort to formal sanctions or issuance of executive orders. In numerous ways a president may bring his personal influence, and

the influence of his cabinet members, to bear on the parties of a
dispute or appeal to other organs for intervention. According to
a competent estimate, presidents between 1902 and 1946 intervened in a purely personal or political capacity in no fewer than
26 strikes.[62] Apart from various actions of Presidents Hayes and
Cleveland, President McKinley in 1898 appointed an industrial
commission to investigate the causes of labor disputes. In 1902
Theodore Roosevelt brought the influence of his office to bear on
the parties of a bitter anthracite strike which lasted five months.
President Wilson twice appealed to Congress urging enactment
of legislation to end industrial disputes. Toward the end of the
war, Wilson called a labor-management conference to review
national policy with regard to labor relations. Subsequently, the
president appealed to the parties in the steel strike of 1919,
stopped a bituminous-coal strike of the same year by appointing
a commission, and induced the parties in the anthracite dispute
of 1920 to submit their wage differences to arbitration.

During the following Republican period, President Coolidge in
1925 sent a special message to Congress asking for increased
power of the executive branch to deal with another anthracite
strike of that year. The influence of Franklin D. Roosevelt
on legislation dealing with industrial relations is a matter of
common knowledge. Apart from many other forms of intervention, President Truman in 1946 imitated Wilson's earlier example
by calling a labor-management conference to examine the problems of the reconversion period. The Eisenhower administration
also resorted to many forms of indirect intervention or persuasion.
In 1955, a brief steel strike was settled when the Secretary of the
Treasury, George Humphrey, prevailed upon his former col-
leagues on the management side to seek an agreement. Also,
Vice-President Nixon's role in negotiations during the steel strike
of 1959 was described as an "urgent kind of governmental intervention." [63] The impact of President Kennedy's intervention in
April, 1962, after the boost of steel prices, is still fresh in memory.

A more institutionalized, although comparatively mild, form of
nonstatutory intervention by the president can be found in the

[62] Edward S. Corwin, *The President: Office and Powers*, 4th ed. (New
York, 1957), pp. 408-410.
[63] Fleming, *op. cit.*, p. 270.

appointment of fact-finding or mediation boards. The experience with nonstatutory fact-finding boards dates primarily from the end of the second World War. However, boards with similar functions but of longer duration had been used previously in wartime and in periods of defense emergency. President Wilson in 1917 established a National War Labor Board attached to the Department of Labor and composed of representatives of employers and workers with the function of mediating labor disputes during the war. During the period of the defense emergency prior to World War II, President Roosevelt on March 19, 1941, created the National Defense Mediation Board whose effective operation continued until November of the same year. Subsequently, the National War Labor Board was established by the president on January 12, 1942. The board was clearly a nonstatutory agency whose orders were not enforceable by traditional legal sanctions and which derived its influence from a voluntary no-strike pledge given by representatives of unions and management at a labor-management conference called by the president shortly after Pearl Harbor. The War Labor Disputes Act of June 25, 1943, simply recognized the prior existence and authority of the board, but did not change its non-legal character or the absence of strict enforceability of its orders.

The termination of the dispute-settling functions of the National War Labor Board at the end of hostilities in 1945 created the need for an alternative mechanism. During the reconversion period, between November 1945 and September 1946, President Truman and his Secretary of Labor appointed nonstatutory boards in thirteen instances. The boards dealt with major reconversion controversies, including the meatpacking, nonferrous metals, electricity, telegraph, longshore, and sugar refinery disputes of 1946.[64] The end of the reconversion period and the enactment of the Taft-Hartley procedures did not entirely eliminate the recourse to nonstatutory boards. In December, 1947, a fact-finding board was created to mediate the dispute between the Western Union Telegraph Company and three AFL unions. Similar boards were established in spring and summer of 1949 in connection with disputes in the railroad facilities of the Kennecott Copper

[64] U.S. Department of Labor, *Work Stoppages, Federal Fact-Finding Boards and Boards of Inquiry,* Series 5, No. 1 (July, 1952), pp. 2, 5-17.

Corporation and in the steel industry. During the Eisenhower administration, the atomic energy disputes of 1954 witnessed the activity of a special labor-management relations panel prior to the appointment of boards of inquiry under the Taft-Hartley Act. A fact-finding board was also created in October, 1954, in a dispute between the United Steelworkers of America and the American Smelting and Kennecott Copper companies. The frequent resort of the Kennedy administration to nonstatutory boards and commissions in a variety of disputes has already been discussed.

All of these boards were *ad hoc* teams established under the general powers of the president without congressional authorization and were usually appointed either by the president directly, by the Secretary of Labor, or by the Director of the Federal Mediation and Conciliation Service. The functions of the boards were to investigate the facts of the dispute, to mediate between the parties and to recommend terms of settlement. The effectiveness of the procedure was based on a voluntary agreement of the parties to appear before the boards and recommendations were not legally binding on the parties. The authority of the president to establish such nonstatutory boards has never been seriously questioned. The procedure acquires new significance in the light of the recent recommendations of President Kennedy's advisory committee which, if adopted by Congress, would furnish a statutory basis for the appointment of similar boards. One might add that, during the Truman administration, the use of the procedure did not always evoke favorable response. Fact-finding boards appointed by President Truman were sometimes criticized by industry representatives as being strongly pro-labor and as being unduly generous in their recommendations. It was partly in response to such criticisms that the Taft-Hartley Act withheld the power to make recommendations from the boards of inquiry.

Use of Federal Troops

A much stronger form of intervention is presented in cases where federal troops or other military services are used to maintain order in labor-management relations. Obviously, this method is an extreme remedy and, in recent decades, has been employed only on comparatively rare occasions. In the majority of cases, federal troops were called in to enforce a court injunction or a prior seizure. In the absence of or apart from pertinent statutory provisions, the use of federal troops by the president in industrial relations must be founded on his constitutional authority as commander-in-chief or, in cases of domestic violence during peacetime, on the "take care" clause and on his power as commander of the militia of the states called into federal service.[65] The earliest intervention of federal troops in labor disputes was based mainly on a combination of the latter powers.

In 1877, the first national emergency dispute occurred on the railroads when strikes erupted spontaneously without union direction in protest against wage cuts. The widespread rioting which resulted was put down when President Hayes ordered the intervention of federal troops. In this case, the use of troops, although it resulted in breaking the strike, was clearly based on the violence and not on the strike itself. The next nationwide emergency dispute was the Pullman strike of 1894, organized by the American Railway Union under the leadership of Eugene Debs. When the union demands for bargaining over employee grievances were rejected, the union called a strike and the railroads retaliated by firing employees on Pullman trains. The railroads' decision to hire replacements bred violence. Despite the objections of Governor Altgeld of Illinois to federal intervention, President Cleveland sent federal troops to the area, provoking further violence which was ultimately crushed. In the meantime the attorney general obtained an injunction not only against the violence but also against the strike effort. The circuit court sustained the injunction on the grounds that the strike constituted a combination in restraint of interstate commerce and thus a violation of the Sherman Antitrust Act of 1890. Without distinguishing clearly between violent or peaceful conduct, the Supreme Court also upheld the injunction and denied Debs' petition for a writ of habeas corpus, claiming that the federal commerce power and an aggregate of statutes gave the federal courts inherent power to grant

[65] Compare "Use of Federal Troops in Labor Disputes," *Monthly Labor Rev.*, 53: 561 (September, 1941); also W.B. Lawless, Jr., "Military Action in Labor Disputes," *Notre Dame Lawyer*, 18: 288 (1943). It should be pointed out that, although the president seems entitled to use troops in an independent manner on the basis of the constitution alone, such use is regularly supported by existing congressional statutes.

the attorney general's petition for injunctive relief.[66] Federal troops were also used by President McKinley in 1899 to suppress disturbances in the Coeur d'Alene mines in Idaho, by President Theodore Roosevelt in 1903 and 1907 during mining disorders in Arizona and Nevada, by President Wilson in several wartime and postwar strikes and especially during the steel and bituminous coal strikes of 1919, and by President Harding in 1921 to quell mining disorders in West Virginia.

The gradual enactment of federal legislation improving the position of labor unions led to a decrease of military intervention on the national level, although it did not immediately reduce the number of martial law declarations on the state level. Federal troops were still called in on several occasions; but their use tended to be restricted to periods of defense emergency, war, or reconversion from war, and to cases where seizure had resulted in government operation of plants or facilities. During the defense emergency in 1941, troops were used in connection with the seizure of the North American Aviation plants at Inglewood, California, in an effort to disperse picket lines and to allow willing workers to return to work. Although President Roosevelt deplored the use of troops as dangerous in a democracy, he considered the case as "not a bona fide labor dispute but a form of alien sabotage." [67] In August of 1944, troops were employed in the Philadelphia Transportation Company seizure to protect workers while enforcing a racial antidiscrimination order. During the seizure of the Chicago Motor Carriers from May to August of 1945, the Office of Defense Transportation had to receive the aid of troops to protect drivers willing to work and also to serve as drivers. In the postwar reconversion period, the Office of Defense Transportation again had to requisition personnel from the Army, Navy and Coast Guard to maintain essential tug service when the seizure of the New York tugboat companies in February of 1946 failed to bring the strikers back to work.

Proposals or threats to induct striking workers into the armed forces were made on several occasions. World War II witnessed

[66] *United States* v. *Debs,* 64 Fed. 724 (C.C.N.D.Ill. 1894); *In re Debs,* 158 U.S. 564, 581-598 (1895).

[67] See Richard B. Johnson, "Administrative Problems of Government Seizure in Labor Disputes," *Public Administration Rev.,* 11: 189, 196 (1951).

occasional endorsements of a "work-or-fight" law in application
to wartime strikes. President Roosevelt came out in favor of such
legislation in 1943 when he vetoed the Smith-Connally Act, and
again in 1945 during the Battle of the Bulge. Refusal of workers
to cancel a strike after the seizure of railroads in May 1946 led to
President Truman's angry request for legislation which would
have permitted him to draft the striking workers into the Army.
Only an indirect relation to military intervention can be found in
the railroad strike of 1948 when the president directed the Secretary of the Army to seize the railroads; in this instance, the
railroads continued to operate largely under the previous management. In August, 1950, however, the seized railroads were placed
under the direction of the Assistant Secretary of the Army while
the entire country was divided into seven regions headed by army
colonels recalled to active military duty. Curiously enough, all
these colonels happened to be railroad presidents in civilian
life.[68]

Seizure

Government seizure of plants during labor disputes has frequently been defended as a strong but balanced form of public
intervention which, while avoiding the onerous side effects of
compulsory arbitration or injunction, protects the public interest
in the maintenance of an essential service. This estimate appears
to have merit especially where the measure is not intended to
enforce a recommended settlement but to function as a holding
device permitting negotiations without loss of the strike weapon
on the part of one disputant. Whatever its merits or demerits,
seizure by the president, in order to be valid, has to be founded
on a constitutional basis, such as the president's authority as
commander-in-chief which applies primarily in wartime, or on
specific legislative authorization. In peacetime, on the other hand,
the power of the president to seize a plant without legislative
permission is very doubtful. If at all, such a measure can only be
justified by a national emergency of severe proportions. It so
happens that emergencies of this nature are not entirely rare in

[68] Marie-Louise Paternoster, "Government Seizure in Labor Disputes,"
Labor L.J., 3: 341, 345 (1952).

the present cold war period with its blending of wartime and peacetime standards. Regularly, of course, any governmental taking of property relies on the constitutional principle of eminent domain. However, in view of the necessity of "just compensation," a compensation which can only be granted by Congress, eminent domain is hardly a sufficient basis of presidential power in the absence of statutory permission, unless there is a justified expectation that Congress will ratify the exercise of seizure by the president by passing a compensation measure.

There is a long succession of congressional enactments authorizing seizure by the president. Beginning with the Civil War period, Congress has passed legislation authorizing seizure of industrial property on at least sixteen occasions,[69] although few of these statutes were framed with a view to permit government intervention in labor-management controversies. During the first World War, some six measures were enacted, the major ones being the Transportation Act of 1916, inserted in the Army Appropriations Act of the same year, which empowered the president in time of war to seize and utilize any system of transportation, and the Joint Resolution of 1918 authorizing the seizure of telegraph and telephone systems. In the period between the two wars only two seizure acts were passed by Congress.[70] Despite a much greater seizure activity, the entire period of World War II from the beginning of the defense emergency in 1940 to the end of hostilities in 1945 witnessed only some five acts authorizing seizure of facilities by the president. The most important of these acts, and the one most frequently used in relation to labor disputes, was the War Labor Disputes or Smith-Connally Act which was passed on June 25, 1943, over the veto of the president. Two major statutes were added in the postwar period: the Selective Service Act of 1948 and the Defense Production Act of 1950, with amendments. Under the Selective Service Act, the president is empowered to seize plants whenever the producer from whom the president has ordered goods required by the armed forces or the Atomic Energy Commission for national defense purposes

[69] A list of the various laws in the form of a tabular analysis is attached to Justice Frankfurter's concurring opinion in the steel seizure case; *Youngstown Sheet and Tube Co. v. Sawyer*, 343 U.S. 579, App. I, 615-619; for a table of individual acts of seizure see *ibid.*, App. II, pp. 620-628 (1952).

[70] Federal Water Power Act of 1920 and Communication Act of 1934.

"refuses or fails" to fill the order within a period of time prescribed by the president. The Defense Production Act in its original form authorized the president, upon payment of just compensation, to requisition and take possession of industrial property and production facilities if their acquisition was needed for the national defense effort and if all other means of obtaining use of such property were exhausted. On June 30, 1953, the section of the act dealing with requisition and condemnation was terminated.

In the great majority of cases, seizures by the federal government have followed statutory provisions. Many other instances of seizure were effected during periods of actual warfare under the president's war powers. In a number of cases, however, the basis of the presidential action was not so clear. The history of the colonies and the early period of the United States offer many examples of seizure, but they usually occurred in the theatre of military operations.[71] Without statutory authority but on the basis of a clear emergency, President Lincoln in 1861 seized the telegraph and railroad lines between Washington and Annapolis. Congress subsequently confirmed the president's action by passing the Railroad and Telegraph Act of 1862, and Lincoln again seized the telegraph lines and the railroads in February and May of 1862. Some of President Wilson's seizures during World War I were supported by statutory authorization, others were not. One of the earliest actions in the latter category occurred in the summer of 1914 and involved the seizure of the Marconi Wireless Station at Siasconset, Massachusetts, as a result of the company's refusal to pledge compliance with naval censorship regulations. There were several other takings unsupported by statutory provisions,[72] a doubtful case being the seizure of the Smith and Wesson plant at Springfield, Massachusetts, in September of 1918.

The period of World War II witnessed again statutory and nonstatutory exercise of seizure power. During the existence of the National Defense Mediation Board from March, 1941 to January, 1942, the president effected three important seizures without

[71] See *United States* v. *Russell,* 13 Wall. 623 (1872); *Prize Cases,* 2 Black 635 (1862); *Mitchell* v. *Harmony,* 13 How. 115 (1852).

[72] Edward S. Corwin, "The Steel Seizure Case: A Judicial Brick Without Straw," *Columbia L.Rev.,* 53: 53, 59 (1953).

statutory support. One of these seizure orders applied to the North American Aviation plant at Inglewood, California, and resulted from a dispute which was apparently communist-inspired. The other two instances involved a shipbuilding company and an aircraft parts plant. The seizure orders which were signed by Roosevelt "as President of the United States and Commander-in-Chief of the Army and Navy" were strengthened by the fact that the president had declared an unlimited emergency on May 27, 1941. In the North American Aviation case the action of the president was vigorously defended by Attorney General Jackson who stated that "the Presidential proclamation rests upon the aggregate of the Presidential powers derived from the Constitution itself and from statutes enacted by Congress." [73] Following the congressional declaration of a state of war on December 8, 1941, some fifty seizures were effected in connection with labor disputes during the war. After the establishment of the War Labor Board in January, 1942, but prior to the enactment of the Smith-Connally Act, the president issued six seizure orders without express legislative authorization. In these instances, however, the intervention was clearly predicated on the congressional declaration of war and the president's war powers. Later wartime seizures were usually of a statutory nature and, in the majority of cases, were based on the Smith-Connally Act of June, 1943.

The postwar reconversion period from August, 1945 to the end of 1946 brought nine presidential takings of industrial property. Practically all of these seizures continued to be based on the Smith-Connally Act. Among other facilities, the actions applied to oil refineries, meatpacking companies, the New York harbor tugboat services, the railroads, and the bituminous coal mines. Apart from these cases, seizure by the president was unsuccessfully urged in a number of labor disputes, including the General Motors and Allis-Chalmers strikes of 1946. Since the passage of the Taft-Hartley Act and prior to the steel seizure case of 1952, three seizure orders were issued by the president. All three orders involved the railroads and were based on the Transportation Act of 1916, despite the fact that the act was clearly phrased to apply "in time of war." The first order which was issued in May, 1948, directed the Secretary of the Army to take possession of the

[73] 89 Cong. Rec. 3992 (1943).

railroads during a labor-management dispute. The seizure was accompanied by a strike injunction granted on the basis of government operation despite the carrier's continuing management.[74] The other two orders were issued in July and August of 1950. In the latter case which resulted from disagreements over contract terms, strike injunctions were again obtained, but stoppages occurred intermittently in December and January. On February 8, 1951, the Army ordered all men back to work on pain of losing their jobs, and the workers complied with the order.[75] The seizure lasted until May 23, 1952.

The Steel Seizure Case

The survey of seizures up until the beginning of the Korean crisis reveals that the taking of industrial property by presidential order was, in the majority of cases, supported by legislative authorization. In other instances, a declared state of war and the president's war powers served as adequate justification. However, there were also a number of borderline cases where the president effectively seized property without congressional support or a declaration of war. It is true that with respect to nonstatutory seizure, court decisions of the last century tended to require that the action occurred in the immediate theatre of military operations. More recent court rulings, however, were less explicit on this point and referred more broadly to emergency situations or immediate crisis conditions. As one writer observed after reviewing judicial precedents:

Now does all of this mean that the President cannot seize property where necessary unless there is an actual invasion of the country? Obviously it does not, as is clear from the language of the . . . decisions, as well as many other cases. An immediate and impending danger or the necessity of urgent action for the protection of the public does not mean that the enemy must have a foothold on our shores or even be within our territorial waters. In these perilous times when man has harnessed fantastic speeds and liberated gargantuan forces of nature

[74] *United States* v. *Brotherhood of Locomotive Engineers,* 79 F.Supp. 485 (D.D.C. 1948).
[75] The union was subsequently fined for contempt of court despite the claim of union leaders that they had exhorted workers to return to work; *United States* v. *Brotherhood of Railroad Trainmen,* 95 F.Supp. 1019 (D.D.C. 1951), 96 F.Supp. 428 (N.D. Ill. 1951).

to encompass his own destruction, an air fleet poised or being readied on the banks of the Volga could well be interpreted as more "immediate and impending" a danger, necessitating even more urgent action, than was true of the grey clad cavalry patrols of Jeb Stuart reconnoitering to the north of the Potomac.[76]

Such was then the historical and constitutional background when President Truman, on April 8, 1952, issued the order to seize the steel mills at the height of the Korean crisis. The facts of the case have frequently been recounted and permit a summary treatment in the present context.[77] The basic issues involved in the dispute were union security and labor demands for wage increases. At the end of 1950, the principal steel producers and the United Steelworkers of America, CIO, had agreed upon a wage increase of about sixteen cents per hour pursuant to a wage reopening clause in the existing contracts. During January of the following year, the wage rates were more or less "frozen" by regulations of the newly established Economic Stabilization Agency and its Wage Stabilization Board. New settlements, however, were expected and necessary in view of the impending expiration of collective bargaining agreements between the union and the steel companies on December 31, 1951. In an effort to open negotiations, the steel workers union, during November, submitted to the companies a list of twenty-two general demands whose terms were subsequently specified in over 100 items. As no progress was made in bargaining conferences, the union set a strike deadline for December 31, the day of the expiration of the old contracts. On December 22, President Truman intervened and, on the basis of the Defense Production Act, directed the Wage Stabilization Board to investigate the dispute and to report back with recommendations. In response to the president's request to defer strike action during the period of the board's investigation, the union temporarily postponed the announced stoppage.

[76] Arthur M. Williams, "The Impact of the Steel Seizures Upon the Theory of Inherent Sovereign Powers of the Federal Government," *South Carolina L.Rev.*, 5: 5, 22-23 (1952).

[77] Compare Robert F. Banks, "Steel, Sawyer, and the Executive Power," *University of Pittsburgh L.Rev.*, 14: 467 (1953); see also Alan F. Westin, *The Anatomy of a Constitutional Law Case* (New York, 1958), pp. 1-20; Smith and Cotter, *op. cit.*, pp. 134-139; Bernard J. Hasson, Jr., "The Steel Seizure Cases," *Georgetown L.J.*, 41: 45 (1952).

On January 3, 1952, the Wage Stabilization Board appointed a tripartite panel, consisting of two representatives each of industry, labor, and the public, to hear the evidence. At the same time, the board requested both parties to maintain production pending a report to the president, with the understanding that if no agreement was reached by April 4, the union could strike upon giving prior notice to the companies. On March 20, the board issued its recommendations which, among other things, provided for staggered wage increases, additional fringe benefits and a union shop clause in the new contracts. The recommendations were accepted by the union but promptly rejected by the companies which claimed that the proposed increases would result in additional costs of over one hundred million dollars in 1952 and one hundred forty-one million dollars in 1953. A period of intense negotiations followed but produced no agreement. On April 4, the union served notice of an industry-wide strike, to become effective at 12:01 A.M., April 9. Thereupon, on the evening of April 8, President Truman announced that he had ordered his Secretary of Commerce, Sawyer, to take possession of the steel plants by midnight.[78]

The seizure order produced immediately a frantic activity on the part of management to prevent its implementation. While the union cancelled its strike call, counsel for the Youngstown Sheet and Tube Company and the Republic Steel Corporation—on the same evening of April 8—visited District Judge Bastian of the District of Columbia at his home, but the latter merely set a hearing on the motion to obtain a temporary restraining order against the government. Secretary Sawyer opposed the motion claiming that an acute emergency existed and that the "President of the United States . . . has inherent power in such a situation to take possession of the steel companies. . . . This power is supported by the Constitution, by historical precedent, and by court decision;" he also argued that the president could not be enjoined.[79] On the next morning Bethlehem Steel Company joined in the action, but

[78] On April 9, the president sent a message to Congress apprising it of his action, but concluding that, in his belief, no immediate congressional intervention was necessary; 98 Cong. Rec. 3962-63 (1952). Congress failed to act either then or two weeks later when the president again raised the problem in a letter; 98 Cong. Rec. 4192 (1952).

[79] Banks, *op. cit.*, p. 470.

District Judge Holtzoff of the same court denied the motion for a temporary restraining order on the grounds that the court could not restrain the president and that the companies had failed to show irreparable damage.[80] The three companies—joined by Jones and Laughlin and U. S. Steel—then asked to have the case heard at the earliest possible moment. After an unsuccessful intervention of the Federal Mediation and Conciliation Service, Secretary Sawyer on April 20 announced plans to grant wage increases during the period of government operation. Since the companies felt that such plans might impair their bargaining position, motions for preliminary injunction both against the seizure and against alteration in terms and conditions of employment were introduced by the counsel for management. The cases and motions were consolidated and set down for hearing on April 24.

On April 29, District Judge Pine of the District of Columbia rendered his decision granting an injunction against the government. The decision was based on two major arguments: first, that the seizure was not supported by a statutory authorization as it should have been in a peacetime situation; and secondly, that in the absence of statutory support the president's action could only be founded on his power as commander-in-chief which, however, did not cover a seizure effected neither in time of war nor in a theatre of war. In addition, the court relied for its ruling on findings that the Secretary of Commerce was not beyond the reach of judicial power and that the damages were shown to be irreparable. Judge Pine concluded his decision by expressing the belief

that the contemplated strike, if it came, with all its awful results, would be less injurious to the public than the injury which would flow from a timorous judicial recognition that there is some basis for this claim of unlimited and unrestrained executive power, which would be implicit in a failure to grant the injunction.[81]

[80] *Youngstown Sheet and Tube Co.* v. *Sawyer,* 103 F.Supp. 978 (D.D.C. 1952).

[81] *Youngstown Sheet and Tube Co.* v. *Sawyer,* 103 F.Supp. 569, 574 (D.D.C. 1952). Rejecting the "stewardship" theory of the presidency, Judge Pine observed: "The nonexistence of this 'inherent' power in the President has been recognized by eminent writers, and I cite in this connection the unequivocal language of the late Chief Justice Taft in his treatise entitled 'Our Chief Magistrate and His Powers' (1916). . . . I stand on that as a correct statement of the law."

Upon the issuance of the restraining order which put the steel companies back in possession of the seized facilities, the union immediately called a strike and, by April 30, the work stoppage was complete.[82] At the same time, Secretary Sawyer requested the Court of Appeals for the District of Columbia to stay the injunction until he filed a petition for a writ of certiorari with the Supreme Court. On the evening of April 30, the Court of Appeals granted a stay of the restraining order until the afternoon of May 2, provided that a petition for certiorari was filed by the government.[83] Both the government and the companies petitioned for certiorari on the designated day. At the same time, in response to an appeal by the president, the union ordered its members to return to work.

On May 3, the Supreme Court granted certiorari and extended the stay of the district court order pending final disposition of the case.[84] In its brief and in oral argument before the Court, the government relied on a series of considerations. After describing the character of the emergency and the existing crisis in military and foreign affairs, the government first attacked the preliminary injunction on the grounds that the companies had a valid remedy for obtaining compensation and that there was no adequate showing of irreparable injury. With regard to the president's action, the government relied both on statutory and nonstatutory authority. On the basis of the constitution alone, the argument was that the president's power to seize property in war or emergency situations, subject to payment of compensation, was supported by prior executive action, legislative consent, and judicial precedent. More specifically, the authority was said to derive from an "aggregate" or combination of his powers as president, commander-in-chief, law-enforcement officer, and such other powers as flow from his position as chief of the executive branch in time of emergency. In addition or alternately, the government claimed to find support for the action in the extensive system of laws providing for national security and in the argument that the proce-

[82] For the foreign policy and cold war implications of the strike compare James Reston's comments in *The New York Times* (May 1, 1952), p. 24, col. 3.

[83] *Sawyer* v. *U. S. Steel Corporation,* 197 F.2d 582 (D.C.Cir. 1952).

[84] 343 U.S. 937 (1952). The Court also stayed any unilateral changes in wages or conditions of employment.

dures of the Taft-Hartley Act were not mandatory and did not preclude seizure in this case. The companies countered by claiming that the seizure resulted in irreparable damage; that Congress had enacted explicit procedures for such disputes which were disregarded by the president; and that the action could not be based on the constitutional powers of the president, on an "aggregate" of such powers, or on vague assertions of an "inherent" authority. In the position of *amici curiae,* the Steel Workers Union was permitted to present brief and argument in support of the government as were counsel for three railway unions, involved in the 1950 railroad seizure, who argued against the president's action.

The decision of the Supreme Court which was handed down on June 2 and resulted in another nationwide strike held that President Truman's seizure was illegal.[85] The opinion of the Court was delivered by Justice Black. Justices Frankfurter, Jackson, Douglas and Burton concurred in the opinion and the judgment of the Court, but each wrote separate concurring opinions which sometimes presented divergent views. Justice Clark limited his concurrence to the judgment of the Court. Chief Justice Vinson, speaking for himself and Justices Reed and Minton, wrote a long and strongly worded dissenting opinion.

The most rigid and narrowly restrictive position was taken by Justice Black's majority opinion. After having affirmed the danger of irreparable injury and the lack of a sufficient remedy for the recovery of damages, Justice Black noted that there was no statute which expressly or impliedly authorized the president to take possession of the steel mills. On the contrary, he found that Congress, in enacting the Taft-Hartley law in 1947, had refused to authorize governmental seizure in labor disputes. The issue was thus narrowed down to the question of whether the president's action, in the absence of legislative support, could be justified in the light of constitutional provisions. Justice Black was unable to discover such justification in the commander-in-chief clause arguing that despite modern modifications of the concept of war, military prerogatives had to be carefully separated from the domestic economy.[86] Nor could the authority be derived from the "take

[85] *Youngstown Sheet and Tube Co.* v. *Sawyer,* 343 U.S. 579 (1952).

[86] "Even though 'theatre of war' be an expanding concept, we cannot with faithfulness to our constitutional system hold that the Commander-in-Chief

care" clause since the law enforcement duty did not include the law-making power. Justice Black was equally emphatic in stating that the seizure could not be validated by reference to an "aggregate" of executive powers under Article II of the Constitution or other assertions of broad executive authority. Even if previous presidents had on occasion exercised similar prerogatives, he argued, such practice had not divested Congress of its exclusive law making power. Justice Black concluded with this famous statement:

The Founders of this Nation entrusted the law-making power to Congress alone in both good and bad times. It would do no good to recall the historical events, the fears of power and the hopes for freedom that lay behind their choice. Such a review would but confirm our holding that this seizure order cannot stand.[87]

A similar restrictive view was expressed by Justice Douglas in his concurring opinion. Taking a strict constructionist approach, the Justice argued that the case could not be decided "by determining which branch of government can deal most expeditiously with the present crisis. The answer must depend on the allocation of powers under the Constitution." Since a governmental taking of property relies ultimately on the eminent domain principle and since under the constitution only Congress can raise revenues for the payment of compensation, he found that

until and unless Congress acted, no condemnation would be lawful. The branch of government that has the power to pay compensation for a seizure is the only one able to authorize a seizure or make lawful one that the President has effected. That seems to be the necessary result of the condemnation provision in the Fifth Amendment.[88]

The argument seemed to overlook the possibility that the power to seize and the authority to raise revenue may be separate and consecutive rather than coterminous. Justice Douglas was unable

---

of the Armed Forces has the ultimate power as such to take possession of private property in order to keep labor disputes from stopping production. This is a job for the Nation's lawmakers, not for its military authorities." *Ibid.*, p. 587.

[87] *Ibid.*, p. 589.

[88] *Ibid.*, pp. 631-632.

to discover a basis for the presidential action apart from statutory support. In his opinion, Article II which vests the "executive power" in the president subsequently defines this power in detail. The commander-in-chief clause granted no authority over domestic civilian affairs, while the "take care" clause was of no pertinence since "the power to execute the laws starts and ends with the laws Congress has enacted."

Somewhat less narrow was the conception propounded by Justice Jackson. According to his concurring opinion, actions by the president fall into three classes: first, actions authorized by Congress where his power is at its maximum; secondly, actions in cases where Congress is silent and when there is a "zone of twilight in which he and Congress may have concurrent authority;" and thirdly, actions incompatible with the express or implied will of Congress where "his power is at its lowest ebb, for then he can rely only upon his own constitutional powers minus any constitutional powers of Congress over the matter." Since Congress had acted in the present case, the first two alternatives were ruled out. The question thus was merely whether there was a remainder of executive power supporting the action. Justice Jackson agreed with Justice Douglas on the interpretation of the first sentence of Article II and with Justices Black and Douglas on the meaning and extent of the commander-in-chief and "take care" clauses. With regard to any broader assertion of executive emergency powers, he stated that they

are consistent with free government only when their control is lodged elsewhere than in the Executive who exercises them. . . . The Executive, except for recommendation and veto, has no legislative power. The executive action we have here originated in the will of the President and represents an exercise of authority without law.[89]

Justice Frankfurter was more careful to limit his considerations to the case at hand and thus avoided some of the broader implications of the described opinions. Reminding his fellow justices that the Court traditionally had abstained from deciding constitutional issues in the absence of actual necessity, he asserted that "the issue before us can be met, and therefore should be, without attempting to define the President's powers comprehensively."

[89] *Ibid.*, pp. 637, 652, 655.

This approach permitted Justice Frankfurter to "put to one side consideration of what powers the President would have if there had been no legislation whatever bearing on the authority asserted by the seizure," and to enter directly upon a documentary review of the legislative history of the Taft-Hartley Act. This review convinced the Justice that Congress had expressed its intention to withhold the seizure power "as though it had said so in so many words." Nor could such a power be derived from the Defense Production Act of 1950 with its amendments. After this conclusion was reached, the remaining arguments had the character of an anticlimax and were not fully consistent with the original approach. Once the existence of a congressional intent to withhold seizure power had been determined, it was not entirely pertinent to inquire whether custom and continued practice, coupled with congressional acquiescence, might have attributed such power to the executive branch. Justice Frankfurter admitted that the powers of the president are not as specific as those of Congress—although the separation of powers principle may give content to undefined provisions—and that "a systematic, unbroken, executive practice, long pursued to the knowledge of Congress and never before questioned . . . may be treated as a gloss on 'executive power' vested in the President." However, a detailed analysis of past executive seizures revealed to the Justice only three cases "in circumstances comparable to the present" and

these three isolated instances do not add up, either in number, scope, duration or contemporaneous legal justification, to the kind of executive construction of the Constitution revealed in the *Midwest Oil* case.[90]

The brief concurring opinion of Justice Burton also attempted to limit itself to the instant case; but it contained some statements which indicated his apparent willingness to concede executive emergency powers under different circumstances. Noting that the validity of the seizure depended on the constitutional distribution of power, he remarked that Congress undoubtedly had the right

[90] *Ibid.*, pp. 597, 602, 610-611, 613. The three seizure cases were those effected by President Roosevelt prior to Pearl Harbor between June to December, 1941. In *United States* v. *Midwest Oil Co.*, 236 U. S. 459 (1915), the Court upheld President Taft's withdrawal of certain lands from public entry without congressional permission.

"to authorize action to meet a national emergency of the kind we face." In the present case, Congress, by enacting the Taft-Hartley law, had failed to provide for presidential seizure power and had "authorized a procedure which the President declined to follow." From this finding which in itself would have been sufficient, Justice Burton ventured briefly into the area of executive emergency powers. The present situation, he indicated, must be distinguished "from one in which Congress takes no action and outlines no governmental policy" or from cases of "an imminent invasion or threatened attack." [91] Apparently the justice did not feel that there was at present such an extreme emergency; in any event, he left open the question of executive power to meet "catastrophic" situations. Justice Clark's opinion was more explicit and affirmative on the latter point. The opinion started with the proposition that the constitution does grant to the president extensive authority in times of grave and imperative national emergency; "in fact, to my thinking, such a grant may well be necessary to the very existence of the Constitution itself." However, the president's independent power to act, depending on the gravity of the situation, may be exercised only in the absence of congressional action defining the procedures to be followed in meeting the emergency. No such independent action was permissible where, as in the instant case, Congress had specified the procedures to be followed by the president. Three pertinent statutes had been enacted; but neither the Taft-Hartley nor the Defense Production Act authorized seizure of the type effected here, while the government made no attempt to comply with the Selective Service Act of 1948.

I conclude that where Congress has laid down specific procedures to deal with the type of crisis confronting the President, he must follow those procedures in meeting the crisis; but that in the absence of such action by Congress, the President's independent power to act depends upon the gravity of the situation confronting the nation. I cannot sustain the seizure in question because . . . Congress has prescribed methods to be followed by the President in meeting the emergency at hand.[92]

[91] 343 U. S. 656, 659. The opinion is ambiguous on the point whether executive power in case of invasion or attack could be exercised with or without congressional action.

[92] *Ibid.*, p. 662. Justice Clark relied strongly on the *Flying Fish* case of

The dissenting opinion of Chief Justice Vinson relied primarily on three points: on the emergency nature of the situation in which the seizure occurred; on the powers of the president in meeting such an emergency; and on the contention that the exercise of these powers was not prevented by existing legislation. Concerning the emergency character of the situation, the dissent stressed such cold war developments as the growing East-West conflict, the obligations of the United States under the United Nations Charter to repel communist aggression in Korea, the congressional enactments of the Truman Plan for assistance to Greece and Turkey and of the Marshall Plan for economic aid to Europe, the Senate ratification of the North Atlantic Treaty and congressional legislation implementing the Treaty, and the passage of the Mutual Security Act of 1951. The president had the duty to execute all these programs whose success depended to a large degree on continued steel production and stabilized steel prices. Against this background, the Chief Justice examined the extent of presidential powers to meet the crisis. He discovered sufficient support for the seizure action in the provision which lodged the whole of the "executive power" in the president and in the commander-in-chief and "take care" clauses of the constitution, noting that "our Presidents have on many occasions exhibited the leadership contemplated by the Framers when they made the President Commander-in-Chief, and imposed upon him the trust to 'take care that the laws be faithfully executed.'" [93] The combination of these constitutional provisions and past executive practice afforded a valid basis for the president's intervention even without express statutory permission.

The dissent emphasized, however, that there was no need to claim undefined authority and no "question of unlimited executive power in this case." Rather, the president acted merely in order to implement the complex structure of congressional policies and to preserve the legislative program from destruction until Congress

1804 where the Court had invalidated a presidential seizure effected in violation of a statute; he added however: "In my view—taught me not only by the decision of Chief Justice Marshall in *Little* v. *Barreme,* but also by a score of other pronouncements of distinguished members of this bench—the Constitution does grant to the President extensive authority in times of grave and imperative national emergency."

[93] *Ibid.,* p. 683.

could act.[94] None of the existing statutes, the dissent argued, prohibited seizure as a method of enforcing legislative programs and this conclusion applied even to the Taft-Hartley and Defense Production Acts. According to the Chief Justice, the injunction provisions of the Taft-Hartley law were permissive, not mandatory and the creation of a new procedure under the Defense Production Act for dealing with defense disputes negated the notion that Congress intended the Taft-Hartley method to be an exclusive avenue. Since Taft-Hartley was a route parallel to the Wage Stabilization Board procedure, the president on April 8 had exhausted available procedures and seizure was the only course open to him for handling the situation.

The decision of the Court in the steel seizure dispute enjoyed immediate popularity and was acclaimed as a landmark case in the development of constitutional law. Many observers praised the ruling as a reaffirmation of the separation of powers principle and as a turning point arresting "the dangerous trend toward concentration of power in the executive branch" and restoring or preserving a government "of laws and not of men." [95] More enthusiastic comments expressed the view that the American way of life had been saved, that national interest and sovereignty had been protected against such international involvements as "Truman's war" and the corroding influences of the United Nations charter, and that the sanctity of individual liberties, especially property rights, was proclaimed against arbitrary intervention of the government. Regarding the latter contention, it requires little skill to show that, at least in the instant case, the individual liberties protected by the decision were those of the companies, and not of the union which supported the president's action as a welcome alternative to the odious Taft-Hartley injunction. Obviously, the decision contained few, if any, constructive contributions to the problem of the solution of labor-management disputes; also, it was relatively unconcerned with the fact that the curtailment of the union's strike weapon in vital industries during emergencies may require a balancing pressure applied to the

[94] *Ibid.*, pp. 701, 703.
[95] See *United States News and World Report*, 32: 18-20 (June 13, 1952); *Christian Century*, 69: 691 (June 11, 1952); *Business Week* (June 7, 1952), p. 180.

management side. However this may be, a Supreme Court decision should perhaps not be evaluated solely on the basis of
ephemeral popular emotions or in the light of partisan commitments to a labor or management point of view.

A cautious and circumspect approach to the case reveals that if
the decision is a landmark, it stands for a much more limited
proposition than the broad language of the majority opinion
would suggest. It may be exaggerated to say that the decision was
in "the same class as a restricted railroad ticket, good for this day
and train only"; [96] but it is undeniable that the ruling did not
resolve the problem of the extent of executive emergency powers
under all circumstances. For a general statement of such executive
powers, the majority opinion conceded too little while the dissent
claimed too much. The majority opinion, fully seconded on this
point by the concurring opinion of Justice Douglas, is unduly
restrictive in holding that, since Congress may act in this field,
seizure by the president must always be based on express legislative authorization. Stated in this broad manner, the opinion dis-
regards executive practice and more permissive judicial precedent,
and erects an excessively high wall between legislative and executive functions; [97] moreover, the statement was not required by the
circumstances and could have profited from Justice Frankfurter's
admonition to hew to the facts of the case. On the other hand, the
position taken by the dissent that the president may exercise
broad emergency powers unless a particular method of action is
expressly denied by Congress claims too much, especially in view
of existing legislation stipulating procedures which the president
could and should have used. The argument that existing procedures were merely permissive is not convincing in the light of
evidence presented in the concurring opinions on the legislative
history and congressional policy of the Taft-Hartley Act. As it appears, the proper basis of the decision, and the only general proposition for which the case may stand, is contained in the view
expressed by Justices Frankfurter, Jackson, Burton and Clark that,
under existing circumstances, the president could not exercise

[96] Jerre Williams, "The Steel Seizure—A Legal Analysis of a Political Controversy," *J. of Public Law*, 2: 29 (1953); the language is taken from Justice
Roberts' opinion in *Smith* v. *Allwright*, 321 U.S. 649, 669 (1944).

[97] See Corwin, *op. cit.* (*supra*, n. 72), pp. 56-62; also Paul G. Kauper,
"The Steel Seizure Case: Congress, the President and the Supreme Court,"
Michigan L.Rev., 51: 141, 180 (1952).

independent powers in the face of statutory procedures prescribed by Congress.

Thus formulated, the proposition is not a final delineation of executive emergency powers and does not encompass cases where seizure is ordered by the president in the absence of pertinent statutes or under entirely different circumstances. The statement obviously does not apply to seizure effected in time of a declared war or in the theatre of military operations. Before the Court, the government in this case did not rely on any war powers of the president which might result from a declared war and the opinions of most justices were relatively explicit that no emergency situation of this type was involved in the instant litigation. Consequently, it is fairly safe to say that in case of an all-out war or the immediate threat of such war the action of the president might have been validated and that even Justices Black and Douglas might have followed this course despite the sweeping language of their opinions in *Youngstown*. It is doubtful, of course, whether a strict limitation to military operations is still consistent with modern cold and hot war developments or justified in the light of previous judicial expansions of the concept of war emergency. Some observers have claimed that in cases of war or catastrophic emergencies the president might act not only in the absence of legislation but in the face of conflicting statutory procedures.[98]

On the other hand, where no declared war is involved or in cases of "less-than-catastrophic" emergencies, the *Youngstown* case teaches that the president should follow existing statutory procedures. However, the case also indicates that a different conclusion might be reached during periods of similar stress in the absence of pertinent legislation. The opinion of Justice Clark strongly endorsed the existence of presidential emergency powers in such situations. Although attempting to be noncommittal, Justice Burton distinguished the case from presidential action taken without statutory support or under more threatening circumstances. Justice Jackson hinted at a "zone of twilight" in situations where Congress is silent and both the president and Congress can validly act. Thus, it appears that, including the dissenters, a majority of five or six justices might have upheld the presidential action in 1952 provided it occurred in the absence of

[98] Compare Jay Murphy, "Some Observations on the Steel Decisions," *Alabama L. Rev.*, 4: 214, 227, 230 (1952).

statutory procedures, permitted the payment of just compensation and otherwise respected the constitutional framework.

With regard to presidential power in industrial relations, the general lesson which can be drawn from the preceding analysis is that the will of Congress is regularly decisive for the exercise of emergency powers. Congress can, and therefore should, normally prescribe the procedures to be followed by the president in emergencies; only timely congressional action can obviate exaggerated or autocratic claims on the part of the executive. Statutory procedures prescribed by Congress must be respected by the president both in peacetime conditions and in "less-than-catastrophic" emergencies or in the absence of a state of war. Where no statutory procedures are stipulated, there is at least a strong presumption that the president can act to meet an immediate emergency provided that constitutional safeguards, such as compensation for seizure, and general congressional policies are respected.[99] The president's authority to exercise independent powers has more solid support in case of declared war, in the theatre of military operations or possibly in modern-type catastrophic emergencies resulting from an intense warming-up of the cold war, although general constitutional provisions and principles would have to be preserved. It must be added, however, that in every instance of an exercise of emergency powers by the president the finding or declaration of emergency remains subject to judicial review by the courts. The latter principle is manifested in all opinions in the *Youngstown* case and expressly conceded by the dissent.[100]

6. EMERGENCY POWERS ON THE STATE LEVEL

The outlined contours of presidential authority find their parallel, at least to a degree, in executive emergency powers on the state level. Obviously the situation on the state level is com-

[99] *Schechter Poultry Corp.* v. *United States,* 295 U.S. 495, 528 (1935).
[100] Chief Justice Vinson: "We also assume without deciding that the courts may go behind a President's finding of fact that an emergency exists." 343 U.S. 579, 678 (1952). Although the Assistant Attorney General had argued before Judge Pine that executive emergency actions were not reviewable, the Solicitor General clearly admitted before the Supreme Court that exercise of emergency powers was subject to judicial review; Kauper, *op. cit.,* pp. 155-156; Westin, *op. cit.,* pp. 62, 120. See also *Duncan* v. *Kahanamoku,* 327 U.S. 304, 329 (1946); *Sterling* v. *Constantin,* 287 U.S. 378, 397, 400 (1932).

plicated by the variety of state constitutions and different forms
of state legislation. Nevertheless, there are many similarities which
permit the formulation of certain general conclusions. In the field
of labor-management relations, any parallel which may be drawn
is seriously conditioned by the steady growth of federal authority
and the comparative decline of state competence and state
activity. In our modern interdependent economy, the emergency
character of industrial disputes tends to be evaluated in a national
perspective; moreover, serious controversies on the local or state
level frequently entail repercussions in interstate commerce, thus
giving rise to federal jurisdiction. The gradual obliteration of state
competence in industrial relations is one of the main distinguishing features of the postwar period when domestic growth combined with international commitments and foreign competition
increasingly challenged the significance of economic boundaries
of the states.

The wave of strikes which swept the country during the reconversion period produced a flurry of legislative and regulatory
activity both on the national and the state level. The Taft-Hartley
Act established procedures for national emergencies, but otherwise relied strongly on the principle of free collective bargaining.
Acting on the assumption that federal laws did not cover local
emergency disputes, a number of states enacted regulations which
frequently were more restrictive than national legislation and
sometimes eliminated the right to strike in public utilities. When
the constitutionality of such restrictive measures, especially compulsory arbitration statutes, was challenged, state courts were at
first prone to uphold their validity on the basis of public need.
As one of these courts said with reference to public utilities:

Where by reason of a strike, work stoppage or lockout, the flow of
services of one of these essentials of community life is halted or impaired, the state not only has the right but a pressing duty to step in
and prevent the continuance of such stoppage or impairment and to
take appropriate measures to restore them.[101]

However, federal courts were less willing to tolerate interference
with the national policy of free collective bargaining. In 1950, the
Supreme Court struck down the mediation procedures and other

---

[101] *State* v. *Telephone Workers Federation,* 2 N.J. 335, 345, 66 A.2d 616,
621 (1949).

pre-strike requirements of a Michigan statute on the grounds that Congress had pre-empted the field of regulation of peaceful strikes.[102] The climax of the conflict was reached in 1951 when the Supreme Court invalidated a compulsory arbitration statute of Wisconsin as violative of federal law.[103] These decisions had an impact on similar state statutes and cast doubt on the validity of other state legislation. Nevertheless, despite persisting uncertainties, many forms of legislation and state action are still predicated on the state police power and state constitutions.

With regard to the role of the executive in labor disputes, the powers of the governor are based either on statutes or on broader constitutional principles. The great majority of states possess statutes or other regulations establishing mediation procedures, and many states have comprehensive labor relations laws either in the form of "Little Wagner" or "Little Taft-Hartley" acts.[104] Usually these statutes or regulations provide for fact-finding teams and for voluntary mediation, conciliation or arbitration. In some cases, the governor is authorized to appoint fact-finding panels or boards of mediation or arbitration; however, these functions clearly do not involve the exercise of emergency powers. More ambitious legislation has been enacted in a number of states for the handling of critical labor disputes in public utilities —that is, industries supplying such necessities as heat, light, gas, water, power, transportation, and communications—and sometimes in hospitals. These regulations usually date from the immediate postwar period, but some have been amended or revised in more recent years. The mildest form of public utility legislation can be found in provisions authorizing investigations and public reports during labor disputes. In Illinois the Department of Labor may resort to conciliation whenever it believes that a public utility strike or lockout is likely to cause injury or inconvenience to the

---

[102] *United Automobile Workers* v. *O'Brien,* 339 U.S. 454 (1950).

[103] *Amalgamated Association of Street, Electric Railway and Motor Coach Employees* v. *Wisconsin Employment Relations Board,* 340 U.S. 383 (1951). Compare Gerard D. Reilly, *States' Rights and the Law of Labor Relations* (New York, 1955); Frederic Meyers, "The Taft-Hartley Act and States' Rights," *Labor L.J.,* 3: 325 (1952).

[104] Compare U. S. Department of Labor, *Growth of Labor Law in the United States* (Washington, D.C., 1962), pp. 229-234, 237-241; also Irving Bernstein, "State Public Utility Laws and Mediation," *Labor L.J.,* 7: 496 (1956); Norene M. Diamond, "Terms of State Labor Relations Acts," *Monthly Labor Rev.,* 71: 214 (August, 1950).

general public; if conciliation fails, the Department may investigate the facts of the dispute and publish its findings with recommendations for settlement. In Minnesota the Labor Conciliator of the state may notify the governor of labor disputes in "any industry, business or institution engaged in supplying the necessities of life, safety, or health"; if, within five days after such notification, the governor appoints a commission to investigate the dispute and report upon it, no strike or lockout can be instituted for a period of thirty days after notification.

Compulsory Arbitration and Seizure

While the described regulations involve only mild forms of public intervention and subordinate executive functions, public utility legislation in some states assigns to the government a more active role. State intervention of a dramatic nature is contemplated in statutes providing for compulsory arbitration, seizure, or a combination of the two. In the immediate postwar period, compulsory arbitration as a method of handling disputes in public utilities was adopted in a number of states including Florida, Indiana, Michigan, Nebraska, Pennsylvania and Wisconsin. At the same time, Virginia enacted legislation making seizure the central emergency measure while New Jersey chose a combination of compulsory arbitration and seizure, Massachusetts a "choice-of-procedures" approach including seizure, and Missouri a mixture of mediation and seizure.

Among possible emergency procedures, compulsory arbitration certainly has the most damaging effects upon free collective bargaining. Even if applied only to public utilities, some observers have expressed the belief that the procedure constitutes a danger to the system of private enterprise. In various studies, the question has also been examined whether compulsory arbitration violates provisions of the federal constitution, especially the equal protection and due process clauses and the protection against involuntary servitude and the impairing of contracts. Although it has been found that postwar statutes would receive a passing mark on this score,[105] the implementation of these statutes might still conflict with constitutional safeguards. The major obstacle to

[105] Clarence M. Updegraff, "Compulsory Settlement of Public Utility Disputes," *Iowa L. Rev.*, 36: 61, 64-66 (1950); Charles Christenson, "Legality of New Jersey's Antistrike Law," *Labor L.J.*, 3: 767, 768-770 (1952).

such legislation, however, resides in its conflict with federal legislation and congressional policy. Not long after the postwar statutes were enacted, federal courts began to discover this conflict and to attack compulsory arbitration provisions impairing the right to strike in industries affecting interstate commerce. In general terms, the decisions of federal courts developed a distinction between the objectives of legitimate strikes—such as wages, hours or working conditions—which are subject to federal jurisdiction and the means employed by the strikers which may be subject to state police power.

In contrast to other compulsory arbitration laws, the Wisconsin statute of 1947 which prohibited strikes and lockouts in public utilities did not directly involve gubernatorial powers; however, it gave rise to significant test cases. If an impasse was reached in collective bargaining, the dispute was to be submitted to conciliation and in case of persisting disagreement, to compulsory arbitration by a panel maintained by the Employment Relations Board of the state. In the year of its passage, the statute was upheld by a state court as a valid exercise of the state police power. Another attack in the following year, however, led a circuit court of the state to the conclusion that the statute was unconstitutional as imposing involuntary servitude by prohibiting collective work stoppages; the court also ruled that the invalidity of this portion of the statute vitiated the compulsory arbitration provision. The Wisconsin supreme court did not follow this argument and, in 1950, decided that the act was not invalid on these or on any other grounds.[106] On certiorari, the Supreme Court of the United States held the Wisconsin statute unconstitutional on the ground that Congress, by passing the Wagner and Taft-Hartley laws, had pre-empted the field of regulation of strikes affecting interstate commerce. In reply to the contention that federal legislation covered only national emergencies but was silent as to local emergencies, the Court stated that the Wisconsin statute was not expressly limited to local emergencies and that in general, peaceful strikes were excluded from state jurisdiction. In a strongly worded dissent, Justice Frankfurter argued that Congress should have been more explicit if it desired to remove such local matters from

[106] *Amalgamated Association* v. *WERB*, 257 Wis. 43, 42 N.W.2d 471 (1950).

state regulation and that the national emergency provisions of the Taft-Hartley Act indicated the possibility of valid limitations of the collective bargaining process.[107] He concluded that the wisdom of state legislation was not for the Court to decide but suggested that perhaps seizure, martial law, or other state action might strike a better balance between the need for continued utility services and the preservation of free collective bargaining.

The attack on compulsory arbitration procedures was not confined to Wisconsin, but extended to other state regulations in which governors were given more prominent functions. Already in 1949, a Michigan statute of 1947 was amended to make arbitration voluntary rather than compulsory in public utility disputes. Similar Indiana and Florida statutes were overturned by state courts on the basis of the Wisconsin decision. The two statutes had provided for appointment by the governor of a board of arbitration whose settlement orders were to be binding upon the parties for one year, subject to judicial review. While most postwar statutes with compulsory arbitration provisions were thus eliminated, legislation of a similar type continued in effect in a few other states despite serious doubts as to constitutional validity. These doubts apply primarily to a Pennsylvania statute of 1947 which copied the Indiana and Florida measures, and to a Nebraska statute which established a Court of Industrial Relations in the manner of an earlier Kansas tribunal. A somewhat different situation obtained in New Jersey due to the curious statutory blending of compulsory arbitration and seizure provisions.[108]

The legal validity of the remaining postwar emergency statutes is hardly less complicated or doubtful.[109] The most diversified

[107] *Amalgamated Association* v. *WERB*, 340 U.S. 383, 406 (1951).

[108] Compare R. R. France and R. A. Lester, *Compulsory Arbitration of Utility Disputes in New Jersey and Pennsylvania* (Princeton, 1951); Louis MacDonald, *Compulsory Arbitration in New Jersey* (New York, 1949).

[109] On June 10, 1963, the Supreme Court struck down the Missouri law of 1947 which authorized a blending of mediation procedures and state seizure of strike-bound public utilities. The Court relied strongly on the argument that the statute violated the supremacy clause of the federal constitution by making unlawful a peaceful strike constituting a protected activity under federal legislation; however, the decision seemed also influenced by the fact that, in this case, the seizure of a Kansas City transit company had been more formal than real and that the employees had not really become state employees: "The short of the matter is that Missouri, through the fiction of 'seizure' by the State has made a peaceful strike against a public utility

combination of procedures is contained in the so-called "Slichter law" of Massachusetts which was enacted in 1947 and subsequently amended in 1954.[110] The law places primary emphasis on free collective bargaining, but supplements the bargaining process by provisions for mediation, voluntary arbitration, and seizure. According to the original act of 1947, the procedures were to be set in motion when the Commissioner of Labor and Industries found that a labor dispute in a public utility threatened a substantial interruption of essential goods and services and when, upon notification, the governor decided that an imminent interruption would curtail essential goods and services and endanger the public health and safety. However, under the amendment of 1954, the governor is required, unless he "deems it impracticable," to hold informal hearings before the invocation of the law at which the parties are heard on the question of whether the interruption is imminent and would lead to a curtailment of essential goods and services to such an extent as to endanger the health and safety of the community. After making the required finding, the governor is authorized to request the parties to submit the dispute voluntarily to a moderator or to an emergency board of arbitration. If these procedures fail, the governor is empowered either to enter arrangements for continuing such part of the production and distribution as necessary to the public health and safety or to declare the existence of an emergency and take possession of plants or facilities for the duration of such emergency. Strikes and lockouts are forbidden during the period of public operation.

Virginia possesses a very effective and straightforward seizure legislation whose provisions have sometimes been acclaimed as a model for other states to follow. The passage of the legislation

---

unlawful, in direct conflict with federal legislation which guarantees the right to strike against a public utility, as against any employer engaged in interstate commerce." As the Court added somewhat quizzically, the decision was not intended to affect "the right or duty of the chief executive or legislature of the State to deal with emergency conditions of public danger, violence, or disaster under appropriate provisions of the State's organic or statutory law." *Amalgamated Association of Street, Electric Railway and Motor Coach Employees* v. *Missouri*, 10 L.ed. 2d 763, 768-769 (1963).

[110] Compare George P. Shultz, "The Massachusetts Choice-of-Procedures Approach to Emergency Disputes," *Industrial and Labor Relations Rev.*, 10: 359 (1957).

was clearly the result of major postwar disputes and disturbances in public utilities, and especially in electric power facilities. Already in 1946, a limited seizure statute was enacted which authorized the state to take over and operate through the state highway commissioner any ferry constituting a link in the state highway system during such period as the owner might, for any reason, be unable or unwilling to operate it.[111] A protracted labor controversy in electricity plants during the same year induced the general assembly to pass in 1947 a general seizure law applicable to public utilities. In a declaration of policy, the general assembly stated at the time:

The continuous, uninterrupted and proper functioning and operation of public utilities engaged in the business of furnishing water, light, heat, gas, electric power, transportation or communication, or any one or more of them, to the people of Virginia are hereby declared to be essential to their welfare, health and safety.[112]

The original statute as passed in 1947 established complicated procedures prior to governmental seizure. In 1952 the statute was repealed and replaced by legislation which retained the seizure provisions in a modified form but eliminated most of the preliminary procedures such as conferences, strike notice, and lengthy waiting periods. The most significant changes with regard to seizure consisted in the stipulation of extensive judicial review of the governor's finding of an emergency justifying the seizure and of the amount of compensation. The alterations were adopted in order to obviate charges of invalidity resulting from the Wisconsin decision of 1951.[113] Under the new act, the desire to change or terminate a collective bargaining agreement involving a public utility has still to be communicated to the department of labor and industry of the state which in turn notifies the governor. An attempt is then to be made by the commissioner of labor to mediate the dispute. If, "in the judgment of the governor," a substantial interruption in public utility services is threatened which en-

[111] Note, "Virginia's Approach to Strikes Against the Public Interest," *Virginia L. Rev.*, 33: 100, 108 (1947).
[112] See Francis V. Lowden, Jr., "Public Utility Seizure in Virginia," *ibid.*, vol. 41, pp. 397, 398 (1955).
[113] Compare Robert R. France, "Seizure in Emergency Labor Disputes in Virginia," *Industrial and Labor Relations Rev.*, 7: 347, 349 (1954).

dangers the public health, safety, or welfare, he is authorized to issue an executive proclamation stating his intention to take possession of the utility for operation by the state at the time of such interruption. The company may contest the seizure if it believes that the governor is mistaken in his finding that an interruption is imminent which would curtail essential services and the issue is to be settled by a court in the city or county where the main offices of the utility are located. The new law provides that after seizure the state is to compensate the utility for its facilities, which in normal situations means that the state turns over to the company eighty-five percent of the net income; however, if the amount of just compensation is contested by the state or the utility, either party may file a petition in court to determine the amount to which the utility is entitled. The procedures of the statute have been applied most frequently to local bus companies and telephone utilities.

Use of State Militia and Martial Law

Apart from authority derived from compulsory arbitration or seizure statutes, governors have sometimes exercised powers which are not, or not clearly, of a statutory character. The problem which most frequently arises in labor disputes is the extent of the governor's power to use the military forces of the state. State constitutions usually designate the governor as commander-in-chief of the state militia and empower him to use the militia to repel invasion and insurrection and to enforce the execution of the laws. These grants of power are sometimes implemented or circumscribed by legislative enactments, sometimes they are not. The use of the militia, of which all able-bodied men are commonly considered to be members, is regularly based upon the governor's finding of "reasonable expectation" that a serious emergency exists or may occur. The occasions for ordering the militia to active duty have included tumult, riot, insurrection, attempts to resist legal process, and other serious disturbances.[114] In the case of labor disputes when a strike or threatened strike imperils the safety or health of the community, the governor may be authorized, at

[114] Compare, *e.g.*, *Brady* v. *State*, 229 Miss. 677, 91 So.2d 751 (1957); *McBride* v. *State*, 221 Miss. 508, 73 So.2d 154 (1954); *McKittrick* v. *Brown*, 337 Mo. 281, 85 S.W.2d 385 (1935); *In re Moyer*, 35 Colo. 159, 85 P. 190 (1904).

least in the absence of statutes to the contrary, to impress the strikers into the state militia if he finds that they will not return to work for the state upon seizure.

Despite the comparative uniformity of state constitutions and despite the wide acceptance in judicial precedents of executive use of the militia in principle, the terms under which the governor may exercise his power and the implications of this exercise are subject to considerable disagreement and ambiguity. Obviously the attitude of courts and the practice of governors have changed with the changing times. Prior to 1932, the prevailing judicial attitude was that the governor's finding of necessity, as expressed in a declaration of emergency or a proclamation of martial law, was final and not subject to judicial control.[115] While conceding that the action of the governor should be based on a "reasonable expectation" of emergency, courts were usually quick to point out that the proper remedy against arbitrary or capricious exercise of power was political retaliation at the polls or the process of impeachment.[116] In 1932 the United States Supreme Court decided to examine complaints of oil companies in Texas where Governor Sterling, under the cover of a martial law proclamation, had imposed oil proration measures in disregard of a temporary restraining order issued by a federal district court. Upholding the claims of the companies, the Court decided that the exigencies of the situation were not such as to permit a governor to use the national guard of the state in defiance of regular court proceedings.[117] The case has served as a guidepost for most subsequent court rulings. Courts still allow the governor a permissible range of honest judgment and will not invalidate an executive action unless it is clearly unjustified or arbitrary.[118] However, a governor's decision to use military force is no longer conclusive and courts regularly examine the factual basis of a governor's finding of emergency.[119]

Apart from the aspect of judicial review, there is a long stand-

[115] Compare *Moyer* v. *Peabody*, 212 U.S. 78, 84 (1909); *Luther* v. *Borden*, 7 How. 1, 14 (1848).

[116] *Hatfield* v. *Graham*, 73 W. Va. 759, 81 S.E. 533 (1914); *State* v. *Brown*, 71 W. Va. 519, 77 S.E. 243 (1912).

[117] *Sterling* v. *Constantin*, 287 U.S. 378 (1932).

[118] *Ibid.*, p. 400; *Powers Mercantile Co.* v. *Olson*, 7 F. Supp. 865, 868 (D. Minn. 1934).

[119] *Hearon* v. *Calus*, 178 S.C. 381, 183 S.E. 13 (1935); *State* v. *Swope*, 38 N. Mex. 53 (1933).

ing controversy concerning the extent to which a governor's use of the militia may interfere with civil rights and with the functions of regular civil authorities. Clearly, as military force is regularly used only in critical situations, some interference with normal rights and procedures is almost inevitable; however, there may be different degrees of intervention. According to one point of view, the militia's powers are always exactly the same as those of civil police under normal conditions, whether or not martial law has been proclaimed.[120] On the other extreme is the conception which grants to the militia any and all powers required by the circumstances, regardless of whether the intervention is in aid of civil authorities or under a declaration of martial law.[121] A third view holds that under normal conditions the powers of the militia are the same as those of civil police, but that military authority is greatly expanded under martial rule.[122] Unfortunately, the situation is even more complicated than this presentation would suggest. Governors in the past have frequently resorted to a hybrid form of intervention, sometimes described as "qualified" or "preventive" martial law, which is placed between assistance to civil authorities and full-fledged or "punitive" martial law. Under this tripartition, state troops acting in aid of civil authorities would normally exercise the same powers as civil police. On the other hand, when active under "qualified" martial law, troops are presumably entitled to place civilians under temporary arrest without otherwise interfering with the regular courts in the area.[123] Under "punitive" martial law, finally, civilians may be subject to trial by court-martial, since and as long as the regular courts are not open and properly functioning.[124]

Although there is merit in the gradation of military powers on

[120] *Franks* v. *Smith*, 142 Ky. 232, 134 S.W. 484 (1911); *Chapin* v. *Ferry*, 3 Wash. 386, 28 P. 754 (1891).

[121] *State ex rel. O'Connor* v. *District Court*, 219 Iowa 1165, 1175, 260 N.W. 73, 83 (1935).

[122] *U.S. ex rel. Palmer* v. *Adams*, 26 F.2d 141 (D. Colo. 1927); *Bishop* v. *Vandercook*, 228 Mich. 299, 200 N.W. 278 (1924).

[123] Compare Robert S. Rankin, *When Civil Law Fails* (Durham, 1939), pp. 69-70, 122-125; see also *Constantin* v. *Smith*, 57 F.2d 227 (1932); *Ex parte Lavinder*, 88 W. Va. 713, 108 S.E. 428 (1921); *Herlihy* v. *Donohue*, 52 Mont. 601, 161 P. 164 (1916).

[124] *United States* v. *Fischer*, 280 F. 208 (D. Neb. 1922); *United States* v. *Wolters*, 268 F. 69 (S.D. Tex. 1920); *State* v. *Brown*, 71 W.Va. 519, 77 S.E. 243 (1912).

the basis of different degrees of emergency, the value of the described tripartition appears doubtful. One does not have to endorse the opinion that there is no third alternative between military assistance and martial law [125] in order to see that declarations of "qualified" martial law are prone to entail factual and legal confusion. Proclamations of "martial law" may well be limited to situations of severe emergency where the courts are closed or seriously obstructed and where military rule supersedes civil authority. This limitation still permits the governor to use the militia in other, "less-than-catastrophic" emergencies. The intervention of the militia in such situations should normally be in aid of regular authorities and its powers should respect the limits set by civil law and legislative enactments. Action which goes beyond such limits might be authorized only in the absence of statutory stipulations and in the face of compelling necessity; but any emergency action would have to maintain basic constitutional principles and be subject to judicial review. As it appears, postwar developments in the states have tended to follow the described approach and to avoid the confusion of hybrid proclamations. This tendency, combined with improved and more detailed labor legislation on both the federal and state level, has led to a sharp decrease in the number of "martial law" declarations in industrial controversies.

One of the earliest labor disputes in the postwar period involving the use of the state militia developed in the Virginia Electric and Power Company in 1946. The company provided electric power and lighting service in an area comprising more than half of the state of Virginia. When early in 1946 a contract dispute between the company and its employees led to several weeks of futile negotiations, the labor union representing the employees gave notice of a proposed strike to become effective on April 1, 1946. On March 22, Governor Tuck of Virginia proposed a conference in his office with the company and union officials; however, the conference did not materialize as the union was unwilling to attend unless the governors of North Carolina and West Virginia were also present, a condition which could not be met at the time. Two days later the governor notified the company and

---

[125] *United States* v. *Adams*, 26 F.2d 141, 144 (1927); *Bishop* v. *Vandercook*, 228 Mich. 299, 309, 200 N.W. 278, 280 (1924).

union officials that unless he was assured by March 28 that the planned strike would not occur, he would declare a state of emergency and take steps to continue operation of the plants, including the possible use of the state militia if the union refused to work for the state. Since negotiations remained deadlocked, an emergency was declared on March 28 and on the following day the employees of the company were ordered embodied into an emergency unit of the state militia for potential service in the plants. The order also stated that in the event of a strike, the state would take possession of the utility and the employees would be transferred to active military service with the duty to seize and operate the facilities together with other members of the militia.

In a lengthy and detailed opinion of April 18, 1946, the attorney general of the state, Abram P. Staples, approved the order of the governor on the grounds that executive emergency powers included the use of the state militia and that the planned intervention of the militia was in aid of regular police and contemplated only the exercise of such powers as a *posse comitatus* would have in the enforcement of law. The attorney general also argued that in view of the public service performed, the employment of the militia would not violate the protection against involuntary servitude and that there was no conflict between the order and federal legislation enjoining interference with free collective bargaining.[126] The opinion was and remains an instructive piece of writing although the occasion required perhaps less effort. The expected strike in the utility did not take place and the governor was consequently not forced to transfer the employees into active militia service. Nevertheless, public apprehension of the danger of utility strikes induced the governor to seek legislation for the handling of future utility stoppages and led to passage of the seizure statute of 1947.

Proposals for emergency legislation were also the result of a similar labor dispute which occurred in 1956 in a part of Ohio's telephone facilities. The controversy which has been described as "one of the longest and most devastating labor disputes in Ohio's industrial history" [127] culminated in a work stoppage which

[126] For critical comments on this opinion see Note, *Virginia L. Rev.*, 33: 100, 108 (1947).

[127] Compare James F. O'Day, "The Portsmouth Strike: Ohio's Hot Potato," *Western Reserve L. Rev.*, 8: 502 (1957).

virtually paralyzed Portsmouth and led to extensive violence, mob riots and vandalism. From October 15 to December 16, the Portsmouth area was completely devoid of telephone service with the result that emergency police, fire and hospital services were rendered practically inoperative. Many efforts were made to bring about an early settlement of the dispute. During the early stages of the controversy, Governor Lausche of Ohio intervened personally but was unable to bring the weight of his influence to bear on the disputants. While mediation of the issues proved fruitless, steps were taken or at least considered to curb the violence. The state highway patrol was of little help in combatting riots as its authority was limited by statute to preventing obstructions of the free use of the state's highways. In this situation Governor Lausche alerted the Ohio National Guard to be prepared to move into the area; however, actual military intervention was prevented by the adverse climate of public opinion. In order to avert disaster, Governor Lausche on November 26 called an extraordinary session of the general assembly and requested the passage of a seizure bill patterned after the Virginia statute. However, the bill was defeated and the special session dissolved without tangible results. In February of 1957, during his first day in office, newly elected Governor O'Neill drew up the necessary papers to send the national guard into Portsmouth if any further violence occurred. The determined attitude of the governor finally resulted in an agreement between the disputants.

While use of the militia was only contemplated or threatened in Virginia and Ohio, more active military intervention was provoked during the past decade in labor disputes in other states, including North Carolina, Indiana and Minnesota. The extent of the intervention ranged from assistance to civil authorities to proclamation of martial law. Quite apart from the problem of legal or constitutional validity, the cases demonstrate that any use of the militia, whether in aid of regular authorities or under martial rule, raises delicate questions of policy since troops can be employed in support of either side of the dispute and thus may tip the balance in favor of one of the parties in the bargaining struggle. A compelling illustration of this fact can be found in the protracted, ugly and extremely violent struggle which raged in Henderson, North Carolina, from late 1958 to the fall of 1959. The conflict witnessed the intervention of the national guard of the state in a law-enforcement or police capacity and almost resulted in a proclamation of martial law. In addition to the usual acrimony of labor disputes, the vehemence of this conflict was nurtured by special problems prevailing in the area. From the union point of view, the dispute was part of a larger battle: a testing ground of organized labor's "Operation Dixie" and its effort to sign up industrial workers in the South. From the management viewpoint, the struggle also assumed the character of a test case: a test whether management was able to stop and, if possible, break the union movement in the South. The state, finally, was in a curious predicament. Although slightly more progressive in the field of civil liberties than many other states in the South, the state government was dedicated to a drive to lure new industry into the area and, consequently, to an effort to make the area attractive to companies.[128]

The dispute, which involved the Harriet-Henderson Cotton Mills and two locals of the Textile Workers Union of America, originated in contract negotiations prompted by the impending expiration of the old agreement on November 10, 1958. The union merely asked that the terms of the old contract be renewed without change while the company presented demands for drastic changes which virtually affected every single clause of the contract. Due to the delaying tactics of the company, the first bargaining session was not held until November 10, the day of the expiration of the old agreement; at the meeting, the company agreed only to an extension of the contract on a day-to-day basis, but in no case beyond November 15. After a few days of futile sparring, the 1,000 members of the union went on strike on November 17 and set up picket lines. The mills closed down and stayed closed for three months. At the beginning of February, 1959, the president of the company, John D. Cooper, Jr., announced that the mills would reopen on February 16 with a single shift; at the some time, he obtained a court order enjoining the union from interfering in any manner with the free entrance to and exit from the mills, from posting more than eight persons in picket lines at either plant, and from approaching closer than seventy-five feet to the gates of the plants. On the morning of February 16, a caravan of state police cars drove up and, under

[128] See "A Town's Bitter Taste," *Newsweek*, 53: 85, 88 (April 27, 1959).

the troopers' protection, a group of strikebreakers entered the gates. While only some fifty union members returned to work, the company had been able to recruit new employees from farms and other towns in the area and some even from Virginia despite federal legislation outlawing the importation of strikebreakers across state lines.

With the partial reopening of the plants, violence flared at the mill gates and in the town. During subsequent weeks, the number of state troopers increased to almost two hundred or one-third of the entire state force. Some two hundred strikers were arrested for violating the court injunction and on other charges. While fines and prison sentences were readily imposed on strikers, attacks on union members were treated lightly.[129] In March, Governor Hodges invited both sides to a conference in Raleigh; but no progress was made. With tensions still mounting, the governor at the beginning of April went to Henderson, held another meeting and, to everybody's surprise, an agreement was signed. After a night of celebration, however, the company suddenly announced the hiring of three hundred additional strikebreakers and permitted only twenty-five strikers to enter the mills. This about-face led to immediate conflicts when the pickets returned to the gates. In the face of spreading disturbances and riots, the irritated governor ordered the intervention of some four hundred members of the national guard, an intervention which had mainly the effect of protecting the interests of the company. In order to equalize the advantages of the parties, the union urged Governor Hodges to declare martial law and to close the mills; but he refused to take this drastic step. Despite the presence of the state militia, violence was rife and manifested itself in nightly explosions and gun fire along the highways. In June, eight of the top union leaders were indicted and subsequently tried on charges of conspiring to burn the general offices of the mills and to blow up plant facilities.[130]

[129] Compare John C. Cort, "Turning the Clock Back," *Commonweal*, 71: 99-100 (October 23, 1959); also "Struggle in Dixie," *Time*, 74: 19 (November 30, 1959).

[130] Boyd Payton and two other union leaders were sentenced to from six to ten years, four others to from five to seven years, and one from two to three years. On appeal, the North Carolina supreme court upheld the convictions, with one judge dissenting as to the sufficiency of the evidence concerning Payton's participation in the alleged conspiracy; *State v. Walker*, 251 N.C. 465, 112 S.E. 2d 61 (1960). Boyd Payton was subsequently pardoned by the governor of the state.

When the national guardsmen withdrew in August, the situation in the town was still tense, but the struggle was basically decided. Although the strike continued, the operation of the mills was expanding with a small minority of union members. Lack of adequate union funds and unfavorable circumstances had permitted the revival of union-busting devices supposedly defunct in industrial societies.

A form of military control which came very close to martial law was instituted in Indiana during a labor dispute in the fall of 1955. The case derives added significance from the fact that it stimulated discussion of the scope of executive power in respect to the state's military forces. Military intervention in Indiana is not a very rare occurrence; during the past forty years, militia units have been called out on over thirty occasions and, in more than a dozen instances, the intervention was prompted by labor troubles.[131] In 1955, the dispute involved the Perfect Circle Foundry in New Castle, Indiana, and the United Autoworkers Union. Unsuccessful negotiations on a new contract, and especially disagreements over the question of union shop, were at the source of the conflict. When the bargaining sessions resulted in deadlock, the union began to strike on July 24, 1955, the day of the expiration of the old contract. Despite a court order enjoining mass picketing and other interference with the company's operation, the foundry between August and September became the scene of intermittent disturbances and acts of violence. In some instances, cars were stoned and overturned while strikebreakers were threatened and attacked. By mid-September, the plant had to shut down completely. At the end of the month, police units removed pickets from the gates and the foundry went back to partial operation. However, on October 5, violence erupted again in the form of a riot between massed pickets and nonstriking workers during which several persons were wounded and a building was set afire.

On the same day, Mayor McCormack of New Castle declared a state of emergency in the city and asked Governor Craig for assistance of the national guard. The situation was slightly complicated by the fact that the governor was out of state at the time.

[131] Note, "Rule by Martial Law in Indiana: The Scope of Executive Power," *Indiana L. Rev.*, 31: 456 (1956).

Although the lieutenant-governor was strongly opposed to military intervention and claimed that the decision was up to him, Governor Craig by telephone complied with the mayor's request and ordered the guard mobilized. The governor's order and his instructions to the national guard made it clear that the guard was to operate in aid of and in subordination to civil authorities. In fact, after their arrival in the city, the guardsmen worked in close collaboration with the New Castle authorities and remained subject to the direction of the mayor. The activities of the guard included the establishment of road blocks around the city, the confiscation of firearms and liquor, the enforcement of evening curfews and, most importantly, the maintenance of an armed guard around the foundry which had been closed by the mayor on October 6. Due to the vigilance of the troops, order was restored, at least for the moment. However, the curbing of violence did not imply that the parties were closer to a settlement, despite repeated efforts of the governor to mediate the dispute. When another meeting of company and labor representatives with the governor failed to produce results, the governor on October 10 proclaimed the existence of a state of emergency in the city and the county, designated the county as military district and declared it to be under military control.[132]

Obviously, the proclamation modified drastically the character and the basis of the military intervention. On face value, at least, the statement purported to establish something very close to martial law in the county. Instead of the previously practiced assistance to civil officers, the civil authorities were expressly transformed into agents of the military. The proclamation also suspended the right of assembly, the right of civilians to carry arms, and the right to enter or depart from the county without permission of the military authorities. Despite the broad range of powers thus conferred upon the military, the national guard did not find it necessary to expand greatly the scope of its activities. The guardsmen continued to guard roadblocks and to enforce curfew, liquor and arms restrictions. Possibly the moderation of the military was prompted by a prevailing uncertainty as to its status and powers under the proclamation; in any event, the policy of the national guard was to interfere as little as possible

---

[132] For the text of the proclamation see *ibid.*, p. 459, n. 16.

with civil authorities and to accomplish its aim with the least possible inconvenience to the civilian population. Nevertheless, the policy of moderation was not expected to apply to all exigencies and harsher methods were held in abeyance pending the development of an actual crisis. In the case of emergency, the military planned and apparently considered itself authorized to try civilians by court martial, to suspend the writ of habeas corpus and the right to jury trial and release on bond. Moreover, the governor's proclamation had serious effects on the civil government of the area. The circuit judge of the county immediately abdicated his bench and refused to hold court on the ground that neither he nor his court had any legal status during the period of military control. After urgent appeals from the local bar association, the judge finally consented on October 20 to reopen the court on a limited basis, shortly before the governor terminated the military control of the county on the same day.

Reviewing the events in Indiana, one observer concluded that the action of Governor Craig was unlawful and that governors are never entitled to proclaim martial law.

The governor of a state has no power to rule by martial law. The governor's power to use the troops in civil disturbances arises from his duty to see that the laws are executed. This duty does not encompass the power to suspend civil government, but requires only the use of that force necessary to quell lawlessness. In carrying out their mission, the troops are bound to follow legal procedures. The extent of their power is that of any peace officer acting under similar circumstances.[133]

The observer based this judgment primarily on provisions of the Indiana state constitution and of state legislation. The writer admitted that, as commander-in-chief of the military forces of the state, the governor was entitled to call out the troops to execute the laws, suppress insurrection, or repel invasion; however, this authority was limited by sections of the Indiana constitution stipulating that the military must be kept in strict subordination to the civil power and that the laws can never be suspended except by the authority of the general assembly. Under the terms of these constitutional provisions, the power to suspend the civil laws in emergency was not an executive but a legislative pre-

[133] *Ibid.*, p. 473.

rogative. However, in the instant case, the Indiana legislature had not only not enabled the governor to institute martial rule, but had actually prevented him from exercising such power under prevailing conditions. Although, under existing statutes, the governor was entitled to decide when a situation called for the presence of troops and although the extent of control over troops in such cases was not precisely delimited, the statutory provisions made it clear that the military was regularly not to supersede police officers but rather to act in aid of and in close collaboration with civil authorities. Nevertheless, the writer conceded that, in case of attack or imminent danger of attack, the commanding officer of the national guard had the statutory power to take *all* necessary steps for the safety of his command, and he concluded with this somewhat enigmatic statement:

> The common law has long recognized that even orderly procedure may be circumvented in case of an emergency. The threat of grave and impending danger may justify actions normally illegal. . . . Domestic disturbance should be met with no greater disruption of normal government and no greater use of power than is necessarily required to deal effectively with the situation.[134]

It remains a matter of speculation to which degree the preceding evaluation was influenced by the Supreme Court decision in the steel seizure case of 1952. In any event, the opinion was based on comparable circumstances and is subject to the same qualifications. As in the steel seizure case, the objection to the executive action was predicated on the existence of legislative procedures which the executive could and should have followed; there was also an implication that the situation was not severe enough to warrant resort to ultimate remedies. In this manner, although correct in the instant case, the evaluation did not cover cases of executive action in the absence of legislative stipulations or in the face of more compelling or catastrophic emergencies.

A more balanced assessment of executive emergency powers was contained in a 1959 ruling of a federal district court in Minnesota. The decision was the outcome of a labor dispute between a meat packing company at Albert Lea, Minnesota, and a local

---

[134] *Ibid.*, pp. 470-471. The writer admitted that his conception was not entirely in agreement with *Sterling* v. *Constantin*, 287 U.S. 378 (1932).

union of the United Packinghouse Workers of America. Following the breakdown of collective bargaining on a new contract, the union went on strike and set up pickets at the plant on October 29, 1959. The company at first attempted to continue its operations with some of its supervisory and maintenance staff; subsequently, however, it began to hire and solicit the employment of new workers, with the announcement that if the strikers did not return to work, their positions would be filled by new employees. The strikebreakers were recruited mainly from rural areas in the county and from contiguous counties but some were residents of Iowa. During November the number of employees increased gradually with the result that by December 8, the plant was operating at about half capacity with some five hundred production workers in addition to the regular supervisory and maintenance staff. With the expansion of the company's operations, acts of violence began to occur on the picket lines. Despite an order issued by the district court of the county restraining the local union from interfering with the free access to the plant and enjoining the strikers from acts of violence, disorders continued and some strikers on the picket lines were cited for contempt of court. Between December 8 and 11, the number of pickets increased substantially and large crowds, sometimes numbering over one thousand persons, gathered at the plant in an attempt to block the entrance. Nonstriking workers were threatened and rocks were thrown at cars carrying employees to and from the plant.

Attempts by the local police and union leaders to persuade the crowds to disperse and refrain from violence were of no avail. On December 10, the county court issued a supplemental restraining order limiting the number of pickets at any one entrance to four; however, the order was not served due to the following events. Shortly after midnight on December 11, the civil authorities of Albert Lea and Freeborn County addressed a letter to Governor Freeman requesting him to assume responsibility of the situation and to close the plant temporarily.[135] Within a few hours after receiving this communication, the governor made a finding that a

---

[135] *Wilson and Co.* v. *Freeman*, 179 F.Supp. 520, 529-530 (D.C. Minn. 1959), Exhibit "A". The police authorities emphasized that, in their opinion, law and order could not be maintained "under their jurisdiction and supervision, even with the assistance of the state militia."

state of insurrection existed and proclaimed that martial law prevailed in the city and county.[136] In pursuance of the governor's action, the commanding officer of the Minnesota National Guard issued a proclamation in which he ordered the suspension of any operation of the plant, stating that continued operation would precipitate riots and acts of violence; he also prohibited any person to assemble in the vicinity of the plant and to enter or leave the plant without the permission of the military. While declaring that the jurisdiction of regular courts of law would continue to operate with full force and effect, the proclamation stipulated as an exception

that any and all court orders pertaining to the dispute between Wilson Company Packing Plant at Albert Lea and the labor union representing the striking workers are hereby suspended and all courts shall be without jurisdiction to issue any further orders or decrees pertaining thereto until further order.[137]

Responding to an action brought by the company against the governor of Minnesota, the federal district court decided on December 22 that the action of the governor placing Albert Lea and Freeborn County under martial rule was unjustified and should be enjoined. The court declared at first that, under provisions of the state constitution, the governor was authorized to call out the military forces of the state to aid the civil authorities in suppressing insurrection and violence, including disorders caused by labor disputes. In the instant case, the order of the governor clearly contemplated a more drastic intervention than mere assistance to local police. However, the court did not find that such action was necessarily beyond the governor's scope of authority; rather, it held that the governor may resort to martial law in cases of severe or catastrophic emergencies.

There is no language in the constitution which specifically empowers the Governor to declare martial law. But obviously where there is

[136] *Ibid.*, pp. 530-531, Exhibit "B".

[137] *Ibid.*, pp. 531-533, Exhibit "C". The order also stated: "All constitutional rights of whatever kind will be held inviolate and will not be disturbed except by direct command of the Commanding Officer of the affected area, as the exigencies of the public welfare may necessitate." Police officers of the city and county were declared "subordinated to the military forces."

actual war in a community, or where insurrection or revolt occurs so
that the duly constituted government is usurped or overcome by the
insurrectionists or mobs, the Governor is impliedly authorized to declare martial law.[138]

The court added that, where dire necessity warranted the imposition of martial rule, "the rights of citizens may be abridged and
greatly restricted."

From this general evaluation of executive prerogatives in extreme emergencies, the court turned to the facts of the case. The
decision recognized that the governor must have some discretion
in such matters and that courts should proceed cautiously before
interfering with a governor's finding of the necessity of martial
law. However, the ruling emphasized that the discretion of the
governor cannot be absolute and that the facts supporting the
finding of necessity must be subject to judicial review. In the instant case, the court found that despite continued disorders,
local government in the area was not seriously disrupted, the
regular courts were open, and peace might have been restored by
using the national guard in aid of civil authorities. Under such
circumstances, the imposition of martial law with its drastic curtailment of civil rights could not be justified. The court was not
oblivious to the fact that the rights involved were primarily the
property interests of the company, and the point was made more
explicit by statements describing the strikers as "mob" and the
proclamation of martial law as abdication to "mob rule." In any
event, the decision clearly established the principle that in "less-
than-catastrophic" emergencies, governors should follow regular
constitutional and statutory procedures and that martial law must
remain an ultimate remedy.

We are . . . mindful of the necessity of preventing bloodshed and that
property rights must at times be sacrificed in order to prevent the spill-
ing of blood. But a free people do not surrender to mob rule by the
expediency of martial law until all means available to the City, County,
and State to enforce the laws have proved futile. The imposition of the
drastic action and the curtailment of constitutional rights of citizens
of a state resulting from a declaration of martial law, cannot be sustained except in situations of dire necessity. We are convinced that that
situation has not yet arisen in Freeborn County. The Governor pos-

[138] *Ibid.*, p. 525.

sesses no absolute authority to declare martial law. Military rule cannot be imposed upon a community simply because it may seem to be more expedient than to enforce the law by using the National Guard to aid the local civil authorities.[139]

[139] *Ibid.*, p. 526.

4

Racial Equality

Viewed in a long-range perspective, contemporary changes in the conception of civil liberties and in the protection of minority rights are perhaps the most significant and lasting contributions of our time to the development of American society in particular and of human society in general. Nonmilitary defense is intimately linked with the international cold war and the East-West conflict; but it is hoped that some day the dangers of war and nuclear attack may vanish or at least diminish and that energies consumed today by defense preparations can be devoted to more positive and beneficial pursuits. Emergency procedures applied to labor disputes are also geared toward the maintenance of a strong economy and of production facilities essential to national safety and health; however, the elimination of cold war tensions would not necessarily or basically alter labor-management relations. Governmental action or inaction in the field of civil liberty and equality, on the other hand, is bound to shape the face of society in a manner which transcends the international power constellations of the atomic age. Even though originating in large measure in the cold war period, contemporary advances in civil rights in all probability will continue to influence society at a time when the cold war has become a mere memory.

The fact that some of the most dramatic developments in the field of civil rights since the Civil War have taken place in the cold war era must be viewed at least as a curious coincidence. The relationship of the two aspects is, of course, subject to a wide range of possible interpretations. Some observers have stressed the extensive and perhaps excessive impact of cold war considerations on domestic civil rights problems and race relations.

Reflecting on postwar rulings of the United States Supreme Court, Fred Rodell pointed to the "little noticed" fact "that all the Vinson-into-Warren (or Truman-into-Eisenhower) Court's big decisions, and a disproportionately large part of all its decisions, dealt with, stemmed from, or were mainly motivated by the cold war (or the Korean hot war) with Communist Russia." In Rodell's opinion, this motivation was definitely apparent in the 1951 convictions of native communists under the Smith Act, in the steel seizure case of 1952, and in the Rosenberg spy trial of 1953; nor, he continued,

is there any doubt that the pro-Negro pronouncements—as many Southerners have accurately, if angrily, charged—although following the New Deal Court's direction, were pushed to such unprecedented lengths to help counter Communist propaganda in Asia and Africa about American maltreatment of people whose skins are not white.[1]

Apart from these widely publicized rulings, Rodell also perceived the "dark shadow of the U.S.S.R." hovering "over the U.S.S.C." [2] in free speech and loyalty matters, in controversies over admitting or deporting aliens, and in cases involving Fifth Amendment pleas or the non-communist affidavit for union officers. "If there was ever any question," he concluded,

that the Justices were primarily political figures, the past five or six years should have dispelled it, and never in the long history of this political group of men—not even when, acting separately on circuit, they were ruthlessly enforcing the Sedition Act at the end of the eighteenth century—did international politics, on a world scale, so overweigh and dominate their work and their decisions.

While containing some grains of truth, this interpretation obviously has its drawbacks. Above all, the concept of external motivation or causation lends support to the familiar charge of segregationists that the equal rights decisions of the Supreme Court were predicated on alien doctrines and not on constitutional

[1] Fred Rodell, *Nine Men* (New York, 1955), p. 303. He added that, in comparison with other decisions, the antisegregation rulings of the Supreme Court are "destined to affect more deeply, over a snowballing period of time, the day-to-day lives of the greatest number of citizens." *Ibid.,* p. 302.
[2] *Ibid.,* p. 303. U.S.S.C. obviously stands for United States Supreme Court.

principles and the law of the land. It is not necessary, however, to embrace the described interpretation in order to acknowledge a legitimate and relevant infusion of international considerations in domestic litigations. In probing the meaning of the law of the land, courts do not merely rely on dead parchment but, in the words of Chief Justice Marshall, it is "a constitution we are expounding." [3] In an age when the world is rapidly shrinking and the interdependence of all nations becomes increasingly manifest, the living constitution of the United States is bound to reflect international developments in the same measure as world politics are influenced by domestic events in this country. This growing interdependence of nations makes it at least plausible that a period of worldwide ferment and revolution in which so many colonial territories in Africa and Asia are quickly gaining independence should be accompanied by a domestic re-evaluation of race relations and civil rights policies. Thus, without endorsing the concept of external motivation, it is possible to view recent advances in the field of civil rights both as a manifestation of constitutional principles and as a reflection of parallel and contemporaneous developments of the international cold war era.

1. A NEW DOCTRINE OF SOCIETY

When in 1954 the Supreme Court ruled that racial segregation in public schools was unconstitutional, a new chapter in social relations and community standards was opened. Yet, despite the dramatic change in traditional concepts and habits inaugurated in 1954, the decision was not an entirely sudden and unprepared event. In fact, ever since the formation of the New Deal court and the gradual abandonment of isolationism, federal tribunals and the national administration had displayed a growing concern with civil rights and the principle of the "equal protection of the laws." [4] Already in 1938, the Supreme Court invalidated a

[3] *McCulloch* v. *Maryland*, 4 Wheat. 316, 407 (1819).

[4] Compare John P. Frank and Robert F. Munroe, "The Original Understanding of 'Equal Protection of the Laws'," *Columbia L. Rev.*, 50: 131 (1950); Morroe Berger, "The Supreme Court and Group Discrimination," *Columbia L. Rev.*, 49: 201 (1949); Edward F. Waite, "The Negro in the Supreme Court," *Minnesota L. Rev.*, 30: 219 (1946).

Missouri law under which a Negro applicant had been refused admission to the law school of a state university and which provided funds for Negro students to finance their legal education in adjacent states which offered unsegregated facilities. In the words of Chief Justice Hughes, speaking for the Court, the constitutional validity of "laws separating the races in the enjoyment of privileges afforded by the state rests wholly upon the equality of the privileges which the laws give to the separated groups within the state." [5] A year later, Attorney General Frank Murphy established a Civil Liberties Section within the criminal division of the Justice Department which was charged with the task of discovering and, in certain instances, prosecuting violations of civil rights. The second World War witnessed many advances in the field of civil liberties, advances which were not surprising in view of the fact that the war was precipitated by state systems whose major feature was the disregard of civil liberties and minority rights. In 1941, President Roosevelt in a message to Congress sought to redefine prevailing concepts of civil rights by including freedom from want and fear among fundamental freedoms. In the same year the Supreme Court castigated the practice of furnishing accommodations of inferior quality to Negro first-class passengers on the nation's railroads. [6]

The beginning of the cold war coincided with determined efforts on the part of the government and the courts to invigorate civil rights and to strengthen the principle of equal protection. Early in 1947, President Truman set up a Committee on Civil Rights to study ways and means of achieving a more complete protection of constitutional guarantees. In its report of the same year, the committee recommended the adoption of regulations to insure equality of opportunity in education, employment and transportation. [7] On the basis of this report, the president in 1948 transmitted to Congress a legislative message endorsing many of the committee's recommendations. Also in 1948, the Supreme Court ruled that qualified Negro applicants had either to be admitted to a state law school or be furnished equivalent pro-

[5] *Missouri ex rel. Gaines* v. *Canada,* 305 U.S. 337, 349 (1938).
[6] *Mitchell* v. *United States,* 313 U.S. 80 (1941).
[7] President's Committee on Civil Rights, *To Secure These Rights* (Washington, D.C., 1947).

fessional education in the state,[8] and that a state court action enforcing restrictive covenants in property deeds was a clear violation of the equal protection principle.[9] Two years later, the Court decided that, once a Negro student had been admitted to the graduate school of the University of Oklahoma, state efforts to segregate the student at the school were unconstitutional.[10] A serious challenge to segregated education itself was posed in another case of 1950 involving a Negro student who had been denied admission to the University of Texas Law School on the basis of color and who claimed that the instruction available at a newly established state law school for Negroes was inferior to the instruction at the University. The Court found that the complaint was justified and that it was very difficult for a new Negro college to match the tangible and intangible assets of an established and highly respected institution.[11]

The Brown Case and Aftermath

In the mentioned rulings, the Court had not yet directly attacked the "separate but equal" principle, although there was a strong implication that the maintenance of equal facilities on a separate basis was hardly possible in practice. The principle had been enunciated in 1896 in a decision which branded as fallacious the "assumption that the enforced separation of the two races stamps the colored race with a badge of inferiority," claiming that any alleged inequality arose "solely because the colored race chooses to put that construction" upon segregation.[12] In the 1952 term a group of new public school segregation cases was presented to the Court, but the justices were unable to reach an immediate decision. During 1953, the Court directed counsel to examine and furnish additional information on such questions as the proper interpretation of the Fourteenth Amendment and the desirable speed of implementation in case the amendment required

[8] *Sipuel* v. *University of Oklahoma,* 332 U.S. 631 (1948).

[9] *Shelley* v. *Kraemer,* 334 U.S. 1 (1948).

[10] *McLaurin* v. *Oklahoma State Regents,* 339 U.S. 637 (1950).

[11] *Sweatt* v. *Painter,* 339 U.S. 629 (1950).

[12] *Plessy* v. *Ferguson,* 163 U.S. 537, 551 (1896). Compare Note, "Separate-but-Equal; A Study of the Career of a Constitutional Concept," *Race Relations L. Reporter,* 1: 283 (1956); Paul G. Kauper, "Segregation in Public Education: The Decline of Plessy v. Ferguson," *Michigan L. Rev.,* 52: 1137 (1954).

integrated school systems. While counsel for the states argued that segregation did not violate the amendment and that the separate-but-equal doctrine was correct, Thurgood Marshall, acting as Negro spokesman, urged the Court to reject the doctrine as "a faulty conception of an era dominated by provincialism." [13]

On May 17, 1954, in a unanimous decision, the Court ruled that "in the field of public education the doctrine of 'separate but equal' has no place. Separate educational facilities are inherently unequal." In reaching this conclusion, the Court expressed the view that the legislative history of the Fourteenth Amendment was "inconclusive" with respect to the question of school segregation. Due to the elusive character of the amendment's history, primary attention had to be turned to the effect of segregation on contemporary public education.

In approaching this problem, we cannot turn the clock back to 1868, when the Amendment was adopted, or even to 1896, when *Plessy* v. *Ferguson* was written. We must consider public education in the light of its full development and its present place in American life throughout the nation.

The Court recognized that, in regard to tangible assets, white and Negro schools were being increasingly equalized. The issue was thus narrowed down to the question of whether segregation, despite the equality of tangible factors, deprived Negro children of the right to equal treatment. Relying in some measure on psychological and social considerations, the Court answered the question in the affirmative.

To separate them from others of similar age and qualifications solely because of their race generates a feeling of inferiority as to their status in the community that may affect their hearts and minds in a way unlikely to be undone.[14]

As was to be expected, the decision and its implementing decrees of 1955 [15] immediately gave rise to heated and embittered

[13] See Alpheus T. Mason and William M. Beaney, *American Constitutional Law* (New York, 1954), p. 459.

[14] *Brown* v. *Board of Education of Topeka,* 347 U.S. 483, 495, 489, 492 (1954).

[15] On May 31, 1955, the Court supplemented its decision by ruling that desegregation had to be carried into effect "with all deliberate speed"; *Brown* v. *Board of Education of Topeka,* 349 U.S. 294 (1955).

argument. On a more sophisticated and scholarly level, the debate centered primarily around the questions of whether educational policy was subject to federal intervention and whether integrated school systems were contemplated by the Fourteenth Amendment. With respect to the first question, it was pointed out that despite the delegated character of federal powers, the required adherence by state laws to the standard of equal treatment was not dependent on the content of the laws. The problem of the correct interpretation of the Fourteenth Amendment remained a highly controversial issue, but the preponderant weight of scholarship endorsed the Court's conclusion that historical materials were basically inconclusive and that the future effect of the amendment was left to future determination.[16] In relying on the contemporary significance of education and the likely effects of segregation on Negro children, the Court opened itself to the charge that its decision was based on modern sociology and psychology rather than on law. In this respect, it was properly observed that the findings of social scientists were not of a determining but only of a corroborative character.[17] Nevertheless, the Court's reference to harmful effects and a "feeling of inferiority" was criticized even by scholars otherwise strongly in favor of desegregation, mainly on the grounds that, in the absence of demonstrable injury, the Court's approach would render segregation presumably constitutional.[18] An answer to this criticism may be found in the argument that the Court's decision invalidated any state laws employing racial classification in the field of public education and that harm or injury were used simply as relevant illustrations of the necessity of such a ruling.[19]

The debate, of course, was not always conducted on the ele-

[16] Louis H. Pollak, "The Supreme Court Under Fire," *J. of Public L.*, 6: 428, 435 (1957); Alexander M. Bickel, "The Original Understanding and the Segregation Decision," *Harvard L. Rev.*, 69: 1 (1955).

[17] Jack Greenberg, "Social Scientists Take the Stand: A Review and Appraisal of Their Testimony in Litigation," *Michigan L. Rev.*, 54: 953 (1956).

[18] Louis H. Pollak, "Racial Discrimination and Judicial Integrity: A Reply to Professor Wechsler," *University of Pennsylvania L. Rev.*, 108: 1 (1959); Herbert Wechsler, "Toward Neutral Principles of Constitutional Law," *Harvard L. Rev.*, 73: 1 (1959).

[19] See Ira Michael Heyman, "The Chief Justice, Racial Segregation, and the Friendly Critics," *California L. Rev.*, 49: 104, 105 (1961).

vated level of scholarship. The emotional furor engendered by the Supreme Court decision was exemplified, among others, by Senator Byrd who assailed "the modern Thaddeus Stevens, now cloaked in the robes of the Chief Justice of the United States Supreme Court" who "has done and is doing more to destroy the form of government we have in this country than has any Chief Justice in the history of the United States." [20] These and similar statements were hardly more than verbal exercises, serving as a relief for intense frustration but otherwise of little practical significance. The same description applies to various countermeasures adopted by state governments and state legislatures at the time, and especially to their frantic efforts to revive the specter of "interposition" or "nullification." According to the doctrine of interposition—whose constitutional inadequacy has not been improved or cured by its frequent invocation in the history of federal-state relations—a state is allegedly entitled to suspend the application of federal laws or court decisions within its territory.[21] The first state to invoke the doctrine in the wake of the *Brown* case was Alabama whose legislature, in January of 1956, approved a resolution nullifying the Supreme Court edict. During the same month, the governors of Mississippi, South Carolina, Virginia and Georgia agreed to fight the ruling of the Court with the weapon of interposition. In February, the legislatures of Virginia, South Carolina, Georgia and Mississippi adopted resolutions declaring the Supreme Court decision "null, void and of no effect." These pioneering achievements were seconded by the Louisiana lawmakers in July, and by the legislatures of Tennessee and Florida later in the same year and in early 1957. Not to be outdone, some ninety-six Southern congressmen in March of 1956 adopted a Declaration of Constitutional Principles pledging the use of "all lawful means to reverse the Supreme Court edict." [22]

[20] 103 Cong. Rec. 672, 675 (July 16, 1957). Senator Eastland attributed the Supreme Court ruling to the "left-wing brainwashing of Court members"; *The New York Times* (January 30, 1956), p. 17, col. 1.

[21] See Note, "Interposition vs. Judicial Power," *Race Relations L. Reporter,* 1: 465, 466 (1956); Symposium, "The Doctrine of Interposition: A Round Table," *J. of Public L.,* 5: 2 (1956).

[22] For the texts of some of the state resolutions see *Race Relations L. Reporter,* 1: 437, 438, 440, 443, 445, 755, 948 (1956), and vol. 2, pp. 481, 707 (1957); for the text of the declaration see vol. 1, p. 435 (1956).

Growing Defiance

The prospects of gradual integration of public schools were not seriously impaired by verbal deprecations or paper resolutions. However, the danger of active resistance arose immediately when, with the opening of the new school year in the fall of 1956, the *Brown* decision was slowly transferred from the realm of theory to the plane of social reality. This process of implementation was in many cases more peaceful and orderly than had been expected; but in some instances violence or the threat of violence led to the adoption of emergency measures and even to military intervention. There can be no doubt that the developments in Southern school districts were followed attentively by the entire nation and by many observers abroad. Reflecting on the international repercussions of the beginning school integration in the South, one writer asserted that

today the attention of the human family has shifted southward to focus on Mansfield, Montgomery, Birmingham, Atlanta, Tallahassee, Clinton, Americus, Sturgis, Clay and Henderson, for these have become the frontier towns in an age of world revolution. Men and women in India, Egypt, Morocco, Kenya and elsewhere, already battle-scarred veterans in the fight for first-class citizenship, are watching with interest this new frontier in American life.

The writer added that "the race relations frontier calls for pioneering in the most exalted and courageous sense. . . . First, however, the frontier line that runs through every human heart must be crossed." [23]

In a number of Southern states, violence or active defiance was definitely anticipated, a fact which induced some state legislatures to adopt emergency statutes endowing the governor with extraordinary powers in case of disorder. As it appears, statutes of this kind were not entirely necessary since, during emergency, governors are already vested with broad authority by state constitutions and under the police power principle. The adoption of new measures was probably due to the general feeling of excitement

[23] Theodore A. Braun, "The New American Frontier," *Christian Century,* 75: 866, 867 (July 17, 1957).

and worry attending the process of integration. In August of 1956, the Florida legislature passed a law conferring additional emergency powers on the governor to quell disturbances at public parks, buildings or other facilities. As the bill specified, the governor was empowered

to promulgate and enforce such emergency rules and regulations as are necessary to prevent, control, or quell violence, threatened or actual, during any emergency lawfully declared by him to exist. In order to protect the public welfare, persons and property of citizens against violence, public property damage, overt threat of violence, and to maintain peace, tranquillity and good order in the state, these rules and regulations may control public parks, public buildings, or any other public facility in Florida.[24]

In order to enforce the rules and regulations authorized by the bill, the governor was given the "emergency power to call upon the military forces of the state or any other law enforcement agency" on the state or county level. Somewhat redundantly, the bill explained that the "powers herein granted are supplemental to and in aid of powers now vested in the Governor of the State of Florida under the constitution, statutory law and police powers" of the state.

The described act was accompanied by another statute passed on the same day which provided for the issuance of proclamations of emergency by the governor and for the quelling of riots, unlawful assembly or other violence. According to this companion bill, the governor of Florida

when, in his opinion, the facts warrant, shall, by proclamation, declare that, because of unlawful assemblage, violence, overt threats of violence, or otherwise, a danger exists to the persons or property of any citizen or citizens of the State of Florida and that the peace and tranquillity of the State . . . or any political subdivision thereof, or any area . . . designated by him, is threatened, and because thereof an emergency . . . exists.[25]

The proclamation statute stressed again the power of the governor to call out the military forces of the state and to direct these forces "to take such action as in his judgment may be necessary

---

[24] See *Race Relations L. Reporter,* 1: 954 (1956).
[25] *Ibid.,* p. 955.

to avert the threatened danger and to maintain peace and good order in the particular circumstances." Similar emergency provisions were subsequently adopted by the general assembly of South Carolina in the form of a bill conferring broad powers on the governor to protect persons or property from violence or threats of violence. Under the terms of the South Carolina statute, the governor, "when in his opinion the facts warrant," was authorized to issue a proclamation of emergency declaring that "because of unlawful assemblage, violence or threats of violence, a danger exists to the person or property of any citizen." The chief executive of the state was also empowered to use the state militia or other law enforcement forces "to take such action as in his judgment may be necessary" to overcome the disturbance.[26]

As it happened, the states which adopted these emergency measures did not experience major disorders requiring the invocation of extraordinary gubernatorial powers. The centers of active defiance during the first year of sporadic school integration were located in Tennessee, Kentucky and Texas. In these states, the opening of the new school year in the fall of 1956 was attended in some school districts by violent disturbances which, on orders of the respective governors, led to the intervention of state military forces. Although resort to martial law was occasionally proposed or considered in these instances, the military units were uniformly used in a supporting role in aid of civil authorities. Nevertheless, the manner and effect of military intervention differed greatly in the three cases. While in Tennessee and Kentucky, national guard units were employed in a more or less neutral manner which did not basically interfere with the progress of integration, military intervention in Texas was definitely designed to support popular resistance to integration and to obstruct Negro registration at white schools. The different use of state troops did not imply that the governors of Tennessee and Kentucky were personally more in favor of public school integration than was the governor of Texas. Governor Clement of Tennessee stated on one occasion very clearly that he and most of the police of his state disapproved of integration; he added, however, that the law had to be upheld despite such personal feelings.[27] To uphold law and

[26] *Ibid.*, vol. 2, p. 855 (1957).
[27] *The New York Times* (September 16, 1957), p. 1, col. 2.

order meant that, if state troops were employed in integration disturbances, they had to afford equal treatment to Negroes and whites and to protect them both from mutual violence and in their right to proper education. The attitude of Governor Clement earned him little sympathy from the more fanatical elements in his state; some pro-segregation organizations actually urged his impeachment for his use of the national guard. On the other hand, the actions of Governor Shivers of Texas established a pattern of state defiance which was later followed with great relish by Governors Faubus, Barnett and Wallace in the Little Rock, Oxford and Tuscaloosa episodes.

The general unrest which accompanied the beginning of school integration in Tennessee assumed serious proportions in Anderson County and more particularly at Clinton. In fairness to the people of the area it must be mentioned that much of the disorder was due to the agitation of an outsider, a professional troublemaker from the North by the name of John Kasper. Apparently dissatisfied with Southern racial attitudes, this man made it his business to organize white citizens' councils, preach violence, incite riots and spread the gospel of hate and prejudice wherever he went. For his activities in Tennessee, Kasper was repeatedly cited for contempt of court, arrested, sentenced and jailed.[28] In Anderson County, school integration was not entirely a novel issue in 1956. Already prior to the Supreme Court ruling in the *Brown* case, a class action had been filed against the county board of education seeking the admission of Negro children in public schools; at that time, however, the action had been dismissed. Early in 1956, the federal district court of the area ruled that the county board should admit pupils to the Clinton high school on a racially non-discriminatory basis beginning with the fall, 1956, school term. On August 25, John Kasper arrived in the city and immediately set himself to the task of organizing a citizens' council and encouraging demonstrations. Despite the issuance of an injunction by the federal district court against interference with integration efforts, racial tensions spread through the city like a contagious disease. In the last days of August street fights erupted

[28] Compare Wilma Dykeman and James Stokely, "Failure of a Hate Mission," *Nation*, 184: 342 (April, 1957).

in the course of public demonstrations involving at times more than one thousand persons.

The initial response of city authorities was to rely on regular police in attempting to curb the disturbances. In addition, a volunteer citizens' police unit was formed and used to disperse crowds gathered for pro-segregation rallies. However, it became increasingly obvious that local police units were insufficient in the face of growing disorders. On September 1, the sheriff of Anderson County, with the backing of city authorities, asked the governor for state assistance. Governor Clement immediately complied with this request and ordered a contingent of state troopers to the scene to restore order. On the following day, the national guard unit arrived at Clinton and, with the help of several tanks, was able to quell the outbreak of new violence. As commanding officer of the national guard, Adjutant General Henry stated that the guardsmen would remain in the city until peace was restored; he also emphasized that the purpose of military assistance was to maintain order and that the troops would not be used to either compel or obstruct integration.[29] The presence of troops did not entirely discourage or pacify the more fanatical segregationists. In view of persisting disorders and threats of violence, tanks were used repeatedly on the following days and guardsmen were told to fire if necessary. Adjutant General Henry imposed a limited curfew in order to curb demonstrations; he also barred outdoor public speaking and the use of public address systems. Mainly due to the vigilance of the guardsmen, calm was restored at Clinton, at least for the moment, and the opening of the new school term saw nine out of twelve registered Negro children in attendance at the formerly all-white high school, although more than half of the white students were absent.[30]

Beginning on September 5, the limitations and curbs imposed by the national guard were gradually relaxed, while community leaders started to explore ways and means of strengthening local police forces in the event of the withdrawal of troops. On September 8, the number of guardsmen was drastically reduced. At

[29] *The New York Times* (September 3, 1956), p. 1, col. 3.

[30] At the time of these developments, violence erupted at Oliver Springs, Tennessee, over the issue of school integration and 40 guardsmen were ordered to the scene to disperse armed rioters. *Ibid.* (September 5, 1956), p. 1. col. 2.

the same time, following a declaration of emergency for the county, police reserves were mobilized by the local sheriff, including guards from the Tennessee Valley Authority and patrol units from the Oak Ridge facilities of the Atomic Energy Commission. Further reductions in the number of guardsmen occurred on the following days and, by September 12, the last state troops were withdrawn. The remainder of the school year was comparatively uneventful. The segregationists had clearly lost the integration battle in this instance; but they were not immediately ready to admit defeat. John Kasper and his friends were still engaged in their favorite pastime of plotting and scheming. During early December, racial tensions and threats of violence mounted again in the city, with the result that all Negro students left their classes and that the high school itself had to be temporarily closed. In this case, however, local police were able to handle the situation and classes were resumed a few days later without incidents on an integrated basis. The opening of the next school year in the fall of 1957 witnessed new efforts of segregationists to create disorders and obstruct integration. Regular police units were assigned to all high schools as the term started. The white citizens' council announced plans to picket the schools and asked white parents to keep their children at home. Governor Clement was urged by a parents' committee to use the National Guard in order to bar Negroes from white schools and to "prevent violence"; however, the chief executive answered very correctly that he lacked such authority.[31] Despite several acts of violence, the attempted boycott of integrated schools failed as class attendance of white and Negro children increased during the subsequent weeks of the school term.

Developments in Kentucky were very similar to those in Tennessee, except for the fact that local segregationists were more successful in their attempts to boycott schools and obstruct integration. The major hotbeds of violence in Kentucky were the school districts of Sturgis and Clay. The scheduled admission of eight Negro pupils to the formerly white high school at Sturgis led to frantic efforts on the part of white parents' groups to thwart the opening of integrated classes at the beginning of the fall, 1956, school term. On September 6, Governor Chandler ordered four

[31] *Ibid.* (September 10, 1957), p. 1, col. 8.

units of the Kentucky National Guard and a number of tanks to the Sturgis area.[32] The purpose of the guard intervention was clearly to curb violence and to protect the orderly admission of Negro pupils to the high school; it was not surprising, therefore, that the presence of guardsmen was immediately protested by white parents. The strategy adopted by the parents' groups was to boycott integrated classes and to intimidate Negro children seeking admission. When the scheduled number of Negroes enrolled under military protection, the majority of white students left the high school; after classes, the guardsmen had to charge into a hostile crowd to clear the path for the Negro pupils. On September 8, it was reported that no Negroes attended the school despite the offer of military escort, a fact which was obviously due to threats of physical and economic retaliation. In the face of spreading disorders, Governor Chandler on the same day signed a stand-by order proclaiming that martial law would be declared if necessary. Although the stand-by order was not implemented, an additional battalion of the National Guard was mobilized to serve as reinforcement of the units stationed at Sturgis and possibly as shock troops at Clay where white crowds were at the time barring Negroes from entering the elementary school.

Despite the presence of troops at Sturgis, the prospects of integrated education remained dim. During the following days, the high school building was surrounded by guardsmen and Negro pupils were escorted into their classes. However, the entrance of the Negro children led to a renewed walkout of white students which left only one-sixth of the enrolled student body at the school. On September 13, National Guard troops and state police units began to occupy Clay on orders of Governor Chandler. The arrival of the guardsmen was greeted with intense hostility by the local population. The attempt of the militia to protect the entrance of Negro children into the Clay High School resulted in an immediate boycott of the school by the majority of white students and teachers. Class attendance during the following week did not rise above the level of one-fourth of the students at the Sturgis and Clay high schools. On September 19, the school board of Union County decided to bar Negroes from the Sturgis school despite the fact that they had already been enrolled. The

[32] *Ibid.* (September 7, 1956), p. 1, col. 6.

move was immediately challenged by the National Association for the Advancement of Colored People through a petition for permanent injunction against the ouster. In view of the prospect of protracted litigation, Governor Chandler on September 22 decided to withdraw the troops from Clay and Sturgis. The school year opening in the fall of 1957 witnessed an improvement in the chances of integrated education. State troops were again deployed at Sturgis to curb violence and to prevent interference with the enrollment of Negro students. Although Governor Chandler was called upon to adopt a policy of "interposition" and to use the National Guard to enforce state segregation laws, the neutral character of the military intervention was retained and Negro students were soon able to enter Sturgis high school without guard or police escort.

Events took an entirely different turn at the Mansfield High School in Texas. The school was the first educational institution in Texas below the college level whose integration had been ordered by a federal court for the school term starting in fall, 1956.[33] In the weeks preceding the opening of the fall term, the announcement of the scheduled registration of Negro pupils at the high school provoked local demonstrations and growing threats of violence. On August 31, after a crowd of some 400 demonstrators had gathered near the high school to bar the enrollment of Negroes, Governor Shivers ordered the Texas Rangers into Mansfield. A statement of the same day accompanying the order left little doubt as to the governor's intentions and the purpose of the military intervention. In his statement, Governor Shivers explained that "under the general powers of the Governor to enforce the laws and see that order is kept in Texas, I have instructed Colonel Garrison to send Texas Rangers to Mansfield to cooperate with local authorities in preserving the peace." Although it was obvious that the only possible threats of violence stemmed from local segregationists trying to prevent the admission of Negro pupils, the statement reported somewhat facetiously

---

[33] *Jackson v. Rawdon*, 135 F.Supp. 936 (N.D. Tex. 1955), *rev'd*, 235 F. 2d 93, 96 (5th Cir. 1956), where the appellate court stated that the plaintiffs were entitled to a prompt start of integration, "uninfluenced by private and public opinion as to the desirability of desegregation in the community."

that the governor had contacted the school authorities at Mansfield and urged them to

go ahead and transfer out of the district any scholastics, white or
colored, whose attendance or attempts to attend Mansfield High School
would reasonably be calculated to incite violence. These transfers
should be for the general welfare, to preserve peace and orderly conduct, and not for any other reason.

The actual purpose of the governor's action was more clearly
revealed in another part of the statement which emphasized that
"it is not my intention to permit the use of state officers or troops
to shoot down or intimidate Texas citizens who are making
orderly protest against a situation instigated and agitated by the
NAACP." [34]

The order of the governor was duly implemented by the Rangers after their arrival at Mansfield. Although the commanding
officer of the Rangers reported that the situation was under control, none of the scheduled Negro children enrolled at the school.
This failure to register was obviously due to the absence of adequate military protection of the Negroes seeking admission and
to the Rangers' support of local segregationists. After thus having
"pacified" the situation, the Rangers quit Mansfield in the first
week of September. The withdrawal of troops left the city entirely in the control of pro-segregation elements. At the opening
of the fall term, no registration of Negroes took place due to the
presence of a large crowd at the site of the high school. In
accordance with the governor's wishes, school authorities adhered
to the policy that any Negro seeking admission would be transferred to other schools "to maintain order." Federal courts, of
course, were not so easily satisfied with the handling of the situation by state and local officials. A petition for a temporary stay
of the federal court order requiring integration of the high school
was denied by Justice Black of the Supreme Court. On December 3, 1956, the Supreme Court ruled that the order of the lower

[34] See *Race Relations L. Reporter,* 1: 885 (1956). In the performance of
their tasks, the troops were given broad powers including the authority "to
arrest anyone, white or colored, whose actions are such as to represent a
threat to the peace at Mansfield," despite the fact that this authority ac-
corded ill with the stated intention to cooperate with local civil auhorities.

court was a valid and proper implementation of the *Brown* decision and in full accord with the principle of "deliberate speed" applicable to public school integration.[35]

2. THE LITTLE ROCK CRISIS

The reported disturbances were minor and relatively uncomplicated in comparison with the disorders which erupted at Little Rock in the fall of 1957. Little Rock and Central High School have become synonyms for racial prejudice in the field of education; but the city was not the only troublespot in the state. From the beginning of the school integration movement, many parts of Arkansas were beset with unrest and racial tensions. A good illustration of these tensions may be found in the developments which occurred during 1955 and 1956 in the Hoxie school district in Lawrence County, near the northern border of the state. The developments in Hoxie derive additional significance from the court action which resulted from the disturbances. Shortly after the Supreme Court rulings in the *Brown* case, the school authorities of the district had voluntarily started a program of integration of the local schools without any prior court order. Although the integration program was initially successful, agitation against the school authorities developed in late 1955, an agitation which manifested itself primarily in mass meetings of white citizens' councils and parents' groups. As a result of threats of violence and other mob action, the school board was finally forced to close the schools. The school district, its directors and superintendents subsequently brought action in a federal district court for a declaratory judgment and injunction against further interference with the operation of the schools on a desegregated basis. In their action, the plaintiffs claimed that they were entitled to federal protection against violent acts of private individuals, mainly on the basis of the constitutional guarantees of a republican form of government and of protection against domestic violence.

In granting the injunction, the federal district court agreed that the school authorities had a right to be free from interference although it was clear that the activities of the mob leaders could not properly be considered as "state action" under the terms of

[35] *Rawdon* v. *Jackson,* 352 U.S. 925 (1956).

the Fourteenth Amendment.[36] Despite a long line of cases which had held that the constitutional guarantees of a republican form of government in the states and of protection against domestic violence were not properly subject to judicial control, the court asserted that the guarantees could be invoked in a situation where state officers were obstructed in the performance of a federal duty.[37] The injunction was immediately appealed by the defendants. At this juncture, the Justice Department was alerted to the case and requested the appellate court to protect the integration efforts of the local school board. The decision of the court of appeals upholding the injunction relied mainly on the concept of a federally protected right deriving from a constitutional duty. As the court stated, the school authorities "being bound by a constitutionally imposed duty and their oaths of office to support the Fourteenth Amendment and to accord equal protection of the laws to all persons in their operation of the Hoxie schools" must be deemed "to have a right which is a federal right to be free from direct interference in the performance of that duty." [38] As it appears, the court conceived the right as one of the privileges and immunities of federal citizenship, a privilege subject to protection both against private individuals and against states. In any event, the decision constituted an important precedent for future integration proceedings.

In the Hoxie case, local school authorities were certainly not hostile to integration or recalcitrant in their duty to implement the Supreme Court edict. A similar attitude prevailed among school authorities at Little Rock in Pulaski County. Already on May 20, 1954, the school board of the Little Rock school district had issued a statement to the effect that it was the board's

[36] *Hoxie School District* v. *Brewer*, 137 F. Supp. 364 (E. D. Ark. 1956). On the requirement of "state action" compare Theodore J. St. Antoine, "Color Blindness but not Myopia: A New Look at State Action, Equal Protection, and 'Private' Racial Discrimination," *Michigan L. Rev.*, 59: 993 (1961); Thomas P. Lewis, "The Meaning of State Action," *Columbia L. Rev.*, 60: 1083 (1960); Note, "State Action: A Study of Requirements Under the Fourteenth Amendment," *Race Relations L. Reporter*, 1: 613 (1956).

[37] Compare Clarence C. Ferguson, "The Inherent Justiciability of the Constitutional Guarantee Against Domestic Violence," *Rutgers L. Rev.*, 13: 407, 423 (1959).

[38] *Brewer* v. *Hoxie School District*, 238 F.2d 91, 98-99 (8th Cir. 1956).

responsibility to comply with federal constitutional requirements and that it would make the needed studies for implementation.[39] On instructions of the school board, the superintendent of the Little Rock schools, Virgil T. Blossom, prepared a plan for the gradual integration of the public schools in the district over a period of six or seven years, starting with the senior high school level in the fall of 1957. The plan was approved by the school board on May 24, 1955. In February of 1956, the parents of a group of Negro school children brought a class action in the federal district court of the area against the members of the local school board. The action requested immediate integration of public schools and the issuance of an injunction against the enforcement of Arkansas constitutional and statutory provisions requiring segregation. In answer to the action, the school board submitted to the court its plan of integration which it contended was in agreement with the *Brown* decision. On August 27, the district court accepted the plan as a "prompt and reasonable start" toward full integration and, without issuing an injunction, retained jurisdiction of the case to supervise the further implementation of the plan.[40] Claiming that the plan did not amount to a reasonable start and that there were no valid reasons why full integration should not be accomplished by fall of 1957, the Negro plaintiffs appealed the district court ruling. On April 26, 1957, the court of appeals held that, under existing circumstances, the plan of the local school board was not unreasonable and constituted a bona fide compliance with the Supreme Court mandate.[41]

Governor Faubus and the National Guard

Developments at Little Rock had so far moved rather smoothly; certainly there was nothing in the background of the case which foreshadowed the coming disorders and the necessity of military

---

[39] For details of the entire Little Rock episode see Wilson Record and Jane C. Record, *Little Rock, U.S.A.; Materials for Analysis* (San Francisco, 1960); Brooks Hays, *A Southern Moderate Speaks* (Chapel Hill, 1959); Virgil T. Blossom, *It Has Happened Here* (New York, 1959); U.S. Senate, Hearings before the Committee on the Judiciary, *Nomination of W. Wilson White*, 85th Cong., 2d Sess. (1958); and *Race Relations L. Reporter*, 2: 931-966 (1957).

[40] *Aaron v. Cooper*, 143 F. Supp. 855 (E. D. Ark. 1956).

[41] *Aaron v. Cooper*, 243 F.2d 361 (8th Cir. 1957).

intervention. In late August of 1957, shortly before the opening of the school term, a petition was filed in a state court by a white parent seeking to enjoin the school officials from integrating the high school. It was in the course of this action that Governor Faubus made his first appearance in the case. Despite a past record of relatively peaceful race relations at Little Rock, the governor offered testimony seeking to show the likelihood of bloodshed and mob violence in the event of school integration. Mainly on the basis of this testimony, the state court ordered a discontinuance of the integration plans. On the request of the city school officials, the federal district court immediately enjoined the enforcement of the state court's order. On September 2, the day before classes were to begin, Governor Faubus reiterated his fears of violent disorders and possible bloodshed. Acting on this vague anticipation, the governor on the same day proclaimed the existence of an emergency and ordered national guard troops into active state service with the mission of maintaining "law and order and to preserve the peace, health, safety and security of the citizens of Pulaski County." Simultaneously, the chief executive directed the adjutant general of the National Guard, Sherman T. Clinger, to station the guard units, under the command of Lieutenant Colonel Marion E. Johnson, at and around Central High School.

The necessity of the militia intervention is open to serious doubt as the troops were called out to prevent a violence which had not yet occurred and in the absence of a clear threat of violence. Governor Faubus, of course, insisted very strongly that there were sufficient danger signals to warrant the use of state troops. In a later statement designed to justify his action, the governor asserted that

I placed the Guard about Central High School to prevent the almost certain blood-shed that would have ensued. I had placed them there because there had been purchased in Little Rock 1,150 of these umbrellas with metal points which are sharpened into weapons by the colored people. Switch blade knives had been sold in almost every store to the extent that in three weeks a three years' normal supply had been sold. It went on from that to many other things.[42]

[42] "Address of Governor Orval Faubus," *Mississippi L. J.*, 30: 520, 536 (1959).

The immediate danger of violent disorders was denied, however, by local authorities at the scene, especially by Superintendent Blossom and the mayor of the city, Woodrow W. Mann. In the words of the mayor, the governor called out the national guard to "put down trouble where none existed. . . . If any racial trouble does develop, the blame rests squarely on the doorstep of the governor's mansion." [43] It is true that, out of an abundance of caution, local school authorities had conferred with the mayor and the chief of police about appropriate steps to prevent disturbances. Nevertheless, the mayor considered that even in this unlikely eventuality, the local police force could adequately handle the situation. In any event, neither the mayor nor the chief of police made any request to the governor for state assistance in maintaining order at the high school. The denial of initial threats of violence does not conflict with the fact that, subsequent to the stationing of troops, a disorderly crowd began to assemble at the high school. As one observer commented, a prophecy of disorders "tends to become self-fulfilling. The governor's prediction had the effect of a call to violence." [44]

If the necessity of military intervention was highly doubtful, its purpose was not. In his order to Adjutant General Clinger, the governor stated his intentions very clearly. "You are directed," the order read,

to place off limits to white students those schools for colored students and to place off limits to colored students those schools heretofore operated and recently set up for white students. This order will remain in effect until the demobilization of the Guard or until further orders.[45]

The directions of the governor were promptly executed by the guardsmen. Standing shoulder-to-shoulder at the school grounds, the troopers prevented the admission of the nine Negro students eligible under the school board plan. While failing to protect the colored students in their right to attend classes, the guardsmen permitted the white children to enter the school. Although the primary duty—the exclusion of Negro students—was well defined,

[43] See Robert McKay, "Little Rock: Power Showdown," *Nation*, 185: 189 (1957).
[44] *Ibid.*
[45] *Race Relations L. Reporter*, 2: 942 (1957).

the general authority of the militia in its relation to local civil authorities was not specified in the governor's order. On request of the mayor of Little Rock, the attorney general of the state subsequently attempted to assess the respective responsibilities. The statements of the attorney general were not a model of clarity. Regarding the problem of jurisdiction for the purpose of law enforcement, the opinion merely asserted that local, state and federal laws may or may not be applicable to law enforcement and that local police, state police and military forces "might have exclusive, concurrent or overlapping jurisdiction as a particular factual situation might develop." In answer to the question as to what legal remedies the city might have if the troops should interfere with the city police, the attorney general expressed the illuminating thought that "if you have any legal remedy, it, of course, would be through the courts." [46] The opinion admitted, however, that the governor's authority over the militia was not unlimited, but constitutional and statutory, and that the decision to use the guard was subject to court review. Despite the vagueness of the opinion, it appears that the militia was definitely employed in support and aid of civil authorities.

The action of the governor of Arkansas was a clear defiance of the federal court order and the Supreme Court mandate. Orval Faubus, of course, was not the first governor to use the state militia in an attempt to obstruct federal laws and court rulings. In 1857, Governor Brigham Young of Utah had called out the militia in defiance of federal laws and officers and even battled the troops of the United States. Since 1930 and not counting the Little Rock episode, governors and their guards have fought at least four wars against the United States. In 1932, Governor Sterling of Texas dispatched the national guard to frustrate the execution of a court order temporarily ending controls on oil production. In 1934, the governor of Arizona used the guard to prevent a construction firm which was under contract with the national government from continuing work on Parker Dam. The state militia was mobilized by Governor Kraschel of Iowa in 1938 to stop hearings of the National Labor Relations Board at the Maytag plant. In protest against unsatisfactory reimbursements for the flooding of state roads, Governor Phillips of Okla-

[46] *Ibid.*, p. 1045.

homa in 1940 called out guardsmen to halt construction of a federally-financed dam at Grand River. To be sure, these and similar acts of defiance by state governors were not silently condoned by federal authorities. It is true that federal courts are hesitant to proceed against state officials and will do so only under pressing circumstances.[47] Nevertheless, there are sufficient precedents for the principle that misuse of power by a state officer, especially actions violating the federal constitution or depriving a person of a federal right, are not beyond the pale of judicial control.[48] In 1936, a federal district court ruled in a famous Minnesota case that the governor could not use the state forces to assist disorderly crowds and deprive citizens of their lawful rights.[49] The most famous precedent, however, was the Sterling case of 1932 where the Supreme Court stated without ambiguity:

The applicable principle is that where state officials, purporting to act under state authority, invade rights secured by the Federal Constitution, they are subject to the process of federal courts in order that the persons injured may have appropriate relief. . . . The Governor of the State, in this respect, is in no different position from that of other state officials.[50]

In accordance with these precedents, federal courts did not remain inactive in the Little Rock crisis. Already on September 3, the day after the arrival of the guardsmen, Judge Davies of the federal district court asked the school authorities to show cause why the integration plan should not be implemented. On discovering that, due to the stationing of military guards at the high school, the school board had requested the eligible Negro students to stay away from school, the court ordered the school authorities to proceed with the integration. When the school officials subsequently filed a formal petition for a temporary suspension of the

[47] Compare, e.g., *Hawks* v. *Hamill,* 288 U.S. 52, 60 (1933).

[48] *Screws* v. *United States,* 325 U.S. 91 (1945); *United States* v. *Classic,* 313 U.S. 299, 326 (1941).

[49] *Strutwear Knitting Company* v. *Olson,* 13 F. Supp. 384, 391 (D.C. Minn. 1936).

[50] *Sterling* v. *Constantin,* 287 U.S. 378, 393 (1932). The case was frequently invoked in public debate during the Little Rock crisis; see, e.g., *The New York Times* (September 6, 1957), p. 1. col. 8; *ibid.* (September 8, 1957), p. 66, col. 6.

integration plan, Judge Davies on September 7 called their attitude "anemic" and denied the petition. Two days later, the court requested the Attorney General of the United States and the federal district attorney to enter the case as "friends of the court" and to file a petition for injunction against the governor and other state officials. The petition of the legal officers of the United States asserted that units of the National Guard were still forcibly preventing eligible Negro students from entering the school and that the state authorities should be enjoined from using the guard in this manner. In response, the governor filed motions and a brief contesting the participation of the United States and the court's jurisdiction; he also claimed that the court was without power to question his judgment and discretion in the use of the national guard of the state. Following a hearing on the petition of the United States, the district court on September 20 issued an injunction restraining the state officials from obstructing or preventing the attendance of Negro pupils at the high school by use of the National Guard or any other means.

In granting the injunction, the district court rejected very firmly the claim of Governor Faubus that he was the final judge of the use of the National Guard. The court did not deny that a governor has a broad area of discretion in matters relating to public welfare and safety within his state. "As the chief executive of the state," the opinion stated, "he is appropriately vested with the discretion to determine whether an exigency requiring military state aid for that purpose has arisen." [51] However, the court held that in the instant case the governor had acted outside the area of his authority. For this conclusion, the court relied primarily on findings that there was no real necessity for military intervention at the time of the governor's decision and that, even if the intervention had been necessary, the troops should have been used in support and not in defiance of the federal court order. Regarding the question of necessity, Judge Davies stated in court that it was "demonstrable from the testimony here today that there would have been no violence in carrying out the plan of integration, and that there has been no violence." From this assessment of the emergency character of the situation, the court proceeded to an examination of the activities of the guard. Ac-

[51] *Aaron* v. *Cooper,* 156 F. Supp. 220, 226 (E. D. Ark. 1957).

cording to the court, these activities were illegal and un-constitutional.

> The Governor does not . . . have lawful authority to use the National Guard to deprive the eligible colored students from exercising their right to attend Central High School, which right is guaranteed by the Federal Constitution, the School District plan of integration and the Court's orders entered in this case. If it be assumed that the Governor was entitled to bring military force to the aid of civil authority, the proper use of that power in this instance was to maintain the Federal Court in the exercise of its jurisdiction, to aid in making its process effective and not to nullify it, to remove, and not to create, obstructions to the exercise by the Negro children of their rights as judicially declared.[52]

The decision of the district court was affirmed on appeal and a petition for certiorari was denied by the Supreme Court.[53]

The President's Use of Federal Troops

Following the issuance of the injunction by the district court, Governor Faubus immediately withdrew the National Guard troops from the school. This action, of course, was merely part of the governor's general strategy and not a sign of his respect for federal court orders. The injunction had merely restrained him from violating federal rights and not from using the guard in case of necessity to preserve peace and order and to protect the admission of Negro pupils to the school. When the injunction was issued, there were definite signs of impending disorder and mob violence. The withdrawal of troops by the governor thus compounded his earlier defiance of the integration mandate. While the National Guard had been called out in the absence of clear necessity in order to prevent the school integration, the governor now withdrew the troops in the face of emergency conditions, thereby abandoning the environs of Central High School to the control of a crowd of segregationists and agitators. The abdication of the law enforcement function by the governor clearly demon-

---

[52] *Ibid.*, p. 226. The language is almost identical with that used in *Sterling v. Constantin*, 287 U.S. 378, 404 (1932).

[53] *Faubus* v. *United States*, 254 F.2d 797 (8th Cir. 1958), *cert. denied*, 358 U.S. 829 (1958).

strated the need for federal action, possibly in the form of military intervention.

There was ample precedent for the president's authority to use federal troops to quell domestic disorders either with or without the consent of the state governor. It is true that only in few instances had this authority been exercised to protect federally guaranteed civil rights; but no compelling reason can be found to differentiate this protection from other historical incidents of federal intervention. In the early days of the Republic, President Washington called forth the militia and sent the troops to western Pennsylvania to suppress the Whiskey Rebellion and to protect the federal judiciary over Governor Mifflin's objection. In 1799, President John Adams employed the militia in eastern Pennsylvania to quell the Fries Rebellion without direct invitation from the state. During his controversy with the South Carolina Nullifiers, President Jackson at least threatened to use troops to uphold the supremacy of federal law. In 1851 and 1854, President Fillmore dispatched troops to Boston on several occasions to enforce the Fugitive Slave Law in the face of Boston mobs. President Buchanan in 1857 sent troops to Utah to put down domestic violence led by Governor Brigham Young. After the Civil War, President Rutherford Hayes in 1878 employed troops in New Mexico at the request of the territorial governor to assist marshals in the execution of federal court processes. In 1894, President Cleveland dispatched troops to Chicago to enforce a federal court injunction against Eugene Debs over the strong protest of Governor Altgeld.[54] After the Pullman strike, troops were used by presidents most frequently in connection with industrial violence, as has been discussed in another context. Nevertheless, military intervention was not always directly related to industrial disputes. Throughout these historical examples the principle has asserted itself that the authority to decide whether the exigencies require the use of troops is vested in the president,[55] although the decision would today appear to be subject to judicial review.

[54] On these cases see Daniel H. Pollitt, "Presidential Use of Troops to Execute the Laws: A Brief History," *North Carolina L. Rev.*, 36: 117, 139-141 (1958).

[55] *Martin* v. *Mott,* 12 Wheat. 19 (1827); compare George H. Faust, "The President's Use of Troops to Enforce Federal Law," *Cleveland-Marshall L. Rev.*, 7: 362, 364 (1958).

In the Little Rock crisis, President Eisenhower and his administration were ill prepared for military action or any form of federal intervention. Despite numerous indications of Southern resistance following the *Brown* decision, the Justice Department had developed no concrete plans to meet contingencies similar to that in Little Rock. The president's own states' rights sentiments and his distaste for the use of federal power to change social habits were common knowledge. On frequent occasions, the president had refused to endorse personally the spirit of the *Brown* ruling and had opposed intervention by the federal government. In July of 1957, President Eisenhower still asserted that troops would be used to enforce school desegregation only "over my dead body." [56] It should be mentioned, however, that the president was not alone in his objection to military action and that similar sentiments were shared by spokesmen of the opposition party. Although criticizing the lack of presidential leadership in the field of civil rights, these spokesmen repeatedly questioned the desirability of the use of federal troops in integration disorders. After the stationing of militia forces by Governor Faubus at Little Rock, the president assumed a somewhat firmer attitude. In a telegram to the governor of September 5, 1957, he informed Faubus of his intention to uphold the federal constitution "by every legal means at my command." [57] The impact of this declaration, however, was seriously diluted by the conference of September 14 between the president and Governor Faubus at Newport, Rhode Island, a conference which created the impression that the implementation of the federal integration order was a matter of negotiation and bargaining. The subsequent withdrawal of guardsmen by the governor in the face of growing disorders created a sudden emergency and, in view of the lack of alternate plans, the use of federal troops appeared as the only remedy.

On September 23, President Eisenhower issued a proclamation which recited the existence of unlawful assemblages in Arkansas obstructing the integration orders of the district court and making it impractical to enforce the laws "by the ordinary course of judicial proceedings." The proclamation called on all persons "en-

[56] See Richard P. Longaker, *The Presidency and Individual Liberties* (Ithaca, 1961), pp. 153, 168.

[57] *The New York Times* (September 6, 1957), p. 1, col. 8.

gaged in such obstruction of justice to cease and desist therefrom and to disperse forthwith." [58] On the following day, due to continued disturbances, the president issued an executive order directing the use of armed forces to enforce the proclamation and the court rulings. The order authorized the Secretary of Defense to call the Arkansas National Guard into active federal service and to employ such parts of the "armed forces of the United States as he may deem necessary." [59] The Secretary of Defense immediately implemented the presidential order and units of the federalized national guard and of the 101st Airborne Division were dispatched to Little Rock. The president made it clear that the purpose of the military intervention was not so much to compel integration but to uphold the sanctity of federal courts and federal law. In an address to the nation on the evening of September 24, he stated that "our personal opinions" about the *Brown* decision "have no bearing on the matter of enforcement" and that "in the present case, the troops are there . . . solely for the purpose of preventing interference with the orders of the court." He also stressed that the "proper use of powers of the executive branch to enforce the orders of a federal court is limited to extraordinary circumstances," but added that the "very basis of our individual rights and freedoms rests upon the certainty that the President and the executive branch" will support federal courts "when necessary, with all the means at the President's command." In closing the president commented on the international implications of the Little Rock episode.

At a time when we face grave situations abroad because of the hatred that Communism bears toward a system of government based on human rights, it would be difficult to exaggerate the harm that is being done to the prestige and influence—and, indeed, to the safety—of our nation and the world. Our enemies are gloating over this incident and using it everywhere to misrepresent our whole nation. [60]

The use of federal troops in Little Rock immediately provoked

[58] *Race Relations L. Reporter,* 2: 963-964 (1957).
[59] *Ibid.,* pp. 964-965.
[60] *U.S. News and World Report,* 43: 64-65 (October 4, 1957); Record and Record, *op. cit.,* pp. 65-66. On the international implications and repercussions of the episode see also Anthony Sampson, "Little Rock and Johannesburg," *Nation,* 188: 23 (1959); Max Ascoli, "Central High and Quemoy," *The Reporter,* 19: 12 (No. 4, 1958).

a torrent of invective and criticism in the South. Some Southern states went so far as to pass legislation designed to prevent or at least discourage future military intervention by the federal government within their boundaries. In October 1957, a resolution of the Florida legislature memorialized Congress to censure the president for the use of federal military forces in Little Rock and to outlaw such use in the future, claiming that the intervention was "reminiscent of Hitler's storm troopers" and an act "indelibly impressing upon the minds and hearts" of school children "the imprint of Fascism and military arrogance." A very different brand of ideological parentage was discerned by the Georgia lawmakers. In a resolution of January, 1958, the general assembly of Georgia censured the president's action, charging that "in so doing the President sacrificed the honesty and integrity of our highest executive office on an altar of political expediency to appease the NAACP and other radical, communist-sympathizing organizations." A House resolution of the Texas legislature of December 2, 1957, contained the following admonition:

That, in order that there be no misunderstanding as to the desires of the Legislature of the State of Texas in regard to the military occupation of the public schools of this state, the President of the United States be advised that the Legislature of the State of Texas requests that he desist and refrain from sending Federal troops into Texas.[61]

The legislatures of Florida, Texas, Mississippi and Virginia also passed laws at the time authorizing the governor of the state or local school boards to close any public schools where federal troops are stationed or which are faced with the threat of federal military intervention.[62]

The legal arguments used by the opponents of the president's action were for the most part not very solid or persuasive. Governor Faubus himself struck the pose of a "defender" of the federal constitution and charged that the military intervention was in violation of constitutional provisions. In attempting to substantiate this charge, the governor did not display particular legal sagacity. The order federalizing the National Guard was portrayed as a violation of the Second Amendment according to which "a

[61] For these state resolutions see *Race Relations L. Reporter,* 2: 1171 (1957); also vol. 3, pp. 97, 357 (1958).
[62] *Ibid.,* vol. 2, p. 1149 (1957); vol. 3, pp. 87, 341 (1958).

well regulated militia, being necessary to the security of a free state . . . shall not be infringed." [63] The governor had apparently not noticed the provisions of the constitution which entitle Congress to call forth the militia and designate the president as the commander-in-chief of the militia in such instances. The presence of federal troops in Little Rock was claimed to conflict with the Third Amendment which prevents the quartering of soldiers in time of peace without consent—although the amendment adds that such military action is possible if supported by law. Somewhat less facetious arguments were advanced by the attorney general of Georgia, Eugene Cook. In a memorandum to the governor of his state, the attorney general contended that intervention of federal troops was only possible by request of the governor of the state or the state legislature and that the order to federalize the national guard had to be issued "through" the state governor. The memorandum also asserted that the dispatching of troops violated the Posse Comitatus Act of 1878 which prohibited the use of the military as a *posse comitatus* or otherwise to execute the laws. Even if it was assumed that the president still possessed the authority to employ troops to enforce the "laws of the United States," such "laws"—according to the attorney general—were only acts of Congress and not court decisions; moreover, the authority extended only to "state action" and not, as in the Little Rock case, to the agitation of private individuals. The attorney general concluded that the president's power to enforce court orders through military intervention, provided it had ever existed, had in any event been repealed by the Civil Rights Act of 1957; since that time, authority to enforce court orders rested exclusively with federal marshals.[64]

From a review of these and similar attacks on the president's action it is possible to distill four or five major objections which deserve consideration: the contentions that the president was prohibited from sending troops into the state without the gover-

[63] "Address of Governor Orval Faubus," *Mississippi L. J.*, 30: 520, 524 (1959).

[64] Memorandum of October 17, 1957; *Race Relations L. Reporter*, 2: 1206 (1957). The arguments were reiterated by the general assembly of Georgia in January of 1958; *ibid.*, vol. 3, p. 357 (1958). For similar arguments see R. Carter Pittman, "The Federal Invasion of Arkansas in the Light of the Constitution," *Georgia Bar J.*, 20: 325 (1958).

nor's request; that his intervention conflicted with the Posse
Comitatus Act, the Civil Rights Act of 1957, and the requirement
of "state action"; and that his authority is limited to acts of Congress. None of these arguments present a serious challenge to the
president's action, although some are more complicated and
thought-provoking than others. The first contention can be dismissed rather easily. The constitutional provision which stipulates
the invitation by the governor or the state legislature refers only
to cases where the federal government protects a state against
domestic violence. The provision has been implemented by a congressional statute dating back to the Militia Act of 1792 which
requires a request on the part of the legislature or governor of the
state before the president may intervene to suppress a revolt
against a state government. The factual conditions of the statute
were not present in the Little Rock case; nor was the provision
invoked by the president in support of his action. In both his
proclamation and the executive order, the president recited as
authority "the Constitution of the United States" and several sections of the United States Code. The pertinent clauses of the
constitution were obviously the provisions which describe the
president as the "Commander-in-Chief of the Army and Navy of
the United States, and of the militia of the several states" and
which enjoin him to "take care that the laws be faithfully executed." The sections of the federal code permit the president to
send troops when disorders "make it impracticable to enforce the
laws . . . by the ordinary course of judicial proceedings" or when
conditions exist which hinder or obstruct the execution of the
laws and which result in the inability or unwillingness of state
authorities to protect a constitutional right. Before calling out the
militia or the armed forces, the president is required to order the
insurgents by proclamation "to disperse and retire peaceably to
their abodes within a limited time." [65]

The argument based on the Posse Comitatus Act of 1878 can
have validity only if this act somehow abrogated the statutory

[65] 10 U.S.C. 332, 333, 334 (1958). On the history of these sections see
Pollitt, *op. cit.*, pp. 122-131; also Robert H. Elliott, Jr. and Richard I. Singer,
"Use of Troops to Enforce Federal Laws," *Michigan L. Rev.*, 56: 249, 260-
261(1957). The legal basis of the president's action is further explained in
an opinion by Attorney General Herbert Brownell of November 7, 1957;
41 Ops. Att'y Gen. 67 (1957).

authority invoked by the president in his proclamation and executive order. The act which, as indicated, prevents the use of the armed forces as a *posse comitatus* is a result of the historical requirement that the president issue a proclamation prior to dispatching the troops. Since the proclamation requirement tended to render military intervention ineffective due to the prior notice of the arrival of troops, federal marshals—acting pursuant to an opinion of Attorney General Cushing [66]—resorted to the device of summoning not only private citizens but also the armed forces to act as a *posse comitatus*. The practice soon led to excesses and, in 1878, Congress passed the Posse Comitatus Act to stop this evasion of the proclamation requirement. However, both the legislative history and the language of the act make it clear that the framers did not intend to interfere with the regular power of the president to employ troops. Referring to then existing legislation authorizing military intervention by the president, one of the sponsors of the act stated that the proposed bill "does not conflict with that." [67] As passed by the House, the bill made it unlawful to use the armed forces as a *posse comitatus* except as "expressly authorized by act of Congress." In the Senate, the proviso was further expanded to read "except in cases and under circumstances expressly authorized by the Constitution or act of Congress." The words "by the Constitution" were inserted so that "the Executive would not be embarrassed by the prohibition" of the act.[68] In this form, the bill was passed by Congress and is still in effect today. Consequently, the president's action in the Little Rock crisis was clearly within the exceptions stipulated in the act.[69]

The reference by the president's opponents to the Civil Rights Act of 1957 [70] does not rest on a more solid foundation. It is true that the 1957 act repealed a statutory provision dating back to the civil rights legislation of the reconstruction period which empowered the president to employ the armed forces to aid in the execution of judicial process issued under the reconstruction legis-

[66] 6 Ops. Att'y Gen. 466 (1854).

[67] 7 Cong. Rec. 3849 (1878).

[68] *Ibid.*, pp. 3856, 4648.

[69] 18 U.S.C. 1385 (1958); see Faust, *op. cit.*, p. 368; Elliott and Singer, *op. cit.*, pp. 262-263; and 41 Ops. Att'y Gen. 67 (1957), pp. 18-19.

[70] 71 Stat. 634 (1957), 42 U.S.C. App. 1975a (Supp. 1957).

lation. Since the Civil Rights Act of 1957 was phrased in terms of an amendment to federal code provisions conferring jurisdiction on federal district courts for cases arising under the reconstruction statute, it was noted in Congress that the president would have been entitled to enforce the new act by military intervention in the same manner as the post-Civil War legislation. During the Senate debate, opponents of the new bill soon centered their attack on the aspect of military enforcement. In an effort to clarify the debate, an amendment was introduced by Senators Knowland and Humphrey eliminating the military enforcement provision. However, the introduction of the amendment was merely a strategic device designed to focus attention again on the substantial provisions of the bill [71] and not to remove the president's power to use troops in other civil rights areas not covered by the repealed section. The limited range of the repeal was repeatedly stressed by many Senators and it was with this understanding that the amendment was finally accepted. As Senator Clark observed, he supported the amendment because

independently of the proposed civil rights bill, the President already is vested with ample authority to deploy the Armed Forces to meet concerted popular resistance designed either to obstruct enforcement of judicial process issued pursuant to constitutional and statutory provisions or to interfere with enforcement of statutory law by Federal officers.[72]

According to Senator Lausche, the particular section was repealed "notwithstanding the provisions of the Constitution which give the President the power to enforce judicial decrees when they are resisted by armed revolution or otherwise."[73] These and similar statements demonstrate that the Civil Rights Act of 1957 did not affect other constitutional or statutory authorizations of military intervention.

The most complicated arguments against the president's action involve the Fourteenth Amendment requirement of "state action" and the interpretation of "laws of the United States." Under the terms of the Fourteenth Amendment, the federal government

[71] See 103 Cong. Rec. 11128, 11131 (1957).
[72] *Ibid.*, p. 11130.
[73] *Ibid.* Compare Pollitt, *op. cit.*, pp. 137-138.

may protect civil rights against infringement by state authorities; on numerous occasions the Supreme Court has insisted on the requirement of "state action" as a condition for the enforcement of Fourteenth Amendment rights.[74] In the Little Rock case, federal troops were used to enforce a court decree not against the state but against individual agitators. One possible method of obviating the "state action" requirement has been indicated by the federal court in the previously mentioned Hoxie school case.[75] In that instance the court asserted that the school board had a federal right—apparently conceived as a privilege or immunity of federal citizenship—to be free from interference in the performance of its constitutional duties. It might well be argued that the implementation of a federal court order is accompanied by a similar privilege of citizenship to be free from interference. Other analytical approaches designed to satisfy or bypass the "state action" requirement have been suggested by observers commenting on the Little Rock episode. One approach is predicated upon the proposition that, once a federal court has issued an order against state action, such an order can be protected against obstruction from anyone. The difficulty involved in this line of reasoning is that, on the same basis, a congressional statute could be aimed directly at interference by private individuals, a device which would clearly circumvent the Fourteenth Amendment limitation. Another approach would establish an analogy with Supreme Court rulings advancing the concept that there is a "peace of the United States" which the president is obligated to preserve.[76] Finally, it appears plausible to contend that, in cases where state officials have reason to believe that civil rights are going to be infringed by disorderly crowds, failure of the state to grant protection amounts to state action and a denial of equal protection under the Fourteenth Amendment.

[74] *United States* v. *Harris*, 106 U.S. 629 (1882); *Civil Rights Cases*, 109 U.S. 3 (1883); *Shelley* v. *Kraemer*, 334 U.S. 1 (1948).

[75] *Brewer* v. *Hoxie School District*, 238 F.2d 91 (8th Cir. 1956).

[76] *In re Debs*, 158 U.S. 564 (1895); *In re Neagle*, 135 U.S. 1 (1890); *Ex parte Siebold*, 100 U.S. 371 (1879). "It should be pointed out, however, that in these cases force was used directly against the officers of the United States who were in the process of attempting to execute their duties. In Little Rock no force was directed against the court itself, but against private persons attempting to comply with the court order." Elliott and Singer, *op. cit.*, p. 268.

The constitution directs the president to take care that the "laws" be faithfully executed. The statutory provisions invoked by President Eisenhower in the Little Rock crisis are also aimed at obstructions to the enforcement of the "laws of the United States." In view of the language of these provisions, it is not surprising that the president's decision to dispatch troops to enforce a court decree should have been attacked as an unconstitutional and illegal exercise of power. The attack was ably led by a member of the bar who arrived at what he termed "the inevitable legal conclusion that the President has no power derived from Congress to enforce federal court decrees." Claiming that, in 1957, "there was repealed the only statute in the United States Code giving the President power to use military force 'to aid in the execution of judicial process,'" this particular writer concluded that "under existing congressional legislation, only the U.S. Marshal has power to enforce court decrees." [77] It must be recognized that the argument is not entirely spurious and that, if it were correct, the conclusion that only federal marshals can enforce judicial decrees would seem to impose itself. Nevertheless, there is impressive authority speaking against the argument, authority derived both from the legislative history of pertinent congressional statutes and from Supreme Court rulings. At least one of the existing statutes gives the president the power to use the armed forces in case of disorder which "impedes the course of justice." [78] When this statute was originally passed in Congress in 1871, Senator Edmunds pointed out that the bill would interpose "the calm force of law, through the judiciary, aided by the lawful executive power of the nation" and would

lend the strong arm of the nation to the assistance of the judiciary. . . . Whatever rights are secured to the people . . . must be guaranteed to them and made effectual for them at last through the instrumentality of the national government. . . . When the laws are opposed, when the courts are in danger of being unable to carry out their decrees, to

[77] Alfred J. Schweppe, "Enforcement of Federal Court Decrees: A 'Recurrence to Fundamental Principles'," *American Bar Association J.,* 44: 113, 114, 116 (1958). According to 28 U.S.C. 547 (1958), federal marshals are directed to "execute all lawful writs, processes and orders issued under the authority of the United States and to command all necessary assistance to execute" their duties.

[78] 10 U.S.C. 333(2) (1958).

arrest and punish offenders, the executive arm is to go to their assistance, is to oppose force to force.[79]

The predecessor of a second statute was interpreted by President Washington as imposing on him the obligation also to "uphold the judiciary functions." [80]

Even if the history of the mentioned statutes were inconclusive, the president's power to use troops is derived not only from acts of Congress but also directly from the constitution, an aspect whose significance is increased by the fact that federal activity with respect to Fourteenth Amendment rights does not seem to require prior congressional implementation. One might also mention in this context that, during the Constitutional Convention, James Madison introduced an amendment adding the words "not legislative nor judiciary in their nature" to the clause enjoining the president "to execute the laws." The members of the Convention defeated the amendment,[81] thus apparently rejecting the concept that the president's power does not extend to the "judiciary laws." Major support for the president's action, however, can be found in several Supreme Court decisions which attributed a broad meaning to the term "laws" or "laws of the United States." In 1890, a federal marshal who was assigned to guard Justice Field shot and killed a man threatening the justice's life. After being held for trial on a murder charge by the State of California, the marshal petitioned the federal courts for a writ of habeas corpus. Under then existing legislation, the writ could only be granted to a prisoner "in custody for an act done or committed in pursuance of a law of the United States." Although finding that the marshal's action was probably covered by statutory authority, the Supreme Court held that the phrase "a law of the United States" was not strictly limited to statutes.

In the view we take of the Constitution of the United States, any obligation fairly and properly inferrible from that instrument, or any duty of the marshal to be derived from the general scope of his duties under the laws of the United States, is "a law" within this phrase.[82]

[79] 99 Cong. Globe 695-698 (1871).
[80] See Pollitt, *op. cit.*, p. 127.
[81] Jonathan Elliot, *Debates on the Adoption of the Federal Constitution* (Washington, 1845), vol. 5, pp. 141-142.
[82] *In re Neagle*, 135 U.S. 1, 59 (1890).

In a later case, the Court construed the words "laws of the several states" as including decisions of state courts.[83] Regarding the extent to which the law of the land may be enforced by the president, the Court observed in another context:

The entire strength of the nation may be used to enforce in any part of the land the full and free exercise of all national powers and the security of all rights entrusted by the Constitution to its care.[84]

In the light of these Supreme Court decisions and other evidence, the power of the president to enforce federal court orders through military intervention appears at least "highly probable." [85] In any event, federal courts have not voiced any doubt with respect to this power of the president. In a petition for injunctive relief arising from the president's use of troops in Little Rock, the courts seemed to act on the assumption that the president's authority was not only highly probable but unquestionable. The action which was brought in October of 1957 by the mother of children attending Central High School asked the district court to enjoin the commanding officers of the stationed troops from policing the school, on the grounds that the president's use of troops was unconstitutional. The district court dismissed the petition very curtly, holding that there was no substantial question as to the constitutionality of the president's action. While recognizing that the petition challenged the constitutional validity of the statutes invoked by the president in his proclamation and executive order, the court found that the action presented "no substantial federal constitutional issue . . . since the President's power conferred by these and antecedent federal statutes . . . have been upheld by the Supreme Court of the United States." [86] In the absence of other grounds and evidence, the district court asserted that it had both the right and the duty to dismiss the

---

[83] *Erie Railroad Co.* v. *Tompkins*, 304 U.S. 64 (1938). Schweppe castigates the decision as "wrong" and "inexcusable"; *op. cit.*, p. 190.

[84] *In re Debs*, 158 U.S. 564, 582 (1895); see also *Ex parte Siebold*, 100 U.S. 371, 395 (1879).

[85] Elliott and Singer, *op. cit.*, p. 264.

[86] See *Jackson* v. *Kuhn*, 254 F.2d 555, 558 (8th Cir. 1958). The Supreme Court decisions referred to by the district court were *Martin* v. *Mott*, 12 Wheat. 19 (1827); *Luther* v. *Borden*, 7 How. 1 (1849); *Sterling* v. *Constantin*, 287 U.S. 378 (1932).

petition for lack of jurisdiction. A summary motion to remand the case to the district court for retrial was denied by the federal court of appeals. Without considering the constitutionality of the issues involved, the appellate court later affirmed the dismissal of the petition for the reason that the value of the controversy was insufficient to warrant federal jurisdiction.[87]

Irrespective of the question of constitutional validity, it is possible to question the wisdom and propriety of the president's decision to enforce the integration order through military intervention rather than some other device, such as the use of federal marshals and their deputies. The picture of federal troops with unsheathed bayonets certainly added fuel to segregationist emotions in the South. Despite the fact that the physical power of federal marshals may have been weak in the face of mob violence, the moral impact of law enforcement agents could have been strong and their use could at least have been tested. As one observer stated:

If it can be assumed that the public record tells the essential facts of the crisis in Little Rock, the measure most in harmony with the requirement of constitutionalism would have been the use of United States marshals and their deputies to accompany the Negro children to the school. . . . A lone marshal, standing against a mob, is probably not without dramatic force in the traditions of the Southwest. . . . The dangers to the Federal marshals and the children in such a situation were great, but a public announcement of the consequences of interference followed by the stern presence of a marshal and his carefully deployed deputies should, in this case, have been tried as a suitable constitutional alternative.[88]

Moreover, military intervention should always remain an ultimate remedy reserved to extreme emergencies and, especially in situations where the statutory authority is not entirely beyond question, alternate solutions should first be explored. Apparently sensitive to these considerations, the Justice Department decided in 1958 to use marshals in Little Rock in the event of a recurrence of disturbances. Although the president made it clear at the time that troops would be sent to any part of the South if court orders could not be implemented by other means, Attorney General

[87] *Jackson* v. *Kuhn,* 254 F.2d 555 (8th Cir. 1958).
[88] Longaker, *op. cit.,* pp. 165-166.

Rogers initiated a program under which marshals were deputized and sent to Washington for training in police work and riot control. Also, briefs were prepared in anticipation of court actions and officials in the Justice Department were directed to study and keep in touch with developments in the South.[89] These preparations were later put to good use by the Kennedy administration during the integration disturbances in Alabama and Mississippi.

Returning to the Little Rock episode, it must be observed that the president's intervention was not completely successful in promoting the progressive integration of classes in accordance with the court decrees. On orders of the president, the troops were withdrawn and the guardsmen released from federal duty in May of 1958; but the Little Rock schools remained closed until 1959. Already in February of 1958, the school officials filed a petition in the federal district court alleging that the turmoil created by public opposition to integration made it impossible to maintain a satisfactory educational program. The petition which requested a suspension of the integration plan until January, 1961, was granted by Judge Lemley of the district court in June of 1958. The appellate court promptly reversed the suspension order, but delayed enforcement of its decree to allow further action by the Supreme Court.[90] On September 12, 1958, the Supreme Court upheld the appellate court decision and reinstated the original order requiring integration.[91] On the same day, Governor Faubus ordered the closing of the Little Rock schools and signed several new segregation statutes, including bills permitting the closing of schools and the withholding or transfer of public school funds of the state. A petition by Negro plaintiffs to enjoin the leasing of Central High School to a private corporation was denied by the district court. However, when the school board subsequently authorized the lease of the high school property, the federal court of appeals issued an order restraining the transfer of the school and directing the school board to proceed with the integration plan.[92] In April

[89] *Ibid.*, p. 170; see also John Osborne, "Strategist-in-Chief for Desegregation," *Life*, 47: 123-124 (November 10, 1958).

[90] *Aaron v. Cooper*, 163 F. Supp. 13 (E. D. Ark. 1958), *rev'd*, 257 F.2d 33 (8th Cir. 1958).

[91] "No state legislator or executive or judicial officer can war against the Constitution without violating his undertaking to support it." *Cooper v. Aaron*, 358 U.S. 1, 18 (1958).

[92] *Aaron v. Cooper*, 261 F.2d 97 (8th Cir. 1958).

of 1959, the district court invalidated the segregation statutes
authorizing the closing of schools and the transfer of school funds
which had been cited by school officials as the major obstacles to
integration.[93] The ruling of the lower court was affirmed by the
Supreme Court on December 14, 1959.[94]

3. ALABAMA AND THE "FREEDOM RIDERS"

The field of education is not the only arena in which the battle
between racial discrimination and constitutional equality has been
waged in recent years. Other battle grounds are the areas of vot-
ing rights, housing, employment, transportation, and public facilities such as restaurants, motels, theatres, parks, swimming pools
and golf courses.[95] Among these various areas, only the field of
transportation has so far witnessed a resort to executive emergency powers. This fact is probably more than accidental in view
of the sensitive character of travel arrangements; as Gunnar Myrdal has pointed out some time ago, Jim Crow travel is "resented
more bitterly than most other forms of segregation." [96] Progress
with respect to the desegregation of travel facilities has been slow
and even more arduous than the breakdown of Jim Crow practices
in educational institutions. Apart from deeply entrenched segregation habits and evasive tactics, the haphazard nature of this progress can be traced to constitutional and legal complications. In
examining discriminatory practices in the field of transportation,
federal courts may rely on the principle of federal control over interstate commerce, on equal protection and due process guarantees,
and on congressional legislation including the Interstate Commerce
Act, the Common Carriers Act and pertinent civil rights statutes.
The most important avenues are clearly the commerce clause and
Fourteenth Amendment provisions; but the two approaches are
not coextensive. Federal power under the commerce clause ex-

[93] *Aaron* v. *McKinley,* 173 F. Supp. 944 (E. D. Ark. 1959).

[94] *Faubus* v. *Aaron,* 361 U.S. 197 (1959). For subsequent events involving the Little Rock school see *Aaron* v. *Tucker,* 186 F. Supp. 913 (E. D.
Ark. 1960); *Norwood* v. *Tucker,* 287 F.2d 798 (8th Cir. 1961).

[95] For a recent report on some of these areas see U. S. Commission on Civil
Rights, *1961 United States Commission on Civil Rights Report,* 5 vols.
(Washington, D.C., 1961).

[96] Gunnar Myrdal, *An American Dilemma* (New York, 1944), p. 635.

tends only to transportation between the states and to such intra-state regulations as create an undue burden on interstate travel; on the other hand, conflict with the federal commerce power does not have to originate in state action and may be due entirely to private practices. Federal intervention on the basis of Fourteenth Amendment guarantees regularly requires some form of state action or a discriminatory practice performed under color of state law; however, where these conditions are met, the constitutional protection applies not only to interstate but to any type of local transportation.

As in the field of education, the gradual obliteration of the principle of "separate-but-equal" travel facilities dates back to the New Deal court and the second World War. The first advances were based almost entirely on the commerce clause and on stat-utes relating to interstate commerce. In 1941, the Supreme Court held that railroad passengers may not be denied pullman service, even though it was understood that the maintenance of separate and equal facilities for Negro passengers would entail consider-able expenses for the railroads. Another ruling of the same year established the principle that a state statute imposing an undue burden on interstate transportation—in this case, a California statute regulating the entry of indigent persons—constitutes a violation of the commerce clause.[97] In 1946, the Court applied this principle to bus transportation and decided that a state law could not require a bus company to force interstate Negro passengers to move to the rear and abandon their seats to white passengers.[98] Two years later, the Court held that a railroad company cannot escape the obligation to accord equal treatment to its passengers and shippers either by the use of facilities which it does not own or by contractual arrangements with the owner of such facilities.[99] A decision of 1950 castigated the railroad practice of partitioning off, for exclusive Negro use, one table in each dining car, and the corollary practice of refusing to serve Negro passengers at vacant seats elsewhere in the car. As the Court pointed out, ade-quate dining facilities must be provided on all passenger trains

[97] *Mitchell* v. *United States,* 313 U.S. 80 (1941); *Edwards* v. *California,* 314 U.S. 160 (1941).

[98] *Morgan* v. *Virginia,* 328 U.S. 373 (1946).

[99] *United States* v. *Baltimore and Ohio RR. Co.,* 333 U.S. 169 (1948).

and limited demand by Negroes is no justification for limited facilities.[100]

Following the *Brown* ruling of 1954 which invalidated a segregation doctrine originally formulated with respect to transportation, new efforts were made both by government agencies and federal courts to eliminate discrimination in travel facilities. In November of 1955, the Interstate Commerce Commission ordered the end of discriminatory railroad practices and directed railroad terminals to take down "white" and "colored" signs in waiting rooms. At the same time, the Commission ruled that racial segregation in cars, buses, and waiting rooms of bus terminals was prohibited by the Interstate Commerce Act.[101] In 1956, the Civil Aeronautics Administrator declared that federal aid for airports would not be made available for the construction of separate facilities.[102] On the basis of the Interstate Commerce Commission orders, the Southeastern Greyhound Lines company issued instructions—of a half-hearted nature, to be sure—which provided that intrastate passengers might be "courteously requested to comply with the law of that particular state, but if a passenger refuses to comply, then no further action should be taken" and that "existing signs and separations of waiting rooms and restaurants will be maintained as at present, but station personnel must not take any steps to enforce segregation in the use of these facilities." [103] Also in 1956, the Justice Department called a conference of United States attorneys in the Southern states to explore measures which the department might take in order to insure a more scrupulous observance of constitutional and statutory requirements by common carriers.

Although federal courts were perhaps not always as aggressive as they might have been, court rulings soon reinforced the *Brown* decision and the efforts of federal agencies and officials. Cumula-

[100] *Henderson* v. *United States,* 339 U.S. 816 (1950). For service in air terminal restaurants compare *Nash* v. *Air Terminal Service,* 85 F. Supp. 545 (E. D. Va. 1949).

[101] *NAACP* v. *St. Louis-San Francisco Railway Co.,* 297 I.C.C. 335 (November 7, 1955); *Keys* v. *Carolina Coach Co.,* I.C.C., No. MC-C-1564 (November 7, 1955).

[102] See Daniel H. Pollitt, "The President's Powers in Areas of Race Relations, An Exploration," *North Carolina L. Rev.,* 39: 238, 270 (1961).

[103] Jack Greenberg, *Race Relations and American Law* (New York, 1959), p. 124.

tively, the rulings of federal courts amounted to a broad offensive against discrimination in all types of travel facilities including bus terminals, local or inter-city buses, and air transport.[104] A variety of avenues was used by the courts for purposes of this offensive. In some cases, courts continued to rely on the commerce clause or on congressional legislation relative to interstate transportation. A prominent example was the case of a homeward-bound Negro law student who, in 1958, was charged with trespass and convicted by a police court for refusing to eat in the "colored" portion of a bus terminal restaurant in Richmond, Virginia. In his petition for certiorari, the student charged mainly that the segregation imposed a burden on interstate commerce and violated the equal protection clause of the Fourteenth Amendment. Relying somewhat narrowly on congressional legislation, the Supreme Court ruled that, despite the lack of active operation of the terminal by the bus company, the maintenance of segregated terminal facilities was in conflict with the Interstate Commerce Act.[105] In other instances, federal courts used a bolder and more novel approach and attacked discrimination in travel accommodations with such weapons as the Fourteenth Amendment [106] and pertinent civil rights statutes.[107] When relying on Fourteenth Amendment guarantees or civil rights acts based on these guarantees, court rulings frequently adopted a broad concept of "state action" comprising any kind of discriminatory practice which can be traced to state laws or to an official policy, custom or usage.[108]

Federal attacks on Jim Crow transportation were not received with great enthusiasm in Southern states. In some areas, it is true, compliance with federal law was comparatively swift. Already in

[104] Bus terminals: *Boynton v. Virginia*, 364 U.S. 454 (1960); local buses: *Flemming v. S. C. Electric and Gas Co.*, 224 F.2d 752 (4th Cir. 1955), *appeal dismissed*, 351 U.S. 901 (1956); *Browder v. Gayle*, 142 F. Supp. 707 (M.D. Ala. 1956), *aff'd*, 352 U.S. 903 (1956); air transport: *Fitzgerald v. Pan American World Airlines*, 229 F.2d 499 (2d Cir. 1956).

[105] *Boynton v. Virginia*, 364 U.S. 454 (1960). Compare Louis H. Pollak, "The Supreme Court and the States: Reflections on Boynton v. Virginia," *California L. Rev.*, 49: 15 (1961).

[106] *Browder v. Gayle*, 142 F. Supp. 707 (M.D. Ala. 1956), *aff'd*, 352 U.S. 903 (1956); *Garmon v. Miami Transit Co.*, 151 F. Supp. 953 (S.D. Fla. 1957); *Baldwin v. Morgan*, 287 F.2d 750 (5th Cir. 1961).

[107] *Flemming v. S. C. Electric and Gas Co.*, 224 F.2d 752 (4th Cir. 1955), *appeal dismissed*, 351 U.S. 901 (1956).

[108] E.g., *Boman v. Birmingham Transit Co.*, 280 F.2d 531 (5th Cir. 1960).

1955 all railroads in Arkansas followed the order of the Interstate Commerce Commission and removed segregation signs while, in North Carolina, city buses in Durham and Greensboro ended segregated seating. Other states, however, answered the new challenge with open defiance. Governor Kenon of Louisiana soon announced his intention to resist integration on carriers. During 1956, the legislatures of Georgia, Mississippi and Louisiana passed new laws requiring continued racial segregation in stations and waiting rooms at least for intrastate passengers. The Georgia statute provided that a separate waiting room was to be marked for both interstate and colored intrastate passengers. Under the terms of the Louisiana act, separate waiting facilities were to be maintained for white intrastate and for interstate and Negro intrastate passengers.[109] These and similar acts of defiance possessed as much or as little constitutional validity as the interposition resolutions adopted during the same period; however, they served as dilatory tactics effectively postponing the inevitable change until court action was able to expose their futility. As a result, much litigation was required to overcome state defiance and to eliminate state regulations insisting on segregation. In the course of this litigation, courts progressively invalidated existing segregation statutes and regulations in Florida, Louisiana, Tennessee, Georgia, Mississippi, and other states.

One of the states in which the integration of travel facilities was resisted with particular vehemence and stubbornness was Alabama. Beginning in 1956, the City of Montgomery experienced a protracted boycott conducted by Negroes against the city bus lines. When the bus company showed signs of willingness to change its segregation policy, the city obtained injunctive relief in a state court which declared existing state laws and city ordinances to be a valid exercise of the state police power. The Negroes continued their boycott through the operation of independent car pools sponsored by a number of churches and private individuals. On application to federal courts, discrimination on buses and city transit lines was promptly castigated as unconstitutional;[110] but the court ruling did not immediately improve the

---

[109] *Race Relations L. Reporter*, 1: 428, 430, 741 (1956).

[110] *Browder* v. *Gayle*, 142 F. Supp. 707 (M.D. Ala. 1956), *aff'd*, 352 U.S. 903 (1956).

situation of the Negroes. In November of 1956, a state court issued a restraining order against the operation of special car pools by the Negroes, while a federal district court refused to intervene.[111] In order to evade the charge of "state action," the city subsequently chartered a "private" club to operate buses in Montgomery, presumably on a segregated basis; again, the federal district court declined to rule on the constitutionality of this strategy. Similar developments and incidents occurred in Birmingham. In 1957, two colored interstate passengers were arrested while seated in a waiting room for "interstate and white passengers" of the Birmingham railroad station; the couple's suit for a judgment determining their right to use the waiting room was dismissed by a federal district court.[112] In the same year, the city enacted an ordinance which reaffirmed the prior policy of maintaining racially segregated seating on city buses. When the ordinance was later challenged by a group of Negroes, the city repealed the order and delegated the authority to regulate seating to the bus company. A suit by Negroes who had been arrested and convicted for refusing to comply with segregated seating signs of the company was dismissed by a federal district court on the grounds that the company had acted as a private person; however, the ruling was reversed on appeal.[113]

Federal Marshals in Montgomery

By 1961, the law applicable to travel facilities was fairly well established by government regulations and court rulings. There was no longer any legal ambiguity concerning the constitutional invalidity of segregation statutes or other discriminatory practices in the field of transportation. However, the clarification of legal issues did not deter fanatical segregationists from pursuing their aims and, in the absence of more legitimate weapons, physical violence became the ultimate and only available tool of defiance. On the other hand, with the progressive elimination of legal barriers to integration, Negro groups and their sympathizers de-

[111] *Browder* v. *City of Montgomery*, 146 F. Supp. 127 (M.D. Ala. 1956).
[112] *Baldwin* v. *Morgan*, 149 F. Supp. 224 (N. D. Ala. 1957).
[113] *Boman* v. *Birmingham Transit Co.*, 280 F.2d 531 (5th Cir. 1960). For later developments resulting from demonstrations in Birmingham against bus segregation see *Race Relations L. Reporter*, 7: 114 (1962).

cided to press for the full implementation and realization of their legal and constitutional rights. This background explains the dramatic developments which, under the name of "freedom rides," gripped many parts of the South during 1961 and which were simply an attempt to translate constitutional guarantees and federally sanctioned civil rights into reality.

The violence which, in some states, accompanied the freedom rides shocked many moderate people in the South; it also attracted considerable national and international attention. The international repercussions were particularly serious in 1961 in view of the mounting cold war tensions in South America, Europe and Southeast Asia and in the light of successful strides toward independence in a number of former colonies. Communist news media were quick in utilizing the racial violence for cold war purposes. As one observer pointed out:

The Communist press and radio have been exploiting the shocking incidents to the full, sanctimoniously pointing to American "savagery", ironically questioning whether "we are living in the twentieth century or not", asking "who will believe American propaganda after what has happened in Alabama"?[114]

Reflecting on the implications of the violence for the international position of the United States, another writer attributed to the segregationists "the blame for a battle lost to America's enemies" and observed that "once again the American image was seriously scarred." [115] Nevertheless, the incidents in 1961 were not only significant from the perspective of the cold war struggle. Quite apart from international repercussions, the success or failure of the freedom rides constituted a vital test for domestic constitutional developments. In the words of Eugene Rostov:

The changes required to make the Negro the white man's equal before the law must come. They are coming—not because political forces in the North demand them, nor yet to please public opinion in

[114] "Violence in Alabama," *America*, 105: 388 (June 3, 1961).

[115] "Freedom Riders," *America*, 105: 358 (May 27, 1961). Compare also the following comment: ". . . since the Sino-Soviet challenge is a moral as well as an economic and military one, our defenses are further impaired because our confidence in America's humane and egalitarian character has again been assaulted by Americans." "Law in Alabama," *New Republic,* 144: 3 (May 29, 1961).

Africa and Asia and score a point in the cold war. We are struggling to accomplish these social changes because we know they are right. . . . To solve such conflicts through the methods of peace and persuasion is the ultimate function of law and its ultimate test.[116]

The story of the freedom rides opened in April of 1961 when the Congress of Racial Equality and a number of similar organizations, including the Nashville Non-Violent Movement and the Southern Christian Leadership Conference, began to formulate plans for a series of bus trips through parts of the South. On May 5, a group of white and Negro men and women, all members of the Congress of Racial Equality, left Washington, determined to challenge segregation in buses and bus terminals between Washington and New Orleans.[117] Traveling in a Greyhound and a Trailways bus, the group progressed with only minor incidents through the Carolinas and Georgia. The peaceful character of the trip changed immediately when the buses crossed the Alabama state line. On May 14, near Anniston, Alabama, the "freedom riders" met a mob of Klansmen and their sympathizers who attacked the passengers and set fire to the Greyhound bus. When, later on the same day, the Trailways bus arrived in Birmingham, Klansmen and local "toughs" again assaulted and beat the passengers who had alighted at the Trailways bus terminal. Although the city hall was located close to the terminal, Police Commissioner Connor of Birmingham failed to order police to the scene and to protect the bus travelers from violence.[118] Since, for fear of further attacks, the bus drivers refused to take the freedom riders on to Montgomery, the group was forced to abandon the bus and to return to their homes by plane via New Orleans.

Although the original party was dispersed, the freedom ride through Alabama was not halted by this temporary setback. In the meantime, some members of the Nashville Non-Violent Movement had resolved to join the test ride. Arriving in Birmingham from Tennessee after the departure of the original party, the group challenged segregated facilities at the Greyhound terminal and

[116] Eugene V. Rostov, "The Freedom Riders and the Future," *Reporter*, 24: 18, 21 (June 22, 1961).

[117] For a brief account of the trip see Helen Fuller, "We, the People of Alabama," *New Republic*, 144: 21 (June 5, 1961).

[118] The police commissioner alleged that a large part of the police force was off for Mother's Day; *The New York Times* (May 16, 1961), p. 1, col. 2.

was promptly arrested by city police. After seven members of the Nashville student group were taken by police from jail to the Tennessee border, the students borrowed a car and returned to Birmingham. With rare determination the Nashville group— reinforced by twelve followers of the Martin Luther King movement—on several occasions tried to board buses for Montgomery but failed due to the refusal of bus drivers to man the carriers. Clearly, the continuation of the trip would have been impossible if the White House and the Justice Department had not decided to intervene at this stage. John Siegenthaler, a special representative of the president and the attorney general, was sent to investigate and report on the situation. At the same time, profiting from preparations initiated by his predecessor, the attorney general began to lay plans for swiftly assembling a large force of federal marshals and deputy marshals in case of emergency. After several unsuccessful attempts by the attorney general and the president to reach the state governor on the telephone, Governor Patterson finally in a telegram expressed his willingness to negotiate with a presidential representative. On the night of May 18, John Siegenthaler received the governor's assurance that, without requiring federal assistance, he would fully protect everyone in Alabama including the busload of freedom riders on their way through the state. When, at the governor's suggestion, justice officials notified the Greyhound company of this assurance, the freedom ride was finally able to continue.

The governor's pledge was carried out only in part. On orders of the director of the state's Public Safety Department, Floyd Mann, sixteen highway patrol cars and one airplane were assigned to accompany the bus from Birmingham to the city limits of Montgomery. At the city limits, however, the protection came to an end. Although local police officials had been informed of the impending arrival of the bus and of the likelihood of violence, Police Commissioner Sullivan failed to alert the city police department and even stated that the police "have no intention of standing guard for a bunch of troublemakers." [119] Thus, when the riders arrived at the Greyhound bus terminal on May 20, the station was surrounded by a crowd of Klansmen and other segregationists, but no police were in sight. The crowd immediately

[119] *Ibid.* (May 21, 1961), p. 1, col. 6.

began to attack the passengers and in the course of the ensuing riot and disorder, a number of freedom riders and bystanders were injured by the mob. The president's representative, John Siegenthaler, who tried to rescue a young girl being pursued by attackers, was beaten unconscious and left on the street for nearly half an hour. Local police forces arrived more than an hour after the outbreak of the riot. In addition to the mob violence, the riders were greeted by the legal arm of the state. Already on the preceding day, a county court, acting on a petition of the attorney general of the state, had issued a broad injunction against the freedom riders. In the morning hours of May 20, the same judge had issued a contempt citation against twenty of the riders charging them with willful violation of the injunction. When the bus arrived in Montgomery, Attorney General Gallion of Alabama went from the police station to the bus terminal and served a copy of the state court injunction on one of the riders who had already been beaten by the mob.

While the freedom riders were thus forsaken by state and local government officials, federal authorities came to the rescue of the mistreated group and of constitutional rights in general. Already on the day of the group's arrival in Montgomery, a federal district court issued a temporary restraining order enjoining the Klansmen and their sympathizers from interfering with interstate commerce in Alabama and from committing any acts of violence upon interstate passengers.[120] However, the issuance of a mere restraining order was clearly insufficient in the face of open defiance of federal law and in the absence of adequate strength to enforce the court order. As racial tensions continued to mount in the city and posed the threat of renewed violence, Attorney General Robert Kennedy, on May 21, sent some four hundred deputy marshals to Montgomery, led by Deputy Attorney General Byron White. On the same day, President Kennedy in a White House statement deplored the mob attacks and urged Governor Patterson and other state officials to curb further outbreaks of violence. In telegrams to the governor and the mayors of Birmingham and Montgomery, the attorney general explained that his and the president's decision to send federal marshals was based on the need to restore order and to "guarantee safe passage in interstate com-

[120] For the text of the order see *Race Relations L. Reporter*, 6: 529 (1961).

merce." [121] The attorney general also announced his intention to ask the federal district court for a regular injunction—in analogy to the *Debs* ruling of 1895—restraining the Ku Klux Klan and similar organizations from disrupting interstate bus travel.

The purpose of the federal intervention was clear, and so was its legal and constitutional basis. As Byron White pointed out at his arrival in Montgomery, the federal marshals were to be active in a supporting role in aid of local police with the task of safe-guarding federal rights and maintaining the free flow of interstate transportation. To be sure, Governor Patterson and other state officials were not very pleased with the presence of marshals in Montgomery. Repeatedly, the governor charged that the federal agents were unwanted and unnecessary and that state forces were able to keep order in the city; on some occasions he even expressed the view that the federal government had no legal right to inter-vene in Alabama. The "legal objections" to the federal action were formulated more elaborately by the state attorney general, Mac-Donald Gallion.[122] These and similar charges were without merit. The dispatching of federal marshals was a politically prudent move and as such escaped the vehement Southern vituperation which had been heaped upon President Eisenhower during the Little Rock crisis; the action was also clearly within the authority of the federal government. It is probably correct that state forces might have been able to maintain order; but the fact is that, in this particular instance, state and local authorities failed to fulfill their constitutional obligations. Under congressional legislation dating back practically to the beginning of the Republic, federal marshals are entitled to lend their assistance to federal courts whenever the enforcement of court orders is obstructed or frus-trated. As one observer commented at the time:

There are no legal complications or even the slightest doubt about prophylactic action. Federal marshals stand ready to protect—as state authorities refused to do—the enjoyment of federal rights. . . . This is all deeply regrettable, but it is unavoidable in the circumstances and within the President's authority.[123]

[121] For the text of the president's statement and the telegram to Governor Patterson see *The New York Times* (May 21, 1961), p. 78, col. 5.

[122] See *ibid.* (May 23, 1961), p. 1, col. 6.

[123] "Law in Alabama," *New Republic*, 144: 3 (May 29, 1961).

Declaration of "Martial Law"

The task which awaited the federal marshals at their arrival in Montgomery was not an easy one, as Klansmen and other segregationists could hardly be assumed to respect the authority of federal law officers. Tempers flared high and the city resembled a powder keg whose explosion could be touched off by a minor incident. In the evening of May 21, a peaceful group of Negroes gathered in the First Baptist Church to hear the Reverend Martin Luther King and other ministers including the Reverends Albernathy and Shuttlesworth. The Reverend King and his friends and supporters had come to town earlier on the same day at the time of the arrival of the federal marshals. Soon after the opening of the church rally, a large crowd of segregationists began to flock to the area. The federal marshals immediately threw a cordon around the church, determined to protect the members of the rally; but the crowd was in no mood to distinguish between marshals and integrationists or between ministers and laymen. A howling mob of club-swinging and rock-throwing "toughs" soon attacked the cordon of federal marshals and threatened to set the church building on fire. It was at this stage of developments that Governor Patterson decided to declare martial law in Montgomery and to dispatch units of the Alabama national guard to the scene of the church rally. The combined strength of marshals and national guardsmen was able to push back the rioters and to prevent them from storming the church. Nevertheless, in the face of continued threats against guardsmen and marshals, the adjutant general of Alabama advised the Negroes to remain in church for the rest of the night.

The imposition of "martial rule" by the state governor was a belated attempt to demonstrate the ability of state forces to maintain order. The declaration itself was a strange patch-work full of contradictions and inconsistencies. The text of the proclamation entirely misrepresented the reasons of the violence and made it clear that, even at this stage, the governor was little concerned with the protection of federal rights. Although the disorders had obviously been provoked by fanatical segregationists, the opening statement of the declaration asserted that "as a result of outside agitators coming into Alabama to violate our laws and customs, outbreaks of lawlessness and mob action have occurred in Anniston, Birmingham and Montgomery" and that "the federal government has by its actions encouraged these agitators to come into Alabama to foment disorders and breaches of the peace." As a result of these "agitators," the declaration alleged that

there now exists in the City of Montgomery, Alabama, a serious emergency, a defiance of the constitution and laws of Alabama, a state of lawlessness, a breach of the peace, and there is continued and imminent danger thereof, which the local peace officers are unable to subdue.[124]

Thus, while the governor previously through words, actions and his failure to protect the freedom riders had encouraged the acts of violence, his proclamation now depicted the disorders blandly as a "defiance of the constitution and laws of Alabama." On either occasion, the governor displayed a callous disregard of the federal constitution and logical reasoning. The character of the militia intervention also was ambiguous and contradictory. According to the declaration the state chief executive, "as governor of Alabama and commander of the Alabama National Guard," proclaimed "a state of qualified martial rule" in the city and county of Montgomery. At the same time, however, the governor instructed the adjutant general "to assist and supplement the local peace officers" of the city and county and the state highway patrolmen. The latter instruction as well as subsequent developments indicated that the task of the troops was to act strictly in support of regular civil authorities. Under these circumstances, a declaration of "martial rule"—qualified or otherwise—was entirely unnecessary.[125]

[124] For the text of the declaration see *The New York Times* (May 22, 1961), p. 26, col. 2.

[125] A "modified" form of martial law in connection with racial disturbances was also imposed on two occasions in Cambridge, Maryland, during the summer of 1963. The first resort to martial rule occurred from June 14 to July 8 as a result of integration demonstrations which threatened to break into open racial warfare; when violence erupted again in the course of a sit-in demonstration at a restaurant, martial rule was restored and national guard troops were again ordered into Cambridge on July 12. "Modified" martial law was apparently used in view of Maryland's Declaration of Rights which prohibits the exercise of full military control over civilian government and courts under martial law. The martial law proclamation of Governor J. Millard Tawes of June 14 gave to the national guard commander "as his

Following the declaration of "martial law," there were at least three different law enforcement agencies in Montgomery. Local police and guardsmen functioned in close collaboration, while relations between these two authorities and the federal marshals were strained. Officers of the national guard sometimes proposed or directed the detention of integrationists, but the arrests were regularly made by local police officers. On May 24, the freedom riders who had arrived on May 20 went to the Trailways bus terminal in Montgomery, boarded a bus and departed for Jackson, Mississippi. A heavy convoy of national guardsmen accompanied the group which, on its arrival in Jackson, was promptly arrested for attempting to enter a white rest room and restaurant. On the following day, another group of whites and Negroes—some of whom had recently arrived in the city—approached the white lunch counter in the Trailways bus terminal in Montgomery and was arrested and jailed by the county sheriff under instructions from the national guard commander, General Graham. The arrest warrants regularly charged that the individual integrationist came

into Montgomery, Alabama, which was subject to martial rule and did willfully and intentionally attempt to test segregation laws and customs by seeking service at a public lunch counter with a racially mixed group, during a period in which it was necessary for his own safety for him to be protected by military and police personnel and when the said lunch counter building was surrounded by a large number of hostile citizens of Montgomery.[126]

The arrested group, together with counsel for some of the freedom riders, immediately brought action in the federal district court asking for injunctive relief against racial segregation on bus facilities, against the enforcement of the state court order including contempt proceedings, and against criminal prosecutions in state courts

---

judgment shall require" the equivalent "authority of sheriffs, police officers and other civil authorities," but added the ambiguous clause that he might "if necessary take entire charge of the situation." *The New York Times* (June 15, 1963), p. 9, col. 1. In both instances, the guard forces maintained a strictly neutral position and acted in support of and in close collaboration with state and local police in the enforcement of evening curfews and of prohibitions to carry firearms, sell liquor or stage further racial demonstrations. Compare *Time*, 82:17-18 (July 19, 1963), p. 10 (August 2, 1963).

[126] See *Race Relations L. Reporter*, 6: 1155, n.4 (1961).

While guardsmen and local police thus acted in unison with the aim of enforcing state and local segregation orders, the federal marshals were placed in a precarious and uncomfortable position, at least in the absence of additional federal court action. With growing impatience, Governor Patterson on several occasions urged the withdrawal of the marshals; in one instance he even stated that the federal agents would be arrested and jailed if they tried to exert authority before local officials requested their assistance.[127] This extravagant statement has justly been described as "an absurd and empty threat," in view of the marshals' "well-established legal status;"[128] moreover, the state of Alabama, through its director of the Public Safety Department, had in fact requested federal help in restoring order shortly after the arrival of the marshals. In any event, the federal government and its agents were not intimidated or deterred by the unsympathetic attitude of state officials. When it became obvious that continued disorders might require a strengthening of federal forces, Attorney General Kennedy, on May 23, sent two hundred additional marshals into Alabama, emphasizing that the federal government would take "whatever action is necessary" in order to safeguard federal rights. Although the marshals were soon withdrawn from the city of Montgomery, they remained stationed nearby, ready on call for any emergency. The Justice Department also was in no hurry to withdraw the marshals during subsequent weeks. Reminding the state officials that actions and not only words were needed in law enforcement, the attorney general pledged to leave his agents in Alabama as long as federal rights were in jeopardy. On the basis of this pledge, some of the federal marshals actually remained in the Montgomery area longer than the national guardsmen of the state. While "martial rule" was terminated by the governor on May 29, the last marshals left Alabama on June 3.

The day before the departure of the last federal agents, the federal district court had acted on the petition of the Justice Department for injunctive relief against the Klansmen and other defendants. After reviewing the previous developments in Alabama, and especially the events of May 20 in Montgomery, the court in its order of June 2 utilized all available constitutional

---

[127] *The New York Times* (May 22, 1961), p. 1, col. 8.
[128] Rostov, *op. cit.*, p. 20.

weapons in order to end the obstruction of federal law. Noting that the action had been brought by the United States to insure the free movement of interstate commerce and the exercise of federal power over such commerce, the district court referred with approval to the *Debs* ruling of 1895 whose language was termed "particularly applicable" to the situation at hand. From the commerce clause, the order proceeded to a consideration of the equal protection and due process clauses of the constitution. As the court stated, the failure of local police officers

to enforce the law in this case clearly amounts to unlawful state action in violation of the Equal Protection Clause of the Fourteenth Amendment. The fact that this action was of a negative rather than an affirmative character is immaterial.[129]

The court also found that the inaction of the local police department invaded the rights of the freedom riders without due process of law, on the grounds that "the right of a passenger to travel in commerce is a right of citizenship which cannot be deprived without due process of law under the Fifth Amendment to the Constitution of the United States." On the basis of these constitutional arguments, the court issued the requested injunction against the Klansmen, together with an additional injunction prohibiting Montgomery city officials from refusing to provide protection for interstate passengers. Stating that the sponsors of the freedom rides were also causing an undue burden on interstate commerce, the court on the same day issued a temporary order restraining them from sponsoring or encouraging test trips through Alabama. The latter order, however, was allowed to die on June 12 because of a technical error.[130]

Later in the year, the same court granted relief to those freedom riders and other integrationists who had been arrested or threatened with criminal proceedings in state courts for their actions between May 20 and 25 in Montgomery. In their petition for relief, the plaintiffs had asserted that the segregation policy of the state violated the Common Carriers Act, the commerce clause of

[129] *United States* v. *U.S. Klans et al.*, 194 F. Supp. 897, 902 (M.D. Ala. 1961).

[130] For the text of the injunctions, restraining order, and additional orders of June 8 see *Race Relations L. Reporter*, 6: 537-542 (1961).

the constitution and, as a practice under color of state law, the equal protection and due process clauses of the Fourteenth Amendment. The federal district court, in its decision of November 1, affirmed the validity of all these charges. Basing itself on a large amount of evidence and testimony, the court found that racial segregation was an established practice in Montgomery and that the bus companies had maintained segregated facilities, even if they had not directly enforced segregation. Since the Common Carriers Act prohibited carriers from subjecting passengers to "any unjust discrimination or any undue or unreasonable prejudice or disadvantage in any respect whatsoever," the segregation practice was clearly illegal. The court also noted that, at the request of the attorney general, the Interstate Commerce Commission—on September 22, 1961—had adopted new regulations prohibiting discrimination on interstate buses and in bus terminals, regulations which were violated by the maintenance of segregated facilities in Montgomery.[131] Apart from federal statutes and regulations, the court relied on the invoked constitutional provisions. Finding that "the policy, practice, custom and usage which the carriers are following is an official policy, practice, custom and usage of the State of Alabama," the court ruled that the practice constituted "state action" in violation of the Fourteenth Amendment. Since any state effort to regulate seating arrangements of interstate passengers on a racial basis contravened "the need for national uniformity in the regulation of interstate commerce," the practice also was in conflict with the commerce clause. In agreement with these findings, the court issued an order enjoining the continuation of racial segregation on buses and bus terminals and restraining state officers from enforcing segregation through arrests, contempt proceedings or other criminal prosecutions.[132]

Apart from the exploits of the freedom riders, the successful inroads on Jim Crow travel in many parts of the South must be attributed in large measure to the painstaking efforts of federal courts to strike down both open defiance and evasive tactics. In February of 1962, the Supreme Court of the United States was able to observe: "We have settled beyond question that no state

[131] For these new regulations see *ibid.*, p. 902; compare also "I.C.C. Should Act to Protect Travelers," *Christian Century*, 78: 732 (June 14, 1961).

[132] *Lewis* v. *Greyhound Corporation*, 199 F. Supp. 210 (M.D. Ala. 1961).

may require racial segregation on interstate or intrastate transportation facilities. . . . The question is no longer open; it is
foreclosed as a litigable issue." [133] In the Montgomery episode,
however, a considerable and perhaps major part of the credit must
go to the prudent preparations and determined actions of the Justice Department and the president. In past years the presidency
had sometimes lent its force but not always its prestige and persuasion to advances in the field of federally protected civil rights. Yet,
in the absence of the president's personal support, rash emergency
actions are hardly sufficient to promote the rights of disadvantaged
groups. Presidential endorsement, on the other hand, coupled
with a determination to back up this expressed conviction, cannot
fail to exercise a powerful influence on social developments. To
conclude with a comment by Eugene Rostov:

This, I think, is the significance of the Freedom Riders' protest. It would
be a mistake to think of the Freedom Rides as a call to eliminate racial
segregation at lunch counters and toilets in bus terminals. They are
part of a more general demand for human dignity in the wide range
of social situations, North and South, beyond the immediate reach of
the national government. To meet this demand, the President must
function not only as the Chief Executive, faithfully enforcing the
Federal code, but also as the occupant of Theodore Roosevelt's "bully
pulpit", speaking to and for the conscience of America.[134]

4. BARNETT AND WALLACE VERSUS THE UNITED STATES

The Montgomery episode was an illustration of what may be
achieved by the federal government during racial disorders without resort to armed force. The lesson of the Little Rock crisis had
apparently been learned and the disturbances were handled by
regular police authorities and law enforcement agents, especially
by a strong contingent of federal marshals and deputy marshals.
Obviously, the use of federal court officers is preferable in every
respect to military intervention and better adapted to the maintenance of civil government and constitutional safeguards. Nevertheless, despite the general desirability of the Montgomery
procedure, resort to military force may not always be avoidable.

[133] *Bailey* v. *Patterson*, 369 U.S. 33 (1962). The case originated in the
"freedom riders" incidents in Jackson, Mississippi.
[134] Rostov, *op. cit.*, p. 20.

While sufficient and proper in all regular situations and even in less than catastrophic emergencies, reliance on civil agents may on occasion prove inadequate in the face of overpowering opposition to law enforcement or other severe crisis conditions. In such extreme emergencies—and only in such instances—the executive branch of the federal government appears justified in using military power as an ultimate weapon, after all other remedies have been explored and exhausted. These considerations and principles were demonstrated in two of the most dramatic challenges to the federal union since the Civil War: the race riots at the University of Mississippi in the fall of 1962 and the Tuscaloosa incident of June, 1963.

The Oxford crisis was shocking and extremely deplorable from every point of view, but it was not entirely surprising or unexpected. Mississippi had always been considered as one of the staunchest citadels of segregation in the deep South; among other state colleges, the University of Mississippi was viewed by state officials as an ideal training ground for segregationist leadership. As a result, there was hardly any other state in the South in which the *Brown* decision of 1954 was received with more intense hostility. Instead of implementing the Supreme Court mandate of "deliberate speed," state officials from the very beginning exercised extreme vigilance in order to discourage any moderate or "soft" policies at public schools and colleges and especially at the University of Mississippi. In 1956, an angry state legislator prodded the university to cancel the appearance of a speaker who had made a donation to the National Association for the Advancement of Colored People. Following the adoption of a discriminatory speakers' policy by the university, twenty leading faculty members resigned during the summer of 1956; they were followed in 1957 by eleven more teachers. During the following years, academic freedom remained one of the most sensitive, unsettled issues at "Ole Miss." In 1961, a student editor at the university who had covered several lunch counter sit-ins in Atlanta came under heavy attack from state officials and white citizens' councils for alleged "subversive tendencies."[135]

Attempts by Negroes to enroll at the University of Mississippi

[135] For these background events see *Milwaukee Journal* (September 16, 1962), p. 14, col. 3-5.

were resisted by state officials with all means at their command. When in 1958 a former Negro teacher tried to register at "Ole Miss," state officials speedily took him into custody and had him committed to a mental institution. After having been declared sane by a state judge, the Negro applicant preferred to leave Mississippi instantly.[136] In the face of these obstacles and harassments, several Negroes turned to federal courts in order to secure compliance with the *Brown* decision. Among this number was James Meredith, an air force veteran and former student at a Negro state college in Jackson, Mississippi. Although his application for admission had been filed in January of 1961, it was not until the fall of 1962 that Meredith obtained the full backing of federal courts for his enrollment. In the course of the legal battle before the fifth circuit court of appeals, the state attempted to attack the mental stability of the applicant by introducing an air force psychiatric report showing that Meredith was "extremely concerned" with racial problems. Ruling against the state, the court observed that a "nervous stomach" was an understandable reaction among Negroes and, on June 25, 1962, ordered the admission of Meredith to the university.[137] The order of the appellate court was implemented on September 13 by the federal district court which also barred any interference from state and university officials.

The reaction of Mississippi officials to the court rulings was one of open defiance. Immediately after the issuance of the district court order, Governor Ross Barnett invoked the discredited doctrine of interposition to prevent desegregation of the university. Stating that Mississippi faced its "greatest crisis" since the Civil War, the governor directed state officials to go to jail rather than obey federal court decrees. In the words of the governor:

Our state has become the keystone in the fight for states' rights. The day of expediency is past. . . . I hereby direct each official to uphold and enforce the laws duly and legally enacted by the legislature of the

[136] *Ibid.* (September 20, 1962), p. 3, col. 2.
[137] *Meredith* v. *Fair*, 306 F.2d 374 (5th Cir. 1962); on October 8 the Supreme Court denied certiorari, 371 U.S. 828 (1962). See also *Meredith* v. *Fair*, 199 F.Supp. 754 (S.D.Miss. 1961), 202 F.Supp. 224 (S.D.Miss. 1962), *aff'd*, 298 F.2d 696 (5th Cir. 1962), 305 F.2d 341 (5th Cir. 1962), *rev'd*, 305 F.2d 343, 356-357 (5th Cir. 1962). Compare *Race Relations L. Reporter*, 6: 1028 (1961), and vol. 7, pp. 70, 423, 437, 739-765 (1962).

State of Mississippi, regardless of this unwarranted, illegal and arbitrary usurpation of power, and to interpose the state sovereignty and themselves between the people of the state and any body politic seeking to usurp such power.[138]

Subsequently, various other proclamations and directives were issued by Governor Barnett in opposition to the integration mandate. One of these directives ordered that a large number of state and local policemen be sent to Oxford, the site of the university, in order to preserve "peace" and to prevent the admission of Meredith. The governor also directed the trustees of the university to appoint him temporary registrar so that he could personally reject Meredith's application. On September 20, the legislature of Mississippi adopted a resolution fervently supporting the governor in his actions.

The legal barriers established by the state against Meredith's admission were promptly hurdled with a temporary injunction by the federal court of appeals. Despite the restraining order, however, the state persisted in its defiance. On September 20, Meredith—accompanied by three federal officials—made his first attempt to enroll at the university. At this time, Governor Barnett was on hand and, acting as registrar, personally refused to admit the applicant. Under a chorus of boos and catcalls from some 2,000 students gathered on the campus, Meredith and the federal officials left the university. The Justice Department immediately brought action in federal courts asking for contempt citations against the board of trustees and top university officials. In court hearings the university leaders were subsequently cleared of contempt charges, while the board of trustees promised to comply with the federal desegregation order. Upon receiving the board's promise, the federal court of appeals on September 24 instructed university officials as to the actions they were required to take in the admission dispute. The court also issued a sweeping restraining order prohibiting Governor Barnett and a large number of state, county and city officials from interfering with the registration. Unimpressed by this order, the governor and state officials remained adamant. On September 24, Governor Barnett issued an executive order directing the state police to arrest and jail

[138] *Milwaukee Journal* (September 14, 1962), p. 1, col. 4.

any federal officer who tried to arrest or fine a state official in connection with the integration conflict.[139] On the following day, the governor personally prevented Meredith from registering at the office of the board of trustees in Jackson. On September 26, Meredith and a small group of federal marshals were turned away at the gates of the Oxford campus by the lieutenant governor of the state and by a massed array of state and local police officers. A fourth attempt at enrollment, scheduled for September 27, was called off at the last moment because of the likelihood of extreme violence and bloodshed.

In the face of these acts of rebellion against the authority of the United States, the federal government began to explore stronger methods for securing state compliance. At the request of the Justice Department, the federal court of appeals instituted proceedings against the governor ordering him to show cause why he should not be held in contempt.[140] On September 27, the Justice Department ordered several hundred additional marshals to proceed to Memphis to augment the small contingent which had accompanied Meredith on previous occasions. At the same time, the federal government made preparations for another registration attempt on September 30. A detachment of Army engineers was sent to Memphis, ostensibly to give logistic support to the federal marshals, but possibly to serve as a reminder of military preparedness. The determined attitude of the federal government and the stubborn defiance of state officers conjured up the possibility of an armed clash between federal and state forces. In a telegram to the White House, seven congressmen from Mississippi claimed that "the highest state of heat and tension prevails" in the state and that a "holocaust is in the making."[141]

On the eve of the scheduled enrollment date, President Kennedy repeatedly contacted Governor Barnett appealing for the maintenance of law and order in the desegregation crisis; in an urgent telegram, the president asked to be informed as to the intended actions of the governor and state law-enforcement offi-

[139] For the text of the executive order see *Current History*, 43: 307 (November, 1962). The governor also obtained a state court order restraining university officials from enrolling Meredith and forbidding Meredith from seeking enrollment.
[140] For the text of the court order see *ibid.*, pp. 307-308.
[141] *Milwaukee Journal* (September 29, 1962), p. 3, col. 2.

cials during future integration attempts.[142] Under the impact of
federal preparations and pending court actions, Governor Barnett
expressed his willingness to admit Meredith and federal marshals
to the campus on the following day; he also indicated that police
protection might be available, but the latter promise was not
sufficiently specific. Finding that the governor's assurances were
unsatisfactory, President Kennedy in the night of September
29-30 issued a proclamation reciting that, in view of "unlawful
assemblies, combinations and conspiracies," a state of emergency
existed in Mississippi and that the enforcement of federal court
orders "by the ordinary course of judicial proceedings" had become impracticable. This proclamation was implemented, in the
early morning hours, by an executive order authorizing the Secretary of Defense "to use such of the armed forces of the United
States as he may deem necessary" and to call into active federal
service "any or all" of the Mississippi National Guard units. The
order cited as legal basis for this action the federal constitution
and basically the same sections of the federal code which had
been invoked by President Eisenhower during the Little Rock
crisis.[143]

Despite the mobilization of troop units and the federalization
of the National Guard, the federal government was by no means
anxious to use the troops and was still hopeful that federal marshals and regular police might be able to handle the situation.
As a news dispatch stated at the time, strategists at the Justice
Department were willing

to make one more try with federal marshals before calling on military
forces to enforce the court orders in Mississippi. All along, the view of
President Kennedy and the attorney general has been that the government should come to the use of troops only as a last resort, making
clear that it was forced to this step only after giving the state every
opportunity to back down.[144]

The reluctance of the federal government to resort to armed force
was still reflected in President Kennedy's address to the nation on

[142] For the text of the telegram see *Current History*, 43: 309 (November,
1962).
[143] For the text of the executive order see *ibid.*, pp. 309-310. See also
"Kennedy Echoes Ike as History Repeats," *Milwaukee Journal* (October 1,
1962), p. 5, col. 4.
[144] *Ibid.* (September 30, 1962), p. 2, col. 1.

the evening of September 30. Observing that Meredith had in the meantime been placed in residence on the university campus, the president commented with satisfaction that "this has been accomplished thus far without the use of the National Guard or other troops, and it is to be hoped that the law-enforcement officers of the State of Mississippi and the federal marshals will continue to be sufficient in the future." In his address, the president expressed his deep "regret . . . that any action by the executive branch was necessary in this case. But," he added,

all other avenues and alternatives, including persuasion and conciliation, had been tried and exhausted. Had the police powers of Mississippi been used to support the orders of the court instead of deliberately and unlawfully blocking them, had the University of Mississippi fulfilled its standard of excellence by quietly admitting this applicant in conformity with what so many other Southern state universities have done for so many years, a peaceable and sensible solution would have been possible without any federal intervention.[145]

The president's hope that civil authorities might be sufficient to cope with the crisis was disappointed. The appearance of Meredith and a contingent of federal marshals on the evening of September 30 was followed by extensive rioting and mob violence on campus in the course of which two persons were killed, scores of people injured, and some one hundred and twelve rioters arrested. At the time of their arrival, Meredith and the marshals were escorted to the campus by state police. However, with the gathering of a large hostile crowd, practically all the state highway patrolmen withdrew from the area and did not return.[146] The withdrawal of state police left the field to the segregationist mob which gradually swelled to over a thousand rioters and which soon began to attack the federal marshals. On several occasions, massed rioters charged against the federal officers but were turned back by a shower of tear gas grenades.[147]

[145] For the text of the president's address see *Current History*, 43: 310-313 (November, 1962).

[146] The commander of the state police claimed that the patrolmen had defective gas masks. After midnight, a few policemen returned to the campus, but the majority of patrolmen were observed sitting in their parked cars about a quarter of a mile away from the scene of violence. See *Milwaukee Journal* (October 1, 1962), p. 1, col. 3; p. 10, col. 5.

[147] One of the attacks was led by former Maj. General Edwin A. Walker

Before midnight, the federal marshals called for help from the federalized National Guard and some sixty guardsmen of the Oxford unit were sent to the scene of violence. The small contingent was unable to bring substantial relief, however, and marshals and guardsmen remained pinned down at their campus position for several hours. In the early morning of October 1, federal troops were ordered on the campus to use any force necessary to put down the rioting. Moving in with fixed bayonets, the troops slowly cleared the area and dispersed the rioters from the campus. After a night of tragedy and under the protection of massed federal power, James Meredith was finally able to secure enrollment at the university.[148]

The emotions kindled by the Mississippi crisis reached an intensity which was reminiscent of the Civil War period. The unfolding events were followed with considerable interest abroad and immediately became a pawn in the international cold war struggle.[149] With respect to domestic repercussions, it is a fair generalization to say that public opinion in the nation at large and even in many parts of the South endorsed the president's action. As one Southern newspaper editorial observed, Governor Barnett had "learned nothing from the lesson of Little Rock. . . . Mississippi is entitled to better leadership than this." [150] Outside of Mississippi, federal intervention was censured primarily by public officials and newspapers in Alabama, Arkansas, and South Carolina. Some aspects of the crisis became the object of heated charges and countercharges. Governor Barnett, in a nationwide

---

who had commanded federal troops during the Little Rock crisis. Walker was subsequently arrested on charges of rebellion, insurrection and conspiracy.

[148] The enrollment was succeeded on the same and the following days by even more extensive violence and bloody riots in Oxford. The federal troops massed in Oxford and nearby Tennessee were estimated at one time at 25,000. With the progressive restoration of peace, troops and marshals were gradually withdrawn. By October 20, only some 500 troops and a handful of marshals were left to preserve order and to act as bodyguards to Meredith.

[149] Compare "Our Shame Before the World," *ibid.* (September 28, 1962), p. 22, col. 2. On reactions abroad see also *ibid.*, p. 1, col. 3; (October 1, 1962), p. 4, col. 2; (October 2, 1962), p. 2, col. 2.

[150] *Ibid.* (September 28, 1962), p. 22, col. 2 (*Nashville Tennessean*). For Southern press reaction see also *ibid.* (October 2, 1962), p. 14, col. 4; for the reaction of Southern governors compare *ibid.* (October 1, 1962), p. 4, col. 1.

broadcast, put the blame for the entire conflict on the president and the federal intervention. The governor charged that "trigger happy federal marshals" had touched off the violence; he also claimed that he had not ordered the removal of the state police.[151]

These and similar arguments were entirely spurious. The attribution of responsibility for the crisis to the federal government implies that the proper method of maintaining peace and order is to surrender to the demands of lawless mobs. The reference to "trigger happy" marshals was both incorrect and unfair. Certainly, the federal marshals could not be expected to remain impassive in the face of a hostile crowd twice or three times their size armed with bricks, bottles, bombs and firearms; moreover, despite extreme provocation, the federal agents only used tear gas grenades while two marshals were actually injured by sniper bullets. With respect to the withdrawal of the state police, the actions and statements of the governor on the day of the rioting were at least ambiguous; a more determined attitude on the part of the governor and his police officers certainly would have acted as an additional deterrent to the rioters. Regardless of the reasons for the police withdrawal on the particular evening in question, it was clearly the state's policy of defiance which precipitated the federal intervention. The state police at first actively resisted the registration of Meredith and later tolerated the mob violence. In view of this failure of local and state authorities to enforce federal law, the federal government was constrained to explore other methods, both civil and military, of implementing the court decrees.

With the forced desegregation of the University of Mississippi in fall of 1962, the battlegrounds of the school integration movement were shifted to other states, primarily to Alabama which remained one of the last fortresses of total school desegregation. Among the educational institutions of the state, the University of Alabama was treated clearly by state officials as a symbol and mainstay of the segregationist spirit. Following the *Brown* decision, a brief but unsuccessful effort had been made by a Negro student, Autherine Lucy, to invade the hallowed halls of the

---

[151] *Ibid.* (October 2, 1962), p. 2, col. 1. The accusations directed against the federal marshals were seconded by Senator Eastland and other Southern lawmakers; *ibid.* (October 1, 1962), p. 3, col. 1.

Tuscaloosa campus. On the basis of federal court decrees and restraining orders, Miss Lucy had been enrolled at the university early in 1956; however, in the face of continued rioting and mob violence, she was finally expelled from the institution because of alleged "baseless, outrageous and unfounded charges" against some of the college officials.[152] After this interlude the university returned to its regular standards of unstained and unmitigated discrimination.

At the beginning of 1963, a new governor entered the executive mansion in Montgomery, Alabama. The new officer, George C. Wallace, had campaigned on an uncompromising platform of racial segregation and obviously considered it as his primary task to improve on the record of his predecessor, John Patterson. The opportunity for a full display of his abilities offered itself soon in his gubernatorial career. Major cities in Alabama had already been selected by integration leaders as testing grounds for their struggle. In April of 1963, large-scale demonstrations and protest marches against racial discrimination started in the business section of Birmingham. In the course of these demonstrations, some fifteen hundred Negroes were arrested and jailed in early May. Later in the same month, a federal district court issued an order directing the University of Alabama to admit two Negro applicants for the summer session starting on June 10. Governor Wallace immediately rose to the occasion. Despite a restraining order of the federal district court enjoining his interference, the governor announced his intention to prevent the integration of the university with all means at his command, if necessary by posting himself in the doorway of the university. During the first days of June, the governor assembled eight hundred law enforcement officers in Tuscaloosa, including a military police unit of the Alabama National Guard; at the same time, state troopers and the remaining guard forces were put on alert. A few days before the scheduled registration of the Negro students, some five hundred guardsmen were dispatched to the campus.[153]

Faced with this serious threat to federal law and authority, the

---

[152] See *Race Relations L. Reporter,* 1:456 (1956); also *Lucy* v. *Adams,* 134 F.Supp. 235 (N.D. Ala. 1955), *rev'd.,* 228 F.2d 619 (5th Cir. 1955), 350 U.S. 1 (1955).

[153] On these developments compare *Time,* 81:19 (June 7, 1963).

federal government had again to resort to compulsion. In handling the new challenge, the president and the Justice Department followed essentially the procedure which had been used at "Ole Miss": that is, primary reliance on civil officers coupled with an ultimate resort to military force in case civilian efforts proved futile. If there was a difference between the "Ole Miss" and the Tuscaloosa procedure, it resided in the fact that in Alabama the federal government displayed less patience and resorted to military intervention after a short and somewhat lukewarm use of civilian pressure. While, in Oxford, federal marshals attempted to enroll the Negro student on at least three successive occasions, military forces replaced the federal civil officers at Tuscaloosa after their first and only rebuff.[154] However, the action of the

---

[154] Federal resort to some form of military intervention was used in Alabama also on two other occasions during 1963. The first instance occurred in spring in connection with the street demonstrations and protest marches in Birmingham. Following the bombing of two Negro residences and in the face of widespread rioting during which some fifty persons were injured, President Kennedy on May 12 sent federal troops to bases near Birmingham and took all necessary preliminary steps to federalize the national guard. Although the troops were never actually used, Governor Wallace brought suit in federal court charging that the president's action was unconstitutional. On May 27, 1963, the Supreme Court curtly dismissed the governor's motion as baseless; *Alabama* v. *United States,* 10 L.ed.2d 540 (1963). Racial tensions continued in Birmingham during subsequent months. Some eleven hundred Negro students were suspended or expelled from city schools for anti-segregation activities; but the federal court of appeals ordered reinstatement of the students and desegregation of city schools starting with the fall term. For some of these developments see *Time,* 81: 23-25 (May 17, 1963), p. 22 (May 24, 1963), p. 16 (May 31, 1963), p. 19 (June 7, 1963). In September of 1963, Governor Wallace at first used state troopers to close down schools in Birmingham and other cities in Alabama; subsequently, the troopers were directed to admit white students and turn away Negro pupils. When federal courts issued a restraining order against Wallace and his state police and when federal marshals attempted to serve the order on the troopers and the governor, Wallace employed guardsmen of the state to harass and disperse the marshals; he also replaced the state police at school entrances with contingents of the National Guard. In this situation, President Kennedy signed a proclamation federalizing the guard, a measure which finally permitted the desegregation of schools in Birmingham and other cities in Alabama although it did not prevent bloodshed and further acts of violence; see *Time,* 82:30 (September 20, 1963), pp. 17-21 (September 27, 1963). The most atrocious of these acts of violence—the dynamiting of a Negro church in Birmingham and the killing of four Negro girls on September 15—prompted the demand that federal troops be used to restore order and help apprehend the perpetrators of the crime. The president rejected this demand but directed other federal agencies to participate in the investigation.

federal government seems understandable in view of the defiant attitude of Governor Wallace and in the light of the dire experiences of federal marshals at "Ole Miss." Moreover, it can be argued that the Tuscaloosa case had definite overtones of a rehearsed play and that actions on both sides were so readily predictable that the federal government did not find it useful to go through all the motions of the Oxford procedure.

Contrary to bold utterances of state officials prior to the actual confrontation, the desegregation of the University of Alabama occurred without serious disturbances, although not without theatrical gestures. In preparation for the collision, the federal government sent to Tuscaloosa a team of federal marshals and Justice Department officials, headed by Deputy Attorney General Katzenbach.[155] The first attempt to enroll the two Negro students, Vivian Malone and James Hood, was made by Katzenbach and the federal civil officers on June 11. Apparently in anticipation of the governor's reaction, the two students remained seated in a nearby patrol car. Standing in the doorway of the university and flanked by a swarm of state troopers, Governor Wallace awaited the arrival of the federal officers. On their approach, the governor with a grand pose stopped the officers and proceeded to read a five-page proclamation denouncing the federal government and stressing the sovereign rights of Alabama. After this recital, the federal officers asked the governor to step aside and left when he refused. Notified of developments by telephone, President Kennedy at this point ordered the federalization of the Alabama National Guard.[156] Only four and one-half hours after the first confrontation, the assistant commander of the guard division at Tuscaloosa, Brigadier General Graham, approached Governor Wallace and requested him politely to step aside. After reading another statement the governor walked away, and the two Negro students were enrolled at the Tuscaloosa campus on the same day.[157]

[155] At the same time, some four hundred Army troops, especially trained for riot duty, were dispatched to Fort Benning, Georgia.

[156] For the text of President Kennedy's proclamation and executive order see *The New York Times* (June 12, 1963), p. 21, col. 1.

[157] See *Time*, 81:13-14 (June 21, 1963). Two days later, another Negro student was enrolled at the extension center at Huntsville, Alabama, without incidents. During June, the guardsmen were progressively released from active federal duty.

It can hardly be denied that, in the described episodes, the president and his assistants proceeded with great caution and made a determined effort to maintain order through regular law enforcement agents of the federal government. This observation applies primarily to the Oxford crisis. Even after the authority of federal marshals had been defied on several consecutive occasions and after the intervention of federal troops had been sanctioned, the president decided to make another attempt to handle the crisis through an augmented contingent of federal marshals. It was only when this contingent proved insufficient in the face of overwhelming resistance that federal troops were ordered to the scene of violence. No doubt, the federal attitude in these instances was an improvement over the Little Rock procedure and commends itself for future imitation. As a rule, federal law and court orders should be enforced through regular civil authorities including the state police and federal marshals. Only in cases of extreme emergency, when all other alternatives have been tried and exhausted, should the federal government resort to armed force as an ultimate remedy. In such cases, however, it is not only the right but the duty of the president to insure, by every means at his command, the supremacy of federal law and the secure enjoyment of constitutional liberties. To such instances in particular applies President Kennedy's comment on the role of emergency powers, recalled by James Reston at the time of the Mississippi crisis: "In the decade that lies ahead . . . the American presidency will demand more than ringing manifestoes issued from the rear of the battle. It will demand that the president place himself in the very thick of the fight."[158]

---

[158] *The New York Times* (October 2, 1962), p. 26, col. 7. For James Reston's comments on President Kennedy's performance in the Tuscaloosa incident see *ibid.* (June 12, 1963), p. 42, col. 3.

5

Conclusions

THE PROBLEM of maintaining civil rights and the civilian control of the functions of government is as old as democratic government itself. On one hand there are rights to preserve, the guarantee of which is an outstanding characteristic of democratic government. On the other hand we have the responsibility placed upon government of preserving and protecting the constitution and society. On one hand we ask the question, "What is the value of government if it is a police state?" On the other hand the question is raised, "How can rights be continued if the government is not strong enough to guarantee them?" Operational efficiency is placed against the freedom of the individual. And so it goes.

The past two decades have witnessed the development of an almost impassioned devotion in the United States to constitutional rights. The same period of time has also witnessed the occurrence of one international or domestic crisis after another, two wars in which the United States has been involved and now the possible threat of nuclear attack with the resulting death and destruction. In the present study an attempt has been made to review postwar experiences and to explore procedures that would permit the preservance of rights in the face of the task imposed upon government to meet cold war emergencies. A particularly searching glance has been directed to the position of the executive within the United States for it is here where the conflict of the two forces is most dramatically manifest. By studying executive emergency powers in the areas of nonmilitary preparedness, industrial unrest and racial disturbances it has been found that the use of these powers in recent years and the procedures established for such use were sometimes but not always attuned to the goal of maintaining constitutional safeguards in emergency situations.

In the area of race relations resort to executive emergency powers has made its appearance particularly in the days that have followed the *Brown* decision. Most troubles with respect to race relations are complicated for they have moral, economic and legal facets. All these aspects were present in the disturbances which accompanied the efforts to establish constitutional equality in the fields of education and transportation. The major instances of government intervention during racial disorders which have been examined in this study were the Little Rock, Montgomery, Oxford and Tuscaloosa episodes. Different forms of intervention were used in these instances, a fact which permits critical evaluation and comparison.

There is little doubt that the president had the constitutional and legal authority to send troops into Little Rock. Constitutional principles were flouted, decisions of federal courts were disregarded and the safety of law abiding citizens was put in jeopardy. Under such conditions the power of the president to intervene and quell the disorders was hardly questionable. However, legality is not always the same as wisdom. Clearly, the use of military forces against United States citizens remains a distasteful procedure, a procedure which should be used only as an ultimate remedy after all other alternatives have been explored. In this particular case, Governor Faubus received considerable support from other Southern states not necessarily because of agreement with his position on the race issue but for the reason that federal troops were used to coerce inhabitants of a state without prior resort to alternate methods of law enforcement.

A similar disregard of federal law and federal court decisions occurred a few years later in connection with the "freedom ride" in Alabama. There was actually more destruction of property and violence than at Little Rock. In the face of this violence, the use of federal troops might have been justified; however, the lesson of Little Rock had apparently been learned in this case. Instead of using military forces to preserve the peace, federal marshals were sent into the area and, after some difficulties, law and order were restored. While there was some local resentment against the use of the marshals, the response in most parts of the South was not nearly as vehement as during the Little Rock episode. The federal action in Montgomery afforded a good illustration of what may be accomplished by adequate and timely preparations and by the use of civil officers in case of racial disorders. Certainly, federal marshals are better adapted than military forces to the maintenance of civil procedures and safeguards in emergency situations. Nevertheless, as the Oxford and Tuscaloosa crises have demonstrated, resort to civil law enforcement agents may not always be adequate or sufficient. In cases of extreme emergency, the president may be constrained—and is clearly entitled—to use military force to suppress the violence; however, military intervention should remain an ultimate remedy and be contemplated only after all other alternatives of law enforcement have been tried and exhausted.

Proper congressional legislation, it seems, might go far in lessening the causes of racial disturbances. Congress has frequently been criticized for inaction and apathy in the field of civil rights. The criticism is not entirely justified in view of the Civil Rights Acts of 1957 and 1960. Nevertheless, additional legislation and a more determined attitude on the part of Congress would be extremely helpful in reducing the number of instances calling for the use of emergency powers and in obviating charges of "judicial legislation" directed against the Supreme Court and other federal courts.[1] Race relations can be expected to remain a pressing problem in the United States. There is a growing impetus for the Negro to receive his full share of civil rights.[2] The speed by which he obtains these rights according to the Negro is slow motion, while many Southerners think that changes are coming as rapidly as they can be assimilated. These conflicts spell out a disturbed condition that may continue for many months or years. It is hoped

[1] On June 19, 1963, President Kennedy submitted to Congress ambitious proposals for new civil rights legislation, including among other provisions a legal guarantee to all citizens of equal access to privately-owned hotel, restaurant, and amusement facilities and to retail establishements in interstate commerce; see *Time*, 81:14-15 (June 28, 1963).

[2] The spring of 1963 has been termed a period that "will long be remembered as the time when the United States Negro's revolution for equality exploded on all fronts." *Ibid.*, p. 17 (June 7, 1963). In an address to the nation on June 11, President Kennedy asserted that the United States faced a "moral crisis as a country and a people" because of the rising Negro protest; see *ibid.*, p. 17 (June 21, 1963). On June 22, the president held a White House meeting with some thirty Negro and white civil rights leaders. On August 28, over 200,000 demonstrators participated in a civil rights march in Washington, D.C.; *ibid.*, vol. 82, pp. 13-15 (September 6, 1963).

that persons in charge of preserving the peace will ponder and apply the lessons learned at Little Rock, Montgomery, "Ole Miss" and Tuscaloosa. When discussion, conciliation and means of communication break down between the races, peace should be maintained, wherever possible, not by military force but by duly constituted police officials.

In the field of industrial relations, the role of government officials, and of the president in particular, is hardly less complicated and difficult. Each issue is charged with emotional excitement, full of political implications and intermingled with other issues of the day both international and domestic. Whatever course he follows, the president is likely to be assailed as a tyrant if he does act and as a weakling if he does not. Under the federal constitution, the control of interstate commerce and industry is placed in the hands of Congress. Yet, the postwar period has allotted to the president an increasingly important position with respect to labor disputes and industrial relations in general. This development has been due in large measure to congressional delegation of power; at the same time, however, cold war crises have produced, and can be expected to produce in the future, presidential assertions of "inherent" or implied emergency powers.

The great industrial unrest that existed in the reconversion period after World War II resulted in a frequent resort to emergency powers and especially to government operation of industries through seizure. Regularly, the basis of such action was wartime emergency legislation. The excitement caused by reconversion disorders and the growing impact of the emerging cold war struggle led to the passage of the Taft-Hartley Act providing definite procedures to be followed in the handling of industrial disputes endangering the national health or safety. The enactment of this measure demonstrated congressional preoccupation with this problem and an unwillingness to leave such matters entirely to the discretion of the executive. However, as has been pointed out in this study, the struggle in Congress at the time centered not so much around the attribution of executive emergency power but around the proposed procedures for the exercise of such power. A curious aspect of the passage of the Taft-Hartley Act was the fact that a statute granting considerable discretionary authority to the executive was vetoed by a president who otherwise was not hesitant to invoke executive emergency powers in time of crisis.

Since the passage of the Taft-Hartley Act, the chief objection of organized labor to the emergency procedures of the statute has been the provision authorizing the president to seek injunctive relief. The demand for modification of the Taft-Hartley Act has resulted in the introduction of numerous amendments and substitute bills. Under the Kennedy administration, policy proposals have been advanced which, while retaining strong executive emergency powers, omit any reference to the injunctive procedure. As it appears, these proposals reflect a justified and understandable displeasure with a procedure which deprives unions of the strike weapon without imposing an equal burden on the other party in the bargaining process. Nevertheless, it is questionable whether congressional enactment of the mentioned policy proposals would constitute an improvement over existing emergency provisions. Irrespective of congressional silence, there remains the problem of the enforcement of a presidential stay-at-work order. Unless Congress is called upon to intervene in every single instance, the implementation of the cooling-off decree would depend on the availability of the injunction to prevent a stoppage in critical industries. However, resort to injunctive relief in the form of a presidential exercise of "inherent" or independent power is hardly preferable to a clearly defined statutory procedure. If the use of the injunction in labor disputes is really unwanted and undesirable, then Congress should find a substitute more acceptable to all parties concerned.

The insistence on clearly defined statutory procedures does not completely obviate or eliminate the problem of the use of independent or nonstatutory powers on the part of the president in extreme industrial emergencies. The present study has examined several types of independent presidential authority and close attention has been paid to the famous steel seizure case of 1952. In the opinion of the writers, the ruling in this case did not entirely deprive the president of nonstatutory emergency authority derived from the constitution. The *Youngstown* decision was based in large measure on evidence that pertinent statutory procedures prohibited a presidential resort to seizure under prevailing circumstances. To this degree, the case established the principle that the president should follow existing statutory provisions in all situations where no active war is involved or in instances of "less-than-catastrophic" emergencies. However, there is reason to believe that, in the absence of pertinent laws, and possibly even in the presence of conflicting statutes, the president would be entitled to use independent powers in the event of extreme or catastrophic disaster. Majority, concurring and dissenting opinions in the *Youngstown* case admitted that every resort to executive emergency authority is subject to review by courts.

Major instruments at the disposal of the president for maintaining peace in labor disorders are United States marshals and federal troops. It is comforting to know that the use of troops either to seize a plant or to preserve order during strikes has been less frequent within recent decades, especially in view of the fact that such use is virtually impossible without giving aid or support to one or the other side of the labor dispute. The decrease in instances of military intervention at the federal level must be ascribed primarily to improved labor legislation and to the availability of alternate methods of bringing the weight of the public interest to bear on the disputing parties. This improvement—which, unfortunately, is not completely matched at the state level—is an additional illustration of the desirability of congressional action designed to delimit the range of emergency powers and to prevent arbitrary executive action. Congress in the future should continue to devote its attention to industrial relations and to prescribe or improve procedures to be followed by the president in all peacetime disputes that might be given an emergency classification and even in most situations that might occur during a cold war crisis.

The problems occasioned by our perilous atomic age are both numerous and grave. Many of these problems are the concern of the natural scientist. Others, equally important, pertain to the social scientist. One of the most pressing and complicated problems is that of nonmilitary defense. As has been pointed out in the present study, nonmilitary defense is almost entirely a postwar phenomenon and, as such, is a telling demonstration of the postwar revolution in arms and weapons and of the horrible threat of suffering and destruction resulting from this revolution. It is commonly assumed that at least one half of the population of the

United States could be destroyed by a sneak atomic attack. In the face of such danger, preparations for the protection of the population and for the maintenance of civil order in case of nuclear disaster have become a major preoccupation of responsible government leaders and of the public at large.

The development of nonmilitary defense during the postwar period has resulted in an unique form of "cold war" emergency authority at the federal and state levels. In view of existing long-range missiles, this authority—in contrast to traditional war powers—is no longer limited to the scene of actual military operations or to cases of a declared war; nor does it extend only to the military establishment. Nonmilitary, and especially civil, defense manifests a curious blending of military and civilian standards or considerations, and this blending is reflected in the broad and baffling character of executive emergency powers in the field of nonmilitary preparedness. The existence of such broad powers obviously constitutes a serious challenge to customary concepts of civil government and to the maintenance of constitutional liberties.

The present study has examined the many changes and revisions which, in the postwar era, occurred in the administrative structure of nonmilitary defense. The primary aim of this examination was to determine to which extent existing arrangements are compatible with constitutional safeguards. It has been found that, under the terms of the 1961 reorganization, overall direction and coordination of nonmilitary defense programs was vested in the president and the Office of Emergency Planning, while primary responsibility for civil defense was transferred to the Department of Defense. Obviously, the reorganization was inspired by a desire to improve the efficiency of civil defense operations and especially of the national fallout shelter program. Despite the cogency of these considerations, the present study has noted several disconcerting aspects of the new arrangement. One of the questions raised by the reorganization concerns the president's authority to effect the reallocation of powers without the benefit of a prior express change in the statutory basis. As has been shown, it is at least doubtful whether pertinent congressional legislation contemplates the exercise of the power on the part of the president to reallocate major statutory functions through sweeping cross-agency delegations. It must also be observed that the assignment of overall direction to the president and to an agency in the president's office decreases the chances of congressional supervision of emergency functions and powers.

The most disturbing aspect of the new arrangement, however, consists in the combination or integration of military and civil defense functions in the Defense Department. The desirability of such a combination had been frequently questioned or openly rejected during the decade preceding the reorganization. In view of these objections or adverse sentiments, it is somewhat surprising that the transfer of civil defense responsibilities in 1961 produced little criticism both inside and outside of Congress. Despite this apparent acquiescence, it is necessary to observe that the integration of military and civil defense functions has serious implications for the maintenance of civil authority and civil rights in the event of nonmilitary defense emergencies. As the present study has stated, the blending of functions renders ambiguous the traditional concept of military assistance to civil defense authorities. It is also questionable whether the combination permits the development of a "new" type of martial rule in the form of a close cooperation of military and civilian officials and institutions. Past experience, together with the military preoccupations of the Defense Department, would seem to point rather to an increased likelihood of a resort to customary martial law.

To a considerable degree, the ambiguities and shortcomings of the present arrangement must be ascribed to the inaction and lassitude of Congress. At the time of the Korean crisis, in the face of widespread concern with the dangers confronting the domestic population, Congress enacted several important measures, including the Federal Civil Defense Act and the Defense Production Act. However, since that time, Congress has shown little active interest in legislation in the field of nonmilitary defense and has left to the executive branch the responsibility for planning and executing emergency programs and procedures.[3] Obviously, Con-

[3] An example of congressional apathy can be found in the drastic curtailment of civil defense appropriations for the fiscal year of 1963 which had been recommended by President Kennedy. However, in September of 1963, the House of Representatives approved substantial appropriations for construction of fallout shelters in federal buildings and for aid to such construc-

gress is not immune to the common human frailty of disregarding the danger of emergencies until they actually occur; however, congressmen have an additional duty to be alert and to provide for the protection of the public against contingencies beyond the control of individual citizens. Congress also has the responsibility to exercise its legislative function for the purpose of preventing the accumulation of excessive executive or military powers and of maintaining, wherever possible, constitutional and statutory safeguards even in cold war emergencies.

It is certainly difficult to select far in advance the most advantageous method of resisting attack and of preserving law and order in the event of nuclear disaster. There is a strong temptation to say that nothing can be done or that resort to martial law is inevitable. It is not denied here that, in instances of extreme catastrophe, such resort may become necessary; when used properly, martial rule is restorative in nature and may be an effective way of restoring law and order. However, martial law is a drastic measure which should be contemplated only as an ultimate remedy when all attempts to preserve civil authority have failed. The most persuasive objections to martial law are that, once the possibility of its use is admitted, it may be invoked indiscriminately and that, once established, it may be continued far beyond the period of actual necessity. Unfortunately, there are historical precedents which justify these apprehensions and which point to the need for adequate preparations designed to keep military ambitions within proper limits. As Operation Alert of 1956 illustrated, most difficult situations can be handled without resort to martial law by the military acting in support of and furnishing aid to civil police forces.

With respect to state functions, the study has indicated that the emergency powers of governors correspond in many respects to those exercised by the President of the United States. The source of these powers are the constitutions of the states and state legislation. During recent decades, express grants of authority have been maintained and sometimes even expanded; however, due to the national repercussions of most contemporary crisis situations,

---

tion by state and local governments, schools, hospitals, and other nonprofit institutions; see *Time*, 82:21 (September 27, 1963), and 109 Cong. Rec. 16349-16391 (September 17, 1963).

the occasions for the use of granted powers have tended to be circumscribed. This change in federal-state relations was clearly manifested in the field of race relations. When Governor Faubus employed his emergency power to enforce state law at the expense of the federal constitution, the courts promptly declared his action unconstitutional and enjoined him from using the state militia in violation of federal court orders. Similar restraining orders were issued in the Oxford and Tuscaloosa crises; in addition, contempt proceedings were instituted against Governor Barnett and the lieutenant governor of the state. In Montgomery, Governor Patterson declared martial law to enforce the state constitution and state segregation laws which were contrary to federal law. Although, in this instance, the governor was not formally enjoined from using troops in this manner, the language of federal court decisions clearly indicated that actions of any and all state officials designed to maintain or enforce segregation were invalid.

In the area of labor disputes the governor's range of power has been narrowed by the growth of interstate at the expense of intrastate business. It is difficult today to name an enterprise which does not affect interstate commerce or does not in some way concern a federal agency or function. As a result, most emergency disputes tend to be federal matters subject to federal authority. While, initially, civil defense was considered primarily as a local matter subject to state regulation, subsequent legislation made civil defense a joint responsibility of the federal and state governments. In view of the need for financial support and possibly military assistance, the federal government—almost inevitably—exercises the lion's share of these "joint" functions. Despite these changing conditions in federal-state relations, emergency power both of a statutory and nonstatutory character continues to be vested in the governor for use in local emergencies.

Returning to the central theme of the study, it is clear that, from the American viewpoint, the significance and meaning of the cold war struggle revolves essentially around the ability of the United States to maintain the democratic character of her institutions in the face of international and domestic crises. Although there is no easy and ready-made solution to the reconciliation of these conflicting tendencies, the preceding inquiry suggests certain procedures and allocations of functions which may go far in achieving a balance of emergency power and liberty. One of the prime requisites for such balance is the principle that, as far as possible, the legislature should establish emergency procedures to be followed by the executive; in addition, legislative bodies should maintain constant vigilance with respect to administrative performance on the basis of established statutory procedures. Timely and determined action on the part of the legislature is even more urgently required in our time of constant crisis than in normal peacetime situations; and, as was correctly asserted in the *Youngstown* case, only Congress can prevent power from slipping through its fingers. Apart from legislative action, preplanning and other preparations are required on the part of all civil agencies of government in order to obviate the need for excessive executive force in emergencies and to permit civil authorities to preserve peace, if necessary with the assistance of the military. Nevertheless, even a scrupulous observance of these safeguards may not always be sufficient to eliminate the requirement of more drastic action and of a resort to independent or nonstatutory emergency powers by the executive. Legislation cannot provide for all contingencies; an attempt to do so would only produce statutes which are so vague and encompassing as to be superfluous and possibly dangerous.[4] The admission of independent or nonstatutory executive powers does not signify that such powers go beyond constitutional limits; any executive emergency authority must be traceable to express or implied grants of the constitution. Finally, any exercise of emergency prerogatives remains subject to judicial control and review.

These recommendations and principles seem to fit well into our constitutional theory and our framework of government. Separation of powers was highly regarded by our constitutional fathers and remains a basic characteristic of our government today. Distribution and separate allocation of functions does not always produce maximum efficiency, especially in times of crisis; however, without proper safeguards, appeals to maximum efficiency and

---

[4] The proposal that Congress should legislate for all emergency situations was made in J. Malcolm Smith and Cornelius P. Cotter, *Powers of the President During Crises* (Washington, D.C., 1960), pp. 144-146. Such a "generic statute" would either have to be detailed in which case it could not anticipate all contingencies or it would be a blanket authorization which is unnecessary and of doubtful value in view of our written constitution.

overriding necessity easily lead to abuse. As Justice Brandeis, dissenting in the *Pocket Veto* case, pointed out: "The doctrine of the separation of powers was adopted by the Convention of 1787, not to promote efficiency but to preclude the exercise of arbitrary power. The purpose was, not to avoid friction, but by means of the inevitable friction incident to the distribution of the governmental powers among three departments, to save the people from autocracy."[5] By following the above recommendations much can be done to secure a desirable degree of operational efficiency required by our nuclear age and to retain the freedoms which are the priceless inheritance from our forefathers.

---

[5] *Myers* v. *United States,* 272 U.S. 52, 293 (1926).

Index